Economic Geography

This book series serves as a broad platform for scientific contributions in the field of Economic Geography and its sub-disciplines. *Economic Geography* wants to explore theoretical approaches and new perspectives and developments in the field of contemporary economic geography. The series welcomes proposals on the geography of economic systems and spaces, geographies of transnational investments and trade, globalization, urban economic geography, development geography, climate and environmental economic geography and other forms of spatial organization and distribution of economic activities or assets.

Some topics covered by the series are:

- Geography of innovation, knowledge and learning
- Geographies of retailing and consumption spaces
- Geographies of finance and money
- Neoliberal transformation, urban poverty and labor geography
- Value chain and global production networks
- Agro-food systems and food geographies
- Globalization, crisis and regional inequalities
- Regional growth and competitiveness
- Social and human capital, regional entrepreneurship
- Local and regional economic development, practice and policy
- New service economy and changing economic structures of metropolitan city regions
- Industrial clustering and agglomeration economies in manufacturing industry
- Geography of resources and goods
- Leisure and tourism geography

Publishing a broad portfolio of peer-reviewed scientific books *Economic Geography* contains research monographs, edited volumes, advanced and undergraduate level textbooks, as well as conference proceedings. The books can range from theoretical approaches to empirical studies and contain interdisciplinary approaches, case studies and best-practice assessments. Comparative studies between regions of all spatial scales are also welcome in this series. Economic Geography appeals to scientists, practitioners and students in the field. If you are interested in contributing to this book series, please contact the Publisher.
If you are interested in contributing to this book series, please contact the Publisher.

More information about this series at http://www.springer.com/series/15653

Maximilian Benner

A New Arab Social Contract?

Institutional Perspectives for Economic Reform in Arab Countries

 Springer

Maximilian Benner
University of Vienna
Vienna, Austria

ISSN 2520-1417 ISSN 2520-1425 (electronic)
Economic Geography
ISBN 978-3-030-19269-3 ISBN 978-3-030-19270-9 (eBook)
https://doi.org/10.1007/978-3-030-19270-9

This Springer imprint is published by the registered company Springer Nature Switzerland AG.
The registered company address is: Gewerbestrasse 11, 6330 Cham, Switzerland

*In memory
of my great-grandparents,
Paul and Henriette*

Preface

The political economy of the Middle East and North Africa currently enjoys much attention on behalf of scholars and policymakers. The so-called Arab spring sparked a new wave of interest in the socio-economic situation of Arab countries and gave rise to a host of policy recommendations on how to reform Arab countries' economies and governments.

Often, reform proposals remain isolated and tend to ignore the specific institutional context found in Arab countries generally and in each individual country specifically. Following the relational school of economic geography (Bathelt and Glückler 2012, 2014), the present book argues that reform agendas have to be context-specific and thus have to take into account the institutional context they are likely to encounter. In so doing, one may find that some policies are more likely to succeed than others or that for some policies to succeed, longer-term institutional change is needed.

Institutional change can be affected by policies specifically targeting the institutional level of an economy. Doing so requires a thorough understanding of the complex and idiosyncratic relationships between economic structures, policies, agents, and the wider socio-economic institutional context. This is the basic assumption that led to the present book. The book wants to contribute to the formation of a framework for a better understanding of these complex relationships in the case of Arab economies in their present transitional state.

In pursuing my research for this book, I found some of the older theoretical approaches explaining socio-economic regulation such as varieties of capitalism (VoC), national systems of innovation (NIS), and regulation school useful for developing such a framework. Combining these and other approaches into a synthesis appeared more appropriate to me than subscribing to just one of them, given the limits and constraints of each one. Thus, the present book attempts to propose both a unified approach to socio-economic regulation and its adaptation to the stylized case of core Arab economies such as Morocco, Tunisia, Egypt, or Jordan.

Any work on economic structures and policies is confronted with an ever-changing reality. Nevertheless, I believe the theoretical perspective of socio-economic regulation offered in the present book provides a useful tool for scholars and policymakers and can help them understand and facilitate the core Arab economies' transition towards a new equilibrium. In any case, changing the ways of socio-economic regulation in core Arab economies is a long-term process fraught with uncertainty. Doing so will require waves of trial-and-error policymaking. I hope the present book, as well as eventual contributions of the scientific community building on this work, will provide policymakers with guidelines and orientation during their reform efforts.

I want to thank everyone who contributed ideas or comments on my research, both individually and in the framework of sessions at the Global Conferences of Economic Geography 2015 in Oxford and 2018 in Cologne. In particular, I want to thank Johannes Glückler for our thorough discussions on institutional economic geography that led to the definition of the precise subject of this book and Michaela Trippl for our discussions on evolutionary policy approaches that are part of the thoughts on regional development expressed in this book. Further acknowledgments go to Harald Bathelt, Christian Haddad, Robert Hassink, Steffen Hertog, Sami Mahroum, Robert Panitz, Paul Rivlin, and Andrés Rodríguez-Pose for valuable discussions or comments. A special thank you goes to Juliane Brach, Steffen Hertog, Adeel Malik, Marc Schiffbauer, and several interviewees for suggesting and introducing interviewees in Tunisia and Jordan, respectively. I am grateful to my interview partners in Tunisia and Jordan for their willingness to be interviewed. Of course, all remaining errors and omissions are my own.

Most of all, I want to thank my wife, Teresa Maria Guggenbichler, for being part of my life.

I hope the book will be met with interest by scholars and policymakers alike and contribute to the debate on institution-sensitive reform policies in the Arab world.

Vienna, Austria   Maximilian Benner
January 2019

References

Bathelt H, Glückler J (2012) Wirtschaftsgeographie: Ökonomische Beziehungen in räumlicher Perspektive. (Economic geography: economic relations in a spatial perspective), 3rd edn. UTB, Stuttgart
Bathelt H, Glückler J (2014) Institutional change in economic geography. Progr Hum Geogr 38(3):340–363

Contents

Abbreviations

AA	Association agreement
ADC	Aqaba Development Corporation
ANETI	*Agence Nationale pour l'Emploi et le Travail Indépendant* (Tunisian national employment and independent work agency)
ANPR	*Agence (Nationale) de Promotion de la Recherche Scientifique* (Tunisian scientific research promotion agency)
APIA	*Agence de Promotion des Investissements Agricoles* (Tunisian investment promotion agency for the agricultural sector)
API(I)	*Agence de Promotion de l'Industrie et de l'Innovation* (Tunisian industrial and innovation promotion agency)
ASEZ	Aqaba Special Economic Zone
ASEZA	Aqaba Special Economic Zone Authority
CEPEX	*Centre de Promotion des Exportations* (Tunisian export promotion agency)
CERT	*Centre d'Études et de Recherche des Télécommunications* (Tunisian research center for telecommunications)
CETTEX	*Centre Technique du Textile* (Tunisian technical center for textiles)
CIT	*Complexe industriel et technologique* (industrial and technological complex)
CLLD	Community-led local development
CME	Coordinated market economy
CONECT	*Confédération des Entreprises Citoyennes de Tunisie* (independent Tunisian business association)
DCFTA	Deep and Comprehensive Free Trade Area
DFZC	Development and Free Zones Commission
EC	European Commission
EEN	Enterprise Europe Network
EHBP	El Hassan Business Park
EHSC	El Hassan Science City
EJEP	Euro-Jordanian Export Program
EMP	Euro-Mediterranean Partnership

ENI	European Neighborhood Instrument
ENP	European Neighborhood Policy
EPZ	Export processing zone
ERSAP	Economic Recovery and Structural Adjustment Program
EU	European Union
EUR	Euro
FDI	Foreign direct investment
Fig.	Figure
FAMEX	*Fonds d'Accès aux Marchés d'Exportation* (Tunisian fund for export market access support)
FIPA	Tunisian Foreign Investment Promotion Agency
FOPRODI	*Fonds de Promotion et de Décentralisation Industrielles* (Tunisian fund for industrial promotion and decentralization)
FOPRODEX	*Fonds de Promotions des Exportations* (Tunisian fund for export promotion)
FTA	Free-trade agreement
GATT	General Agreement on Tariffs and Trade
GCC	Gulf Cooperation Council
GDP	Gross domestic product
GDF	Governorate Development Fund
GERD	Gross domestic expenditure on research and development
GMG	*Groupement de maintenance et de gestion* (industrial zone maintenance and management entity)
GNI	Gross national income
GVC	Global value chain
HCST	Higher Council for Science and Technology
HEI	Higher education entities (originally higher education institutions)
HSC	El Hassan Science City
IBRD	International Bank for Reconstruction and Development
ICT	Information and communication technology/technologies
IDA	Irbid Development Area
IDRC	International Development Research Centre
IFI	International financial institution
ILO	International Labour Organization
IMF	International Monetary Fund
INNORPI	*Institut National de la Normalisation et de la Propriété Industrielle* (Tunisian national institute for standardization and for intellectual property)
iPark	ICT Business Park
IPCO	Intellectual Property Commercialisation Office
ISET	*Instituts supérieurs des études technologiques* (Tunisian universities of applied sciences)
ISI	Import substitution industrialization
IT	Information technology
JD	Jordanian Dinar

JEDCO	Jordan Enterprise Development Corporation
JICA	Japan International Cooperation Agency
JIEC	Jordan Industrial Estates Corporation
JTB	Jordan Tourism Board
JTTON	Jordan Technology Transfer Offices Network
JUMP	Jordan Upgrading and Modernization Program
JUST	Jordan University of Science and Technology
KHBP	King Hussein Business Park
LEADER	*Liaison entre actions de développement de l'économie rurale* (links between actions for the development of the rural economy)
LFP	Labor force participation
LME	Liberal market economy
MENA	Middle East and North Africa
MES	*Ministère de l'Enseignement Supérieur et de la Recherche Scientifique* (Tunisian Ministry of Higher Education and Scientific Research)
MFA	Multi-Fibre Arrangement
MOTA	Jordanian Ministry of Tourism and Antiquities
MSME	Micro-, small-, and medium-sized enterprise
NDC	Northern Development Corporation
NIE	Newly industrialized economy
NIS	National innovation system
OECD	Organisation for Economic Co-operation and Development
PMN	*Programme de mise à niveau* (Tunisian enterprise upgrading program)
PSUT	Princess Sumaya University of Science and Technology
QIZ	Qualifying Industrial Zone
QRCE	Queen Rania Center for Entrepreneurship
R&D	Research and development
RSS	Royal Scientific Society
S&T	Science and technology
SCIT	*Société complexe industriel et technologique* (management company of an industrial and technological complex)
SHTT	*Société Hôtelière et Touristique* (Tunisian hotel and tourism development company)
SME	Small- and medium-sized enterprise
SOE	State-owned enterprise
SRTD	Support to Research and Technological Development and Innovation Initiatives and Strategies in Jordan project
SSP	Social system of production
STB	*Société Tunisienne de Banque* (Tunisian banking company)
STP	Science and technology park
TFP	Total factor productivity
TNC	Transnational corporation
TTO	Technology transfer office

TVET	Technical and Vocational Education and Training
UAE	United Arab Emirates
UfM	Union for the Mediterranean
UGTT	*Union Générale Tunisienne de Travail* (Tunisian General Labour Union)
UNIDO	United Nations Industrial Development Organization
UNRWA	United Nations Relief and Work Agency for Palestine Refugees in the Near East
UoJ	University of Jordan
USAID	United States Agency for International Development
US	United States (of America)
USD	US Dollar
UTICA	*Union Tunisienne de l'Industrie, du Commerce et de l'Artisanat* (Tunisian federation of business associations)
VET	Vocational education and training
VoC	Variety/varieties of capitalism
WB	World Bank Group
WIPO	World Intellectual Property Organization
WTO	World Trade Organization
ZDR	*Zone de développement régional* (regional development zone)

Chapter 1
Middle Eastern and North African Economies After the "Arab Spring"

Abstract The chapter introduces the subject of the book and defines the research questions.

Keywords Arab Spring · Arab social contract · Arab economies

Since the so-called Arab Spring[1] in 2011, political, economic, and social development in the Arab economies in the Middle East and North Africa has caught

---

[1] The expression "Arab Spring" coined by mass media is unfortunate because it is misleading in a number of ways. First, the nature of political movements towards the end of the first decade of the twenty-first century and at the beginning of the next decade was not solely and simply "Arab." On the one hand, Moghadam and Decker (2014: 73–74) convincingly argue that the "Green protests" in 2009 in Iran were forerunners of the later protests in Arab countries and had a demonstration effect for protesters there. On the other hand, protests in countries such as Tunisia, Egypt, Yemen, Libya, Syria, and Morocco were embedded in their own national contexts. Some common problems and underlying causes do exist across many Arab nations, and the importance of a shared Arab public sphere and "regional demonstration effects" (Lynch 2014: 390) should not be underestimated. Neither should the relevance of specific national political and economic contexts be neglected. To emphasize the heterogeneity of revolutionary phenomena in different Arab nations, it would be far more appropriate to use the term "Arab revolutions." The second major reason why the term "spring" is misleading is because it implies a cyclicity which does apparently not exist. Given the vastly different outcomes of revolutions (e.g., when comparing Tunisia and Egypt) and tragic courses in some countries (notably in Syria, Yemen, and Libya), the uniform idea of a "spring" which is necessarily followed by summer is a misnomer. On the other hand, the term "spring" is reminiscent of the "Prague Spring" of 1968. Apart from the fact that this reminiscence is Eurocentric, the term denies the different contexts of both sets of events and thus suggests a similarity that did not exist. As is argued in the following sections, the Arab revolutions were based on a complex mixture of social, economic, institutional, and political reasons (e.g., Moghadam and Decker 2014: 74). The narrative implicit to the adaptation of the word "spring" from the "Prague Spring" focuses primarily on a struggle for democracy against autocracy and thus masks the complexity of underlying reasons for the Arab revolutions. Despite being a most inappropriate term, "Arab Spring" has unfortunately become a household name. Therefore it is close to inevitable to use it even in scientific discourse. Consequently, whenever used in this book, the term is put in quotation marks to emphasize its highly problematic nature.

Throughout the book, US spelling is used, except for names of organizations or in direct quotes where original British spelling was kept.

© Springer Nature Switzerland AG 2020
M. Benner, *A New Arab Social Contract?*, Economic Geography,
https://doi.org/10.1007/978-3-030-19270-9_1

worldwide attention. While the impact of the political upheavals since 2010/2011 has led to far-reaching political and security-related implications, the economic dimension of the evolutions and revolutions in Arab countries is often represented in a simplistic and superficial manner. Youth unemployment is seen as a major cause of the "Arab Spring," and providing employment opportunities for youth (especially young men) is supposed to solve the prevalent social and security-related problems. Such a popular analysis necessarily ignores the complexity of the multifaceted reasons for demonstrations and protests both in the Arab world as such and in each idiosyncratic case of the countries where they occurred. Further, a too simplistic analysis misses the complex reality of socio-economic regulation in Arab economies. Youth unemployment is a symptom of deeper structural deficiencies in the economic fabric of an economy, and often it is not the only symptom. Other symptoms might be less visible but not less serious. A thorough analysis of these structural deficiencies and their socio-institutional causes is necessary to understand how public discontent could rise to the levels it reached in 2010/2011 and eventually to formulate well-informed strategies to solve structural problems instead of proposing piecemeal, isolated, and one-size-fits-all policy measures.

Indeed, Amin et al. (2012: 1) stress that unemployment was actually decreasing before the revolutions, obviously calling into question monocausal economic explanations. Still, there was an economic dimension to the popular discontent that led up to the protests. Apart from symptoms of structural problems such as high and persistent unemployment, cronyism instead of inclusion and half-hearted and non-inclusive market reforms in the 1990s may well have had their effect on the populations' perceptions of their long-term economic prospects (Amin et al. 2012: 1–4).

The present book does not have the ambition to put forward an all-encompassing explanation of the underlying reasons for the "Arab Spring." Rather, the book starts with the assumption that the underlying reasons for the political upheavals in Arab countries are based on a mixture of exogenous and endogenous reasons. Endogenous reasons include economic aspects or demographic aspects with economic indications such as unemployment and the so-called youth bulge in Arab countries with young and growing populations (Dhillon and Yousef 2009: 2; Moghadam and Decker 2014: 73–74). Yet, the set of economic aspects of the revolutions and evolutions in Arab countries since 2010/2011 are much more complex and multifaceted, not to speak of wider social and political aspects (Cammett 2014: 161, 170–171). This book sets out to discuss the major economic aspects and regards the economic dimension of the "Arab Spring" as a part of the socio-economic history of Arab economies since their independence. From this perspective, the Arab revolutions can be seen as a major regulation crisis that calls for finding a new, consistent, and sustainable regulation regime that allows for solving the major underlying structural problems of Arab economies and their symptoms.

The regulation approaches known from economic sociology and geography such as the regulation school, national systems of innovation, varieties of capitalism, and social systems of production are useful tools to develop a framework to understand the specifics of socio-economic regulation in Arab economies and to apply the framework to propose pathways towards a more consistent and sustainable new regulation regime. A fifth, newer theory proposed by Acemoğlu and Robinson (2012) deals with the interplay of extractive and inclusive institutions and complements the framework.

The present book makes an attempt to propose such an integrated regulation framework to be used in Arab economies as a tool for analyzing how regulation used to work according to the notion of the "Arab social contract" known from the literature in Middle Eastern political economy, for understanding why and how this old regulation regime collapsed, and for elaborating pathways towards a more efficient, consistent, and sustainable regulation regime. As a policy design tool, the framework suggests a comprehensive package of economic policy interventions for core Arab economies.

Such a regulation perspective puts the focus not only on questions of static efficiency but equally on whether a regulation regime allows for achieving sufficiently high levels of dynamic efficiency to cope with economic and social challenges at hand. To do so, a regulation framework has to consider the dynamics of Schumpeterian creative destruction in a given regulation regime because they are drivers of structural change and thus industrialization. Conditions, prevalence, and outcomes of entrepreneurship and innovation are determinants of the efficiency and sustainability of a regulation regime. This is why the present book discusses both the old Arab social contract and a possible new regulation regime for core Arab economies through the lens of entrepreneurship, innovation, and the degree of creative destruction it enables. Corresponding to the socio-economic perspective of regulation approaches, creative destruction is not a strictly economic phenomenon but equally a social and political one. Successful Schumpeterian entrepreneurs are not only economic or technological agents of change but form a social class with political ambitions. The relevance of a politically independent and confident entrepreneurial class is thus an important socio-economic feature of an efficient and sustainable regulation regime, as was emphasized by Acemoğlu and Robinson (2012). Regulation regimes differ in the degree to which they allow for the emergence of such a politically independent and confident entrepreneurial class. The present book assesses the degree of independent entrepreneurial initiative possible under the economic, political, and social conditions of the Arab social contract and discusses the role such an independent entrepreneurial class could play in a renewed regulation regime.

Research for the present book was guided by the motivation of bringing together two bodies of literature which, somewhat surprisingly, have not experience much contact yet. On the one hand, socio-economic regulation approaches from economic sociology or geography and development economies form the theoretical base for the arguments presented and for the consolidated regulation approach proposed. On the other hand, the regulation framework is applied as a lens to understand and elaborate possible policy interventions to solve structural economic problems prevalent in core Arab economies which have for long been analyzed by Middle Eastern political economy. Curiously, while the notion of the "Arab social contract" known from Middle Eastern political economy and its collapse is basically a description of a concrete regulation regime and its crisis, these regulation approaches and Middle

Eastern political economy have not yet been combined, at least to my knowledge. Regulation approaches have rarely been applied to core Arab economies. For instance, the varieties of capitalism (VoC) approach so far focused mainly on industrialized countries,[2] while Acemoğlu and Robinson's (2012) arguments are directed to a large extent towards Latin American economies. Considering both the considerable and pressing structural economic problems in core Arab economies and the closeness of the Arab world to Europe, understanding regulation in these economies and providing a theory-based lens for developing comprehensive socio-economic and institution-sensitive policies (Benner 2017; Glückler and Lenz 2016) are thus highly relevant.

Defining the spatial subject of the book confronts some problems. In the literature, the term Middle East and North Africa (MENA) is often used to describe the total of Arab countries. While there is no commonly accepted definition of which countries with an Arabic-speaking majority and/or a Muslim majority are included under the MENA term (e.g., is Mauritania included? Sudan? Djibouti? Somalia?), the Middle East undoubtedly includes core countries without an Arabic-speaking majority (in any case, Turkey and Iran) and one country without an Arabic-speaking majority and without a Muslim majority (Israel). This is why the term MENA is not suitable to define the focus of this book which is put on Arab economies with their distinctive political economies distinct from those of Turkey (Eder 2014), Iran (Bouroujerdi 2014), and Israel (Ben Shitrit 2014). The focus of the book excludes countries at the fringes of the Arab world such as Mauritania, Sudan, Somalia, or Djibouti and those undergoing civil wars that make an analysis of their economic status highly specific (Syria, Libya, Yemen). These cases certainly merit scholarly attention but will need to consider each country's very peculiar situation (e.g., Gobat and Kostial 2016). Furthermore, the West Bank and Gaza are not covered by the focus of this book because of their special situation and status. The book does focus on resource-poor "core Arab economies" including Morocco, Tunisia, Egypt, Jordan, and, with some reservations, Lebanon. Resource-rich Arab economies such as Algeria and the GCC member states might share some socio-economic characteristics with these core Arab economies but are confronted with a distinct set of challenges and opportunities.

Under the umbrella of such a broad regulation perspective, the present book strives to develop answers to the following five research questions:

1. How does regulation between economic action and institutional context work in Arab economies, notably in relation to drivers of private-sector growth such as entrepreneurship?
2. Which new modes of regulation could help Arab countries in addressing structural economic and social difficulties by facilitating private-sector-led growth?
3. What role can entrepreneurship play in such new modes of regulation?

---

[2] One of the rare attempts to characterize an Arab VoC is made by Hertog (2016) which is presented in Chap. 3.

4. Which implications does the current transitional context in Arab economies hold for regulation, including opportunities implicit in the current regulation crisis?
5. What types of policies are needed to put such new modes of regulation in place?

The book's core aim is to propose a framework model for socio-economic regulation in Arab economies that can be used to describe the institutional context (Glückler and Bathelt 2017) in an Arab economy or possibly in one of its regions and to predict the consistency of policy recommendations with the institutional context and thus, from an institutional point of view, their prospects for success.

While the conceptual part of the book focuses on core Arab economies as such, the regulation framework proposed will be applied to the particular cases of Tunisia and Jordan. Both countries share the fundamental structural problems evident across core Arab economies but at the same time represent interesting cases due to their specific similarities and differences. While both countries are similar in size, resource-poor, and labor-abundant and have achieved relative success in industrialization, tourism, and the transition towards a more knowledge-based economy, political change since 2010/2011 was revolutionary in Tunisia but evolutionary in Jordan. Tunisia's republican political tradition since independence was marked by a short period of Arab socialism and a subsequent long-term opening (*infitah*) to the world economy, while Jordan's conservative monarchical system has permanently left a significant degree of freedom to private entrepreneurial initiative. Tunisia's economy is strongly oriented towards the European Union (EU), and its population is culturally close to European countries such as France and Italy, not least because of the large Tunisian diaspora in Europe. Jordan, in contrast, is embedded in the geopolitical dynamics of the Middle East marked by the Israeli-Palestinian conflict and its consequences including the large share of Jordanian citizens of Palestinian origin, the "cold" Israel-Jordan peace, the labor migration to GCC countries, the precarious political and security situation of Iraq, and the civil war in Syria and the presence of large numbers of Syrian refugees in Jordan. Both the common features and the differences between Tunisia and Jordan allow for refining the regulation framework in these two exemplary cases.

Despite the book's approach of looking at nation-states as the primary scale for regulation, the aspects covered are to a large degree spatially sensitive on subnational levels. Processes of economic growth, innovation, and entrepreneurship are locally or regionally embedded and cannot be considered independently from their institutional context (Glückler and Bathelt 2017) which is to a significant degree local and regional. This is evident first on the empirical level by the spatial dimension of structural problems such as (youth) unemployment which is even more severe in peripheral regions in countries such as Tunisia and second on the policy level by the spatial nature of coping strategies such as regional incubators (such as the Tunisian *cyberparcs*), technology parks and regional cluster initiatives (such as those under the Tunisian *pôles de compétitivité* or *complexes industriels et technologiques* schemes), or special economic zones (such as Jordan's Aqaba Special Economic Zone). Thus, the regional dimension is a cross-cutting aspect in this book. The book therefore takes a multi-scalar perspective which includes a regional-level view and addresses the subnational spatial dimension of empirical realities and policy approaches wherever appropriate.

Methodologically, research for this book is primarily theoretical in nature. The core of the research tasks was combining the abundant literature of Middle Eastern political economy with regulation approaches found in economic sociology, economic geography, and development economics which were consolidated into a unified conceptual framework. This generic theoretical framework is further refined and applied to specific national contexts in case studies on Tunisia and Jordan. Further, the theoretical considerations built deductively on the conceptual framework are enriched with empirical research through triangulation interviews with stakeholders and experts from both countries. However, this work is not primarily an empirical study. The conceptual thoughts developed are based on theoretical and empirical arguments found in the literature, giving this book the character of a meta-study. More elaborate in-depth empirical research testing and applying the theoretical framework proposed here could further contribute to understanding socio-economic regulation in core Arab economies.

The book is structured as follows: Chap. 2 presents major structural difficulties present in core Arab economies on the basis of a detailed review of the literature on Middle Eastern political economy. Chapter 3 introduces regulation approaches known from economic sociology and geography as well as development economies and proposes a consolidated framework for regulation for core Arab economies. In so doing while putting a particular cross-cutting focus on entrepreneurship, innovation, and creative destruction, Chap. 3 attempts to answer the first research question (How does regulation between economic action and institutional context work in Arab economies, notably in relation to drivers of private-sector growth such as entrepreneurship?). Since the breakup of the old Arab social contract is understood as a regulation crisis, Chap. 3 goes on to sketch the transition towards a new regulation regime and discusses how such a future regulation regime in core Arab economies may look like under the assumptions that such a regime be more efficient and sustainable in the long run. The chapter proposes a policy package to address the present structural economic problems in core Arab economies in a comprehensive, socio-economic, and institution-sensitive perspective, thus trying to answer the second, third, and fourth research questions (Which new modes of regulation could help Arab countries in addressing structural economic and social difficulties by facilitating private-sector-led growth? What role can entrepreneurship play in such new modes of regulation? Which implications does the current transitional context in Arab economies hold for regulation, including opportunities of the current regulation crisis?). Chapter 4 applies and refines the regulation framework proposed to the cases of Tunisia and Jordan. Finally, Chap. 5 draws conclusions for policy, based on the comprehensive and institution-sensitive policy mix elaborated in Chap. 3 and on the insights from the Tunisian and Jordan case studies, thus suggesting answers to the fifth research question (What types of policies are needed to put such new modes of regulation in place?).

References

Acemoğlu D, Robinson JA (2012) Why nations fail: the origins of power, prosperity and poverty. Profile Books, London

Amin M, Assaad R, Al-Baharna N, Derviş K, Desai RM, Dhillon NS, Galal A, Ghanem H, Graham C, Kaufmann D, Kharas H, Page J, Salehi-Isfahani D, Sierra K, Yousef TM (2012) After the spring: economic transformations in the Arab world. Oxford University Press, Oxford

Ben Shitrit L (2014) Israel. In: Lust E (ed) The Middle East, 13th edn. CQ Press, Thousand Oaks, pp 537–563

Benner M (2017) From clusters to smart specialization: tourism in institution-sensitive regional development policies. Economies 5(3):26. http://www.mdpi.com/2227-7099/5/3/26/pdf. (29.07.2017)

Bouroujerdi M (2014) Iran. In: Lust E (ed) The Middle East, 13th edn. CQ Press, Thousand Oaks, pp 478–506

Cammett M (2014) The political economy of development in the Middle East. In: Lust E (ed) The Middle East, 13th edn. CQ Press, Thousand Oaks, pp 161–208

Dhillon N, Yousef T (2009) Introduction. In: Dhillon N, Yousef T (eds) Generation in waiting: the unfulfilled promise of young people in the Middle East. Brookings, Washington, DC, pp 1–10

Eder M (2014) Turkey. In: Lust E (ed) The Middle East, 13th edn. CQ Press, Thousand Oaks, pp 830–865

Glückler J, Bathelt H (2017) Institutional context and innovation. In: Bathelt H, Cohendet P, Henn S, Simon L (eds) The Elgar companion to innovation and knowledge creation. Elgar, Cheltenham, Northampton, pp 121–137

Glückler J, Lenz R (2016) How institutions moderate the effectiveness of regional policy: a framework and research agenda. Invest Reg – J Reg Res 36(2016):255–277

Gobat J, Kostial K (2016) Syria's conflict economy. IMF Working Paper No. 16/123. http://www.imf.org/external/pubs/ft/wp/2016/wp16123.pdf. (30.06.2016)

Hertog S (2016) Is there an Arab variety of capitalism? Economic Research Forum Working Paper No. 1068. https://erf.org.eg/wp-content/uploads/2016/12/1068.pdf. (02.03.2017)

Lynch M (2014) Regional international relations. In: Lust E (ed) The Middle East, 13th edn. CQ Press, Thousand Oaks, pp 367–395

Moghadam VN, Decker T (2014) Social change in the Middle East. In: Lust E (ed) The Middle East, 13th edn. CQ Press, Thousand Oaks, pp 73–106

Chapter 2
Economic Challenges in Arab Economies

Abstract By providing an extensive literature review, the chapter summarizes the major structural challenges core Arab economies are confronted with. In particular, these structural challenges include high and persistent unemployment among youth and women in the context of young and growing populations and insufficient growth to absorb young generations in the labor markets.

Keywords Arab economies · Youth unemployment · Youth bulge · Structural adjustment

The major economic challenge core Arab economies face can be summarized by saying that "the Arab economies are squeezed by the demographically preordained imperative to create jobs on the one hand and the increasingly competitive nature of the global economy on the other," while "some of the channels of development such as manufacturing exports pursued by recent success stories in Asia will be hard to replicate" (Noland and Pack 2007: 11). Simply imitating other countries' previous industrialization successes is thus not an option, both for path dependence and the particular temporal and socio-institutional context found in Arab economies.

Still, comparisons are being made and in some limited aspects probably do merit attention. For instance, the World Bank (2009) states a certain degree of similarity between Arab economies today and Eastern European economies prior to their transformation or with East Asian newly industrializing economies (NIEs), notably in terms of East Asian NIEs' initially weak accountability in governance (World Bank 2009: 172). Yet, the industrialization and development trajectories between Arab economies and Eastern European or East Asian comparators have played out very differently.

It is important to note that Arab economies' long-term economic performance in past decades was not particularly weak (Noland and Pack 2007: 38), and on broader human development indicators, most core Arab economies were fairly successful after independence (Richards and Waterbury 2008). When looking at human development indicators such as life expectancy, infant mortality, or maternal mortality, Arab economies achieved considerable progress since the middle of the twentieth century, much more so than on income. Furthermore, income inequality is not

© Springer Nature Switzerland AG 2020
M. Benner, *A New Arab Social Contract?*, Economic Geography,
https://doi.org/10.1007/978-3-030-19270-9_2

particularly high in contrast to other developing countries. Absolute poverty is low compared to other developing countries, and Arab economies attained strong progress on educational attainment and in narrowing the educational gender gap (Noland and Pack 2007: 60–70, 85).

While Arab oil-producing countries exhibited weak performance in terms of economic growth performance in the 1990s, more diversified economies such as Tunisia, Morocco, or Egypt performed better than Latin America and sub-Saharan Africa but still weaker than comparators in East and South Asia (Noland and Pack 2007: 47–48). Still, core Arab economies have been plagued by severe structural difficulties for a long time. While macroeconomic framework conditions are not so much of a problem in core Arab economies, microeconomic and mesoeconomic conditions are (Noland and Pack 2007: 301). This chapter gives an overview of these structural economic problems apparent in most core Arab economies and relates them to political events, notably to the revolutions and evolutions commonly termed "Arab Spring."

2.1 Structural Growth Problems in Arab Economies

The most visible structural problem in core Arab economies is high unemployment. While caution is advised when looking at unemployment rates in core Arab economies, it is clear that high unemployment, particularly among youth and women, is a long-term and persisting problem in the Arab world (e.g., Amin et al. 2012: 56–57; Moghadam and Decker 2014: 88–89; Richards and Waterbury 2008: 134–138; World Bank 2014b, c, d).

High unemployment especially among vulnerable groups is a symptom of underlying structural difficulties in an economy and society. In core Arab economies, the prevalence of high unemployment cannot be understood without looking at the demographic situation on the one hand and long-term problems of economic growth and structural change on the other hand.

In terms of demographics, while fertility rates in core Arab economies are falling and, thus, demographic change is underway, populations are young and set to grow further for some time, adding pressure on labor markets and giving rise to what is often called the "youth bulge" (Moghadam and Decker 2014: 73). An estimation puts the number of people entering the labor force in Arab economies over the coming two decades at 150 million people (Amin et al. 2012: 58). Demography is thus one of the fundamental determinants of (youth) unemployment in core Arab economies (Amin et al. 2012: 58–59; Noland and Pack 2007; Richards and Waterbury 2008: 71–89).

The other fundamental determinant is the performance of core Arab economies in terms of economic growth and productivity-enhancing structural change. In general, per capita GDP growth in Arab countries in recent decades was not particularly low compared to other developing countries (Noland and Pack 2007: 38; World Bank 2009: 46). However, the basic feature shared more or less by most core Arab economies is their weak rates of industrialization and their lack of dynamism. While

50% of aggregate real GDP growth per capita in core Arab economies over the last two decades were driven by demographic change, productivity growth was significantly lower than in other developing world regions (World Bank 2014a: 9). The trajectories of core Arab economies sharply differ from the development paths of other middle-income countries, with a relatively low share of manufacturing in the economies' total output when compared to Brazil, Chile, China, Malaysia, Mauritius, Thailand, and Turkey at times of comparable development. Even Tunisia, though having become the leading industrializer among resource-poor Arab economies (Cammett 2014: 164), is below the benchmark. The manufacturing sector has stagnated in Arab economies since 1990s or is even declining, although Tunisia has a slightly better performance and has engaged in the task-based global division of labor, thus taking part in global value chains or global production networks. The flip side of the coin is that the agriculture and services sectors are more dominant in core Arab economies than in the benchmarking countries, implying a slow pace of structural change (Amin et al. 2012: 22, 112–117).

Rivlin (2009: 24) confirms that "to a considerable extent the Arab world has failed to industrialize" as is demonstrated by low levels of manufacturing exports and employment. Manufacturing value added per capita in many Arab countries was even lower than the developing-country average with Tunisia as the only non-oil country exceptionally above developing-country average both on manufacturing value added per capita in the period between 1995 and 2005 and on its share of manufacturing in the economy. Still, even there the share of manufacturing value added in GDP declined. Rivlin (2009: 23–26) relates the weak progress of industrialization in the Arab world to underlying causes such as growing populations, inflated public sectors, restrictions to international trade, the absence of reform policies, low productivity, deficiencies in the education systems, the emigration of educated labor, or insufficient technology imports and investments (Rivlin 2009: 23–26).

According to the World Bank (2013: 90–92), in the wake of falling oil prices in the 1980s, structural reform, liberalization, and opening up to world markets notably in Morocco, Tunisia, and Jordan led to higher growth particularly in the early 2000s; industrialization and economic diversification are still incomplete. Lacking dynamism of productivity-enhancing structural change is evident in low rates of enterprise creation (e.g., in Egypt), low rates of transition of entrepreneurs towards higher value-added activities, and slow industrial diversification (Amin et al. 2012: 8).

Arab economies exhibit low rates of firm entry, with non-GCC MENA economies scoring particularly low in international comparison. Morocco and Tunisia have the highest entry densities among non-GCC MENA countries. Firm exit rates are low in non-GCC MENA countries (World Bank 2014a: 26–27).

This evidence implies that the Schumpeterian process of entrepreneurial creative destruction is not working properly and not fast enough in Arab economies compared to other developing world regions, as is evident in the weak export competitiveness of non-oil exports from Arab economies. A burdensome business environment and constraints to SMEs in Arab economies, insolvency laws that in some instances even criminalize bankruptcy, and the social stigma of failure represent considerable disincentives to entrepreneurship and innovation in Arab economies (Amin et al. 2012: 107–112).

Arab countries are not well integrated in the world economy. Their economies perform weakly in manufacturing exports compared to all other developing regions. Most Arab economies are not well integrated into global value chains, although Tunisia is an exception which reflects the country's relative progress in industrial diversification (Noland and Pack 2007: 100–108).

In the same vein, the World Bank (2009: 59–61) states a persistently weak export performance of Arab economies in comparison to other emerging economies despite some limited success in the 1990s. Arab economies' exports are marked by a low-technology content, although Tunisia and Jordan are relatively more successful in exporting medium- or high-technology products with a share of about 25% of total exports compared with just over 6% for Egypt in 2004 (World Bank 2009: 60).

On the macro-level, the World Bank (2009: 79–84) links the lacking industrial and entrepreneurial dynamism found in core Arab economies to deficiencies in an uneven business environment marked by barriers to entry and exit to markets and higher ages of firms and businesspeople (World Bank 2009: 79). Some private-sector growth apparently occurred after reforms took place, particularly in more ambitious reform economies such as Tunisia, Morocco, Jordan, or Egypt (World Bank 2009: 84). Yet and despite partial successes, macro-level reforms in Arab economies produced a weaker private-sector response than in countries such as China, Malaysia, Thailand, Turkey, or Poland (World Bank 2009: 85). One of the reasons behind this lackluster private-sector reaction may be deficiencies in reform implementation as "a large part of the problem seems to lie not with policies as they appear on paper, but with the unequal, discretionary, and preferential implementation of policies" (World Bank 2009: 89).

Apart from macro-level conditions, fundamental conditions in core Arab economies limit opportunities for productivity-enhancing growth. For instance, youth unemployment is not only a consequence of weak industrial development but at the same time one of its causes, suggesting a vicious circle of cumulative causation. Not seizing the production potential inherent to a young labor force limits the possibilities for industrial development and entrepreneurship. Similarly, low labor-force participation of women in core Arab economies is a constraint to industrialization and entrepreneurship. As the World Bank (2013: 63) confirms, "at 25.4 percent in the Middle East and 28.1 percent in North Africa, women's labor force participation (LFP) is lower than the 2008 world average of 51.6 percent." Amin et al. (2012: 40) equally highlight that female LFP in Arab economies is about half the global average and even among female university graduates only half enter the labor market.

On the one hand, not using significant parts of the labor force limits possibilities for skills formation, while on the other hand, it constrains the perspectives for promoting both entrepreneurship and employability. This is because professional experience gained through labor market participation and entrepreneurship are related. For instance, in a survey on "missing entrepreneurs" from economically underrepresented and disadvantaged groups carried out by the OECD and the European Commission, "a substantial proportion of the population reports lacking entrepreneurship skills, particularly amongst women and youth. In the case of youth, this is related to inexperience in the labour market and self-employment"

(OECD and European Commission 2015: 86). In a context marked by low female LFP, the latter argument applies analogously to women (OECD and IDRC 2013: 55–57; OECD 2014: 58–72).

All of these structural deficiencies in core Arab economies suggest a need for deep reform on all levels of the economy but equally, and more fundamentally, in regulation between economy and society. As one would expect, visible and widespread symptoms of the underlying structural problems in core Arab economies such as high (youth) unemployment have led to public discontent. In the regulation perspective taken here, core Arab economies are struggling with a severe regulation crisis and have been so for at least two decades. This regulation crisis can be understood as the collapse of what literature commonly calls the "Arab social contract" (e.g., Amin et al. 2012: 32), a particular arrangement of regulation between economy and society and core Arab economies which has come under intense pressure due to its inherent problems in terms of economic efficiency and sustainability. The next section sheds light on the fundamental characteristics of this Arab social contract, its inherent inefficiencies and lack of sustainability, and its gradual demise and eventual collapse most evident during the revolutions and evolutions since 2010/2011.

2.2   The Collapse of the Arab Social Contract

The revolutions notably in Tunisia and Egypt as well as evolutionary political changes after waves of demonstrations in countries such as Morocco and Jordan can be understood as the political climax of a decade-long process that Amin et al. (2012: 32) call "the unraveling Arab social contract." In the literature on Middle Eastern political economy, the term "Arab social contract" is used to describe a particular configuration of political and economic arrangements dominant in core Arab countries after their independence. Basically, the Arab social contract is a historically specific form of regulation between the social, political, and economic spheres of society.

The unraveling of this regulation regime was a gradual process marked by the fundamental inefficiencies and lack of sustainability of the basic tenets of the Arab social contract. As will be described in the following sections, visible symptoms of these structural deficiencies included high (youth) unemployment, underperforming public services and concomitant public discontent, as well as political interventions including *infitah* policies and structural adjustment supported by the International Monetary Fund (IMF) and the World Bank (Richards and Waterbury 2008). In a sense, public discontent accompanied *infitah* policies and structural adjustment over and over again, resulting at times in riots. However, until 2010/2011 public discontent did not reach the point of seriously threatening regime survival, probably in part because of accommodating regime reactions (Richards and Waterbury 2008: 218–226).

It is important to note the long-term nature of the regulation crisis that meant the breakup of the Arab social contract. Without taking a long-term perspective, it would be difficult to understand the seemingly sudden emergence of revolutionary or evolutionary demands for political and economic change just at the end of the first decade of the twenty-first century. Indeed, when looking at macro-level indicators, the years before 2011 could be seen as comparatively good years for core Arab economies. The average rate of real GDP growth in MENA countries stood at 3.6% annually in the late 1990s and accelerated to 5.8% annually in the period from 2004 to 2008 (World Bank 2009: 46). Amin et al. (2012: 51) call this phenomenon the "unhappy growth" paradox. Economic indicators did improve prior to 2011, but strong popular dissatisfaction with public services and pessimism towards the future characterized the social climate before the "Arab Spring" (Amin et al. 2012: 50–53). This mounting discontent can be understood as the result of years or decades of persisting structural deficiencies in the regulation system, leading "to a perception that while past performance was praiseworthy, future opportunities may be dwindling" (Noland and Pack 2007: 83).

Rather than absolute figures, the relative economic position of core Arab economies in an uneven international context can better explain the reasons for the negative perception of economic opportunities. While per capita GDP growth in core Arab countries in recent decades was not particularly low compared to other developing countries, but it was indeed disappointing when compared to Southern Europe (Noland and Pack 2007: 38). While the spatial proximity among countries on the Northern, Southern, and Eastern shore of the Mediterranean lends itself to such a comparison, it is not entirely fair because Southern European countries such as Portugal, Spain, Greece, Malta, or Cyprus benefited from EU membership and thus had opportunities for economic development not available to their southern neighbors. Equally, comparisons to Turkey tend to ignore Turkey's strong economic integration with the EU due to the customs union and years of intense institutional alignment in the wake of Turkey's EU accession process. Still, it seems that Southern European countries including Turkey are perceived as the benchmark by the populations in core Arab economies. While one might argue that Southern EU member states or, for that matter, East Asian NIEs with their exceptionally quick industrialization in a peculiar historical context that does not exist anymore today are not the right benchmarks to evaluate the economic performance of core Arab economies, public discontent with the pace and results of economic development of core Arab economies is a fact that cannot be ignored. Noland and Pack (2007: 43) argue that the awareness of international gaps in living standards and consumption among populations in core Arab economies may have increased their dissatisfaction. Yet, popular discontent may have deeper social causes such as urbanization and the uprooting of traditional social networks and maybe cannot be countered with higher economic growth alone (Noland and Pack 2007: 59–60). These arguments call for a more comprehensive regulation perspective on the breakup of the Arab social contract instead of a narrow policy focus on simply raising rates of GDP growth.

In any case, the urgency for policymakers in core Arab economies to facilitate the transition towards a new regulation regime capable of overcoming or at least easing the structural difficulties prevalent under the old Arab social contract is clear.

2.2.1   The Arab Social Contract and the Authoritarian Bargain

After gaining their independence, core Arab states followed a state-driven growth model during the 1950s and 1960s. They followed the lead of Atatürk's Turkey and built large bureaucracies, created state-owned enterprises (SOEs), and nationalized privately owned industrial ventures, with Jordan being a partial exception because of the comparatively liberal free-market approach it followed (Richards and Waterbury 2008: 179–210; Moore 2010: 73–77). Public-sector employment was a major part of this postindependence growth model and of the social contract implied which was meant to secure loyalty to regimes. Apart from providing public employment, regimes extended patronage to buy political support, for example, by granting cronies minority stakes in SOEs or import/export licenses or through public land transfers, through politically biased credit allocation, or by allowing for the creation of private monopolies in a system of crony capitalism (Moore 2010: 76). Thus, crony capitalism and mismanaged state-owned enterprises and related inefficiencies became a major element of the prevailing postindependence growth model (Richards and Waterbury 2008: 215–218). Despite these inefficiencies, core Arab economies experienced strong growth from the 1960s to the 1980s, fueled by oil revenues and remittances as well as government-led growth stimulation (World Bank 2013: 90–92).

At the heart of the state-led growth model of the 1950s and 1960s was an "authoritarian bargain," defined as "an implicit arrangement between ruling elites and citizens whereby citizens relinquish political influence in exchange for public spending" (Desai et al. 2009: 93). As Desai et al. (2009) demonstrate, such an authoritarian bargain is not rare among developing nations and tends to exhibit a certain degree of resilience as long as regimes meet citizens' expectations in terms of economic development and public service delivery. If and when economic performance does not satisfy citizens' expectations, in contrast, regimes may be subject to increased pressure from citizens, the opposition, and their own supporters (Desai et al. 2009: 96). Evidence suggests that "in contrast to democratic states, welfare spending and political liberalization are negatively related in authoritarian states" (Desai et al. 2009: 118). In Arab economies with their young populations and demographic trends exerting pressure on public services, Desai et al. (2009: 118) predicted that the authoritarian bargain might come under pressure, which is what eventually happened in 2010/2011.

In the postindependence decades, the authoritarian bargain was still intact and stable, underpinned by cooptation mechanisms such as the large-scale provision of public employment. Either implicitly or explicitly, regimes in core Arab economies promised young high school or university graduates employment in the government or in SOEs. For example, explicit public-sector employment guarantees for graduates of secondary schools and universities were put in place in Egypt and in Morocco, resulting in a share of public-sector employment in total formal employment in Arab countries about twice the worldwide average (Noland and Pack 2007: 32). Another result is the emergence of expectations towards public-sector employment among subsequent generations of students and their families. Public employment has become the aspiration of choice among parents for their children and among students for themselves. The high share of government employment led to a heavy fiscal burden on public wage bills, significant overstaffing and redundancies in the public sector. A dominant public sector came to distort labor market signals and set incentives not linked to productivity, and it created inflated expectations and segmented labor markets. Core Arab economies tend to exhibit high rates of public-sector employment to GDP compared to other developing countries and higher wages in the public sector than in the private sector. Public-sector employment can be understood as a kind of welfare system that may have driven faster progress on human development indicators than on economic growth and income. Thus, while the state-driven nature of economic policy under the authoritarian bargain may have facilitated comparatively rapid human development, it was not conducive to efficient and productive economic growth (Amin et al. 2012: 61–62, 92–93; Dhillon and Yousef 2009: 2; Moghadam and Decker 2014: 77; Noland and Pack 2007: 71; World Bank 2013: 181).

One of the reasons for the lacking economic efficiency of the authoritarian bargain is that authoritarian regimes tend to lack the credibility needed to induce private-sector responses to incentives set by governments (Noland and Pack 2007). Indeed, the authoritarian bargain in Arab economies included rent distribution in favor of regime cronies, typically resulting in a lack of economic openness and liberalization (Noland and Pack 2007: 7–9).

Cammett (2014) confirms the basic tenets of the authoritarian bargain in Arab economies and emphasizes high levels of government spending, although the share of government spending in GDP started to decline during the late 1980s and early 1990s. High expectations of citizens' vis-à-vis governments persist even after revolutions in core Arab economies, suggesting the stickiness of the institutional foundations of the authoritarian bargain. Yet, some variations are observable. While the oil-funded authoritarian bargain appears to be particularly entrenched in Gulf monarchies, conservative resource-poor monarchies such as Morocco and Jordan have traditionally allowed for a significant role of traditional private-sector business elites. Among Arab states, Lebanon is the unique example of a long-term laissez-faire orientation and concomitant importance of its merchant class, owing presumably to the sectarian nature and weakness of the Lebanese state (Salem 2014: 612). Single-party republics were marked by an organization of labor and business in peak organizations or confederations connected to or coopted by authoritarian regimes and by repression of independent entrepreneurialism for more or less extended periods during the second half of the twentieth century. In sum, Cammett (2014: 203) characterizes the kind of authoritarian bargain commonly found in core Arab economies in the second half of the twentieth century as an "interventionist-redistributive development model" and states a lock-in into inefficient development paths due to a cemented social contract, yet to a varying degree in different countries (Cammett 2014: 166–204).

However, the state-driven model core Arab economies followed in the postindependence decades cannot be seen as an expression of any particular political ideology. Indeed, the provision of public-sector employment and the state-driven growth model was found both in countries that followed Arab socialism and in conservative regimes alike during the 1950s and 1960s (Rivlin 2009: 20).

It is important to understand the formation of the authoritarian bargain after Arab countries' independence in its historical context: *dirigiste* policies and rent distribution including the creation of coalitions through means such as public-sector employment guarantees and restrictive labor laws for formally employed workers can be seen as an attempt towards nation building in the context of initially weak Arab states within new borders artificially drawn by the former colonial powers Britain and France, notably under the Sykes-Picot agreement of 1916 (Noland and Pack 2007: 192).

Jamal and Khatib (2014) highlight the associational nature of the authoritarian bargain, evident in the role of associations, trade unions, and parties. This prominent role of state corporatism under the authoritarian bargain in core Arab economies relates to the role of *wasta* (personal connections) within larger organizational structures such as political parties. Jamal and Khatib argue that the main interest of voters in political participation within the Arab authoritarian bargain was not so much the desire to contribute to political decision-making processes in favor of the common good than a desire to benefit from patronage (Jamal and Khatib 2014: 253–257).[1]

Part of the patronage extended by authoritarian regimes in core Arab economies to citizens was the setup and maintenance of a system of generous fuel and foodstuff subsidies (Amin et al. 2012: 86–89). The volume of these subsidies in some cases reached a dimension of roughly 10% of GDP and thus implies another large burden on public budgets, in addition to inflated public sectors (World Bank 2015: 12). In addition to the strain they put on government budgets, these supply-side subsidies set questionable incentives, for instance, against more energy-efficient fuel use, and tend to benefit wealthier strata of society more than poorer ones (World Bank 2014c). For example, the World Bank (2014a: 44) highlights that, in Egypt, subsidies for energy set incentives for more capital-intensive and less labor-intensive industrial production. Furthermore, supply-side subsidies lead to overconsumption with detrimental effects on health and the environment, discourage measures to invest in energy efficiency, and tend to benefit the wealthier strata of society disproportionately (Amin et al. 2012: 86–89).

Rent distribution is an important element of the authoritarian bargain found particularly in the oil-producing economies of the GCC as well as in Libya and Algeria.

---

[1] However, in established democracies, too, the motivation of voters to participate in elections and to vote for a particular candidate or party may be driven by an interest to benefit from a candidate of incumbent's connections and his or her capability to advance the vested interests of voters or narrow constituencies. Public-choice theory with its perception of political campaigning and voting as a mutual bargain makes this presumption plausible.

In GCC countries, oil-funded welfare programs as well as government employment are at the core of the authoritarian bargain (Cammett 2014: 192). Still, non-oil-producing Arab countries for a long time benefitted from oil rents through remittances, tourism, and FDI from oil-producing countries (Noland and Pack 2007: 34).

Rentier state theory as originally proposed by Mahdavy (1970) offers an explanation for the authoritarian bargain found in Arab economies. According to rentier state theory, "since the state receives this external income and distributes it to society, it is relieved of having to impose taxation, which in turn means that it does not have to offer concessions to society" (Gray 2011: 1). The consequence is that authoritarian regimes can use rents to co-opt citizen coalitions in exchange for political acquiescence since "the population in effect is 'bought off,' with democratic input sacrificed by society in exchange for a share of the rental wealth" (Gray 2011: 6). On the other side, opposition to the bargain is met with repression (Gray 2011: 6).

Rentierism and neopatrimonialism (Altenburg 2011) often go hand in hand. Neopatrimonialism is found "when the ruling elites employ patronage and political clientelism systematically to create and preserve their legitimacy" (Altenburg 2011: 1). For instance, in pre-revolutionary Tunisia during the Ben Ali era, the sheer size of economic activities controlled by regime cronies is evident from the fact that the total value of assets confiscated from the Ben Ali clan after the revolution was equivalent to roughly a quarter of Tunisia's 2011 GDP (World Bank 2014a: 84). While these enterprises accounted for roughly 3% of the output of the private sector and 1% of the total of wage jobs, they accounted for 21% of net profits of the private sector (World Bank 2014a: 85). Not surprisingly, the control of industries by members of the Ben Ali clan coincided with entry barriers in these industries (World Bank 2014a: 88). Due to the economic dominance of politically connected firms in Benalist Tunisia, the World Bank (2014a: 90) suggests "that at least in part the distortions to firm dynamics and competition in Tunisia (…) originate from legislative barriers to entry that benefitted a few connected firms."

Marked by its inherent authoritarian bargain, rent distribution, and crony capitalism, the Arab social contract suffered from a number of inefficiencies, causing or exacerbating structural economic difficulties. The next section presents aspects of these economic inefficiencies related to the core features of the old Arab social contract in more detail.

2.2.2 Economic Inefficiencies of the State-Driven Growth of the Arab Social Contract

The World Bank (2015) argues that the Arab social contract marked by inflated public sectors, aspirations and expectations towards government employment, rigid labor market legislation, rent distribution, fuel and food subsidies, corporatism, and limited political voice and accountability under the authoritarian bargain for some time delivered comparatively high GDP growth rates and lower inequality than elsewhere, with other development indicators (e.g., school enrollment, infant mortality, poverty rates) improving considerably as well. However, due to its inherent inefficiencies, the Arab social contract became untenable for governments to fund in the late 2000s or probably much earlier as evidenced by the need for IMF-/World Bank-assisted structural adjustment programs in the 1980s. Public-sector employment consequently had to slow down and the share of the public sector decreased, while the private sector did not grow sufficiently to absorb the growing labor force. This dilemma led to high levels of youth unemployment even in comparison with other developing countries and to the growth of informal employment. At the same time, the quality and equity of education and health systems declined, leading populations to resort to private service providers. Infrastructure deteriorated, too, provoking a dramatic fall of popular satisfaction with public service delivery in years immediately prior to revolutions in Egypt and Tunisia (Amin et al. 2012). This sentiment was expressed during revolutions in 2010/2011 when people demanded "jobs, better public services, and dignity" (World Bank 2015: 16). These revolutions can be seen as the culmination of a long-term deterioration of the Arab social contract due to its unsustainability (World Bank 2015).

Rivlin (2009: 20–21) argues that since the 1980s, Arab countries have moved away from their previously dominant state-driven growth model and have embarked on privatization efforts, but the share of public-sector employment has not decreased. To take Egypt as an example, the share of public-sector employment even increased further in the 1990s. Still, structural crisis in the 1980s meant that "governments that previously guaranteed jobs for graduates could no longer afford to do so" (Rivlin 2009: 22). From the 1980s on, governments began to encourage the private sector by allowing for high market power and protecting private (and remaining public) firms from foreign competition. This is a major reason why despite liberalization in the late 1990s, barriers to trade remain high and Arab economies' integration in the global division of labor and in globalization's benefits is fairly weak. Governments continue to exhibit an attitude of distrust against the private sector, while governments' desire to control the course of economic development has led to intense regulation and constraints in the business environment. As a result, the private sector in core Arab economies tends to be weak, and productivity is low (Rivlin 2009: 20–29).

Yet, the dualism between a large public sectors and weak formal private sector in core Arab economies masks the phenomenon of a large informal sector. Arab economies tend to exhibit large informal sectors, while the formal private sector usually accounts for less than a fifth of employment (World Bank 2013: 1). On the other hand, the public sector dominates formal employment with shares between 60 and 80% of the total in core Arab economies such as Egypt and Jordan (World Bank 2013: 1). Richards and Waterbury (2008: 138–141) argue that large informal sectors lead to a strong dualism on labor markets because of the rigidity of formal labor laws governing the formal sector and the absence of any legal or social protection for workers in the informal sector. Highly regulated, rigid, and inflexible formal labor markets in Arab economies have given rise to a deep insider-outsider division marked by rigid wage and dismissal conditions for insiders and weak protection for outsiders (World Bank 2013: 23). Further, Richards and Waterbury (2008: 140) stress that while the informal sector does offer employment, informal employment is rather unattractive to young graduates and thus does not alter the fundamental structural problem of high youth unemployment among better-educated graduates.

The inefficiencies related to the Arab social contract go well beneath structural symptoms such as high youth unemployment and widespread informality. The World Bank (2013: 6–23) claims that in Arab economies, job placement typically does not follow meritocratic criteria but is often a result of exogenous circumstances such as family connections, location, or gender. Maybe as a consequence, unemployment and economic inactivity among women or the highly educated are more widespread in MENA economies than in comparable middle-income countries (World Bank 2013: 1).

The combination of large public sectors and weak formal private sectors creates an obvious problem of fiscal sustainability. The World Bank (2009: 179–180) reports that in the early 2000s, the public-sector wage bill relative to GDP in most Arab economies was significantly higher than in East Asian NIEs and other developing regions of the world. For instance, in 2001, public-sector wages accounted for 12.0% of GDP in Tunisia and for 19.0% in Jordan (World Bank 2009: 179–180). On average over a number of Arab economies including Egypt, Jordan, Morocco, and Tunisia, the average government wage was significantly above per capita GDP (World Bank 2009: 180).

Not surprisingly, in economies marked by a state-driven growth model and a channeling of resources such as human capital towards government and SOEs, formal private sectors tend to be weak and crowded out. At the heart of this polarization between inflated public sectors and weak formal private sectors seems to be an institutionally based attitude that favors government activity and intervention over private initiative and entrepreneurialism. For example, the World Bank (2009: 3, 6–25) sees an attitude of mutual mistrust between public and private sectors in core Arab economies, fueled by views of the private sector being dominated by rent-seeking behavior on the one hand and by views of the public sector being driven by politicians' interests and co-optation of politically connected firms on the other hand. While on paper there has been a trend towards market-oriented reforms and the private sector has responded to some degree, reform implementation and rule enforcement are uneven and often arbitrary, discriminating particularly against SMEs and new market entrants. The postindependence state-led growth model was characterized by government-led planning, protectionism and traditional industrial policies, nationalizations, redistribution through welfare programs, the widespread provision of public-sector jobs, and a restricted business environment. The state-led growth model was related to a dominance of the private sector by small firms often engaging in rent-seeking behavior. The discriminatory nature of policy implementation led to considerable efforts by enterprises to counter the resulting policy and implementation uncertainty, leading to inefficient outcomes. For instance, there is evidence that discriminatory policy implementation reduces innovation and employment growth in Jordan and Egypt (World Bank 2009: 3, 6–25; 2014a: 47–55).

Structural adjustment and liberalization since the 1980s included subsidy and spending cuts, trade liberalization, exchange rate reforms, export and investment promotion, and privatization of SOEs (World Bank 2009: 26). In consequence, the dominance of the public sector has decreased. Core Arab economies today feature private-sector shares in non-hydrocarbon GDP similar to those found in Eastern European and Asian economies. Yet, this trend did not change the underlying constraints to private-sector dynamism and growth: Often, entrepreneurs who eventually succeed are those politically well-connected and start their ventures in protected and highly regulated sectors before diversifying to other, more competitive sectors. The result is a fairly closed, well-established business elite active in a number of sectors such as real estate, retail, telecommunications, or pharmaceuticals dominated by a limited number of large family businesses (World Bank 2009: 26–29).

Not surprisingly, in such an environment enterprises tend to become accustomed to government support, resulting in a focus on calling for more support and protection by governments (World Bank 2009: 31). The inefficiencies of cronyism give rise to a widely uncompetitive and unproductive private sector more focused on political connectedness and rent-seeking than on enhancing its competitiveness and innovative capabilities (Moore 2010: 82–83). All of this leads to a private sector less dynamic than in other developing world regions because of weak dynamics of Schumpeterian creative destruction (World Bank 2013: 18). These low dynamics of creative destruction are underpinned by lower rates of firm entry, exit, and growth than in comparable countries elsewhere (World Bank 2013: 123; 2014a; 2015: 16–19).

Mirroring the weak dynamics of the private sector, the public sector in Arab economies tends to be inflated and inefficient. Noland and Pack (2007: 71–72) stress the lack of sustainability of this growth model because of the inefficiency of public sectors in core Arab economies and the crowding-out of more efficient private-sector uses of resources. This is because funds invested in the public sector could have been invested more efficiently and growth-inducing elsewhere and because taxes imposed to fund public investments create distortions (Noland and Pack 2007: 71–72).

Sustainability is another fundamental problem of the Arab social contract because of the demographic pressure as well as because of political constraints on raising taxes to fund public spending and limitations to borrowing on financial markets. Thus, the state-driven growth model probably reached the limit of what it could achieve. Consequently, the performance of core Arab economies in terms of income growth and employment in past decades was weak (Noland and Pack 2007: 72–78).

Given the limits of the previous state-driven growth model, it seems reasonable to assume that the private sector should take over the role of growth engine in Arab economies. However, weak dynamics of creative destruction severely limit this prospect, as do obstacles to independent entrepreneurship linked to the authoritarian bargain. In the cases of pre-revolutionary Tunisia and Egypt, Rijkers et al. (2014) suggest the prevalence of protective practices in favor of politically well-connected firms. For instance, "sometimes, connected firms received construction permits faster; and they were inspected by tax officials less frequently" (World Bank 2015: 19).

However, in spite of its inherent and long-standing structural inefficiencies, the Arab social contract is not a monolithic and static pattern. Its development has to be placed in its historical context which demonstrates that efforts at maintaining and reforming the Arab social contract have occurred throughout the past decades. Cammett (2014: 189–194) relates the buildup of large state sectors and SOEs during the 1960s and 1970s to the general growth model pursued at the time, import substitution industrialization (ISI). This policy trend left little space for the private sector but instead crowded out private-sector initiative. In Egypt, for example, during the ISI period, SOEs came to assume a dominant role in the economy both in terms of value added and employment. The subsequent *infitah* policy created an export-import class but still failed to stimulate broad-based private-sector initiative. Somewhat more liberal economic policies were pursued in the conservative monarchies of Morocco and Jordan which left more room for the private sector, but public sectors still dominated these economies. In other countries, more or less extended periods of Arab socialism resulted in tight regulation of the private sector. In the 1980s and 1990s, macroeconomic stabilization policies and IMF-/World Bank-assisted structural adjustment programs, accompanied by business elites advocating liberalization, created a somewhat different policy climate. Alignment with the EU in the process of negotiating and implementing bilateral free-trade agreements (FTAs) under the umbrella of association agreements (AA) obliged Morocco and Tunisia to open up and liberalize their economies (Benner 2015). Tunisia is commonly seen as the most successful case of structural adjustment because of comparatively early liberalization efforts, notably with its liberal offshore investment regime, its relatively high civil service capacity, and public health and education investments which helped create a comparatively competitive and qualified workforce. The process of structural adjustment and liberalization was aided by EU support, for instance, through the large-scale upgrading scheme *Programme de mise à niveau* (Cammett 2007: 1895; Ghali and Rezgui 2015; Hazboun 2008: 74–75). Morocco is perceived as another relatively successful case of structural adjustment, notably on the macro-level, but results have not been as strong as expected. While the Jordanian model heavily relied on foreign aid and remittances, IMF-recommended subsidy cuts led to unrest, as they did at times in Egypt, Morocco, and Tunisia. Structural adjustment in Egypt had a strong negative impact on the poor due to limited social safety nets, while export-led growth did not take off as hoped. Overall, the success of structural adjustment in core Arab economies during the 1980s and 1990s was mixed. Despite achievements on the macro-level, productivity declined, inequality increased, and cronies strongly benefited from liberalization, while the poor were disproportionately affected. The concomitant perception of inequality may have functioned as a major underlying factor for the revolutions that occurred in 2010 and 2011 (Cammett 2014: 189–200).

The history of the Arab social contract, reform efforts in the 1980s and 1990s, and mixed results of structural adjustment and liberalization suggest that the economic inefficiencies and lack of sustainability of the Arab social contract continue to be a pressing problem. Despite the partial achievements of structural adjustment and liberalization in stabilizing Arab economies on the macro-level, the fundamental inefficiencies of state-driven growth, a private sector lacking dynamism and productivity, and uneven patterns of access to economic opportunity remain at the root of much of the economic distress of core Arab economies.

2.2.3 Demographic Change: The "Youth Bulge" and Aging Societies

Core Arab economies' demographic situation is characterized by a "youth bulge" (Moghadam and Decker 2014: 73; World Bank 2013: 15). While fertility rates are declining in core Arab economies, 66% of population are under the age of 24 and two thirds under the age 30 (Amin et al. 2012: 54–65; Noland and Pack 2007: 2, 86–89; Rivlin 2009: 7–8, 10). According to Moghadam and Decker (2014: 86–87), 35% of the population in Arab states are under the age of 15, and some 60% are under the age of 25. Egypt, Algeria, and Morocco feature median ages of 20 to 21 (Noland and Pack 2007: 2–3). Population growth is continuing, meaning that "within just three generations (…) the region's population will have increased *twelvefold*" (Richards and Waterbury 2008: 45, italics in original). Population growth was particularly high in the 1970s and 1980s. Yet, the continued rapid pace of population growth should not conceal the fact that a profound demographic transition has set in. Since the 1970s, birth rates have fallen significantly, not least because of women's higher labor-force participation and higher marriage age, but so have mortality rates due to health improvements. Morocco was the first country to embark on the demographic transition, which may be due at least in part to the country's encouragement of women to join the labor force (Rivlin 2009: 9–12).

Moghadam and Decker (2014: 84–87) link the massive drop in the total fertility rate for the region to women's (and men's) rising levels of educational attainment and shifts in women's socio-economic status as well as changing urban-rural patterns of life. For instance, Tunisia now has one of the lowest total fertility rates in the MENA region (Moghadam and Decker 2014: 86). Indeed, Tunisia, Egypt, and Lebanon were the first countries where fertility rates began to fall in the early 1960s (Noland and Pack 2007: 87–88). This demographic phenomenon is related to broader socio-economic changes. Richards and Waterbury (2008: 78) confirm the link between female employment outside the home and lower fertility but at the same time stress that female labor-force participation in Arab economies is the lowest worldwide. Both demography and female labor-force participation are critically related to education since higher educational attainment seems to change women's preferences towards having fewer children and looking for outside employment (Richards and Waterbury 2008: 87). Even so, the demographic transition from a previously steady state of high birth rates and high death rates towards an eventual new steady state of low birth rates and low death rates takes time and causes population growth in the meantime (Noland and Pack 2007: 88).

Apart from a high but falling dependency ratio (Noland and Pack 2007: 88, 90), such an extremely young and growing population puts enormous pressure on labor markets: despite solid economic growth in the early 2000s that included high employment growth, the fast growth of the working-age population prevented significant decreases in unemployment (World Bank 2013: 15). Labor market demand did not keep pace with demographic trends in labor market supply because of weak industrialization. Since Arab countries are the world region with the highest population growth and will remain so at least until around 2050, the labor force is set to grow rapidly, a trend further intensified by higher labor-force participation rates of women (Rivlin 2009: 7–8, 10–13).

Paradoxically, while demographic change and the youth bulge put pressure on labor markets, they create a window of opportunity for a limited time until populations grow older. Noland and Pack (2007: 13–14) argue that falling fertility rates will eventually open up the chance of realizing a demographic dividend (Chaaban 2010: 14) for Arab societies as the youth bulge generation enters their most productive years. At the same time, young populations can lead to temporary and potentially beneficial fiscal implications due to lower needs of supporting those not economically active (Rivlin 2009: 34–36; World Bank 2013: 103). However, realizing this demographic dividend presupposes sufficient work opportunities (Rivlin 2009: 34–35). This is another reason to worry about persistently high rates of youth unemployment. The next sub-section therefore analyzes the phenomenon of persistently high youth unemployment in core Arab economies in more detail but addresses the other vulnerable group in core Arab economies, women.

2.2.4   Youth and Women's Unemployment in MENA Countries

Core Arab countries tend to exhibit high levels of aggregate unemployment. However, on aggregate, unemployment in Arab economies is consistent with their levels of development, industrialization, and structural change, and the Arab economies' sensitivity of employment on growth does not seem to significantly differ from other parts of the world (World Bank 2012a: 22–23).

Yet, as the calls for jobs during the revolutions of the "Arab Spring" and subsequent waves of demonstrations (e.g., in Kasserine, Tunisia in 2016, Tataouine, Tunisia in 2017, or Al-Hoceima, Morocco in 2017) imply, unemployment is a much more serious problem than aggregate rates suggest. This is first because figures or rates of registered unemployment may not capture the real size of the problem, not least because of not statistically registered underemployment or people not actively looking for work. A second reason is that unemployment rates vary spatially, implying more pressure in some regional labor markets than in others. Third, the lack of progress on combating unemployment may be another important driver of popular dissatisfaction. Amin et al. (2012: 55) stress that unemployment in Arab economies has remained high in spite of the fastest employment growth in the world which suggests a relationship with demographics because of the large numbers of young graduates entering the labor markets each year. A fourth reason for the severity of the unemployment problem in core Arab economies is that some societal groups suffer disproportionally from unemployment and its wider social and economic consequences than the mainstream. According to the World Bank (2012a), there are three characteristic features of Arab economies' labor markets: (i) low labor participation rates driven particularly by low female participation rates, (ii) high unemployment among women, and (iii) high youth unemployment. This means that women and youth tend to suffer relative economic marginalization vis-à-vis the mainstream of society. Further, the economic marginalization of women means that apart from social consequences, significant economic potential remains untapped since "MENA's female employment to population ratios are the lowest in the world by a wide margin, and MENA simultaneously records the lowest female labor force participation rates as well as the highest female unemployment rates" (World Bank 2012a: 21). Wider social implications of low female labor-force participation and high female unemployment include, inter alia, a link with long-term demographic trends because female unemployment is a major driver of declining fertility rates (Richards and Waterbury 2008: 78).

While the phenomenon of high youth unemployment is similar to female unemployment insofar as it signifies underutilized economic potential, its social consequences are even more immediate and urgent. High youth unemployment may provoke social unrest, and, more fundamentally, it has implications for economic and personal perspectives of a whole generation in societies which still tend to see males as breadwinners and link major transitions in life such as marriage and household setup with unemployment. This connection between employment and the marriage/household setup transition means that a significant part of the young generation and notably young men is stuck in an ongoing and open-ended situation of looking for work, living with their families, and not being able to marry or even enter a relationship perceived as legitimate in society and to found their own families (Amin et al. 2012: 57).

It would be misleading, though, to conclude that core Arab economies do not offer employment perspectives at all. Rather, part of the complex picture is that available jobs do not conform to the expectations of young people and their families. The formal private sector could provide quality jobs for young graduates but, as was argued in Sub-section 2.2.2, is too weak and lacks dynamism. The informal sector does offer employment opportunities, but these jobs usually lack quality and security (World Bank 2007, 2013, 2014c: 17–18). Indeed, the informal sector or low-paid parts of the formal private sector represent the last resort for youth whose families do not have the means to support long-term unemployment (World Bank 2007: 31), a phenomenon exacerbated by the absence of fully developed unemployment insurance schemes (World Bank 2011: 182). As educational levels rise, private-sector employment below the educational level achieved becomes unattractive, adding to young people's and their families' preference for waiting for public-sector jobs rather than accepting lower-level private-sector jobs. Paradoxically, youth unemployment in core Arab economies thus has become "something that only those with some means, however modest, can afford" (Richards and Waterbury

2008: 138). A remarkable example is Morocco where unemployment among the ungraduated in 2013 stood at only 4.5%, but the rates rise to 18.8% for higher-education graduates (Haut Commissariat du Plan 2015: 73). Family structures support youth waiting for public-sector jobs because families invest in their children's education in the rational hope that with some probability, their children will get public-sector jobs that will sustain the family, basically representing a kind of "income insurance" (Richards and Waterbury 2008: 121).

Amin et al. (2012: 59) confirm that expectations of young people in core Arab countries are still geared towards public-sector employment. Consequently, parents support their university-educated children during "waithood" (Dhillon and Salehi-Isfahani 2009: 248), the time they spend waiting for public-sector employment opportunities to open up (World Bank 2015: 19). Because waiting for public-sector employment opportunities requires resources, those young people who cannot wait enter informal employment (Richards and Waterbury 2008; World Bank 2015: 19). Another consequence is that given attractive conditions of public-sector employment, reservation wages of young people in core Arab economies tend to be high (World Bank 2013: 8, 77–80; 2015: 19). "Waithood" means that youth and particularly young women spend time "queuing" (World Bank 2013: 7) for public-sector jobs instead of taking private-sector or informal-sector jobs which could enhance their skills (World Bank 2007: 28). The particular emphasis on young women may be related to the fact that in core Arab economies, government employment is particularly attractive to many women because shorter working hours and better benefits such as maternity leave in comparison to private-sector employment allow for balancing job and family duties (Richards and Waterbury 2008: 138). In any case, youth unemployment is particularly high among highly skilled youth and notably among university graduates (Amin et al. 2012: 59–60; Richards and Waterbury 2008: 137).

Dhillon and Salehi-Isfahani (2009: 244) confirm that young (university) graduates in core Arab countries tend to prefer public-sector employment (World Bank 2013: 7) due, inter alia, to job security and benefits afforded by government employment conditions, setting incentives to pursue university education and be awarded a degree and leading to what Amin, Assaad et al. (2012: 62–70) term a "credentialist equilibrium" where educational needs are less geared towards skills formation and more to procuring the formal credentials to access public-sector employment by acquiring any higher-education degree. Richards and Waterbury (2008: 133) confirm the widespread focus of young people and their families on formal credentials instead of skills demanded by the labor markets and notably by private sectors in tertiary education. The situation seems to have worsened over time. In Tunisia, for example, "between 1975 and 2008 graduates of tertiary education have seen their share in the unemployed increasing dramatically to represent a quarter of the unemployed and at the same time their unemployment rate multiplied by ten" (Ghali and Rezgui 2015: 56). Part of the phenomenon of waithood is that tertiary-educated young unemployed may decline job offers due to their high reservation wages, as shown by a considerable prevalence of job refusals that increases with the level of educational attainment (World Bank 2013: 77–78).

While it is tempting to claim that unemployment because of queuing for public-sector jobs is a temporary phenomenon, youth unemployment is of particular concern because of the path dependence involved in young people's career paths (World Bank 2012a: 21). At the same time, youth unemployment is more volatile than aggregate unemployment (World Bank 2012a: 21). Therefore, youth are to benefit particularly from increased economic growth, but this would require changing attitudes since economic growth in the first place creates private-sector employment. In fact, expectations may slowly be shifting, as younger people apparently show somewhat more readiness to accept nonpublic sector jobs (World Bank 2013: 80–81).

The link between the youth bulge and high unemployment is obvious, especially as the MENA region's population is expected to double until 2025 (Moghadam and Decker 2014: 87). Noland and Pack (2007: 93) emphasize that young populations in core Arab economies provide economic opportunities because educational attainment is rising over generations but stress that realizing these opportunities requires absorbing them into the labor market. This assumption calls for growth driven primarily by the private sector. The challenge is that Arab economies have "to generate jobs of a certain type, which local residents would be willing to fill" (Noland and Pack 2007: 94), although public-sector jobs cannot be provided on a large scale anymore in a post-structural adjustment reality. Indeed, Moghadam and Decker (2014: 78) show how structural adjustment in the 1980s led to a deceleration in hiring for public-sector employment. However, the overall results of structural adjustment in employment generation were generally disappointing since unemployment rates did not decrease (Chaaban 2010: 25).

It is not surprising, then, that the underlying reasons for the 2010/2011 revolutions and protests were related to youth unemployment at least to a significant degree. While oversimplified explanations of complex sociopolitical phenomena such as revolutions have to be rejected, public discontent was arguably fueled by a complex mixture of exogenous and endogenous reasons with endogenous reasons including unemployment and the consequences of the youth bulge of the labor market (Moghadam and Decker 2014: 73–74).

Summing up, the labor markets of core Arab economies are marked by fast growth of the labor-force, low female labor-force participation, large shares of public employment, and high unemployment when compared to other developing world regions (Rivlin 2009: 15). If the major challenge facing Arab countries is to create sufficient employment to absorb coming generations into the labor market (Noland and Pack 2007: 1), persistent structural unemployment notably among well-educated youth and women in the current demographic context requires that labor-intensive economic growth be accelerated (Noland and Pack 2007: 300). Doing so is difficult, however, as long as deeper structural problems persist in core Arab economies. In particular, the skills mismatch between demand and supply on Arab labor markets is a major problem that will be analyzed in further detail in the next sub-section.

2.2.5 The Labor Market Mismatch: Education and Youth Unemployment

Paradoxically, high unemployment rates in core Arab economies do not necessarily mean an overall scarcity of employment opportunities. Rather, there is a mismatch between supply and demand on the labor market:

> Jobs are created in areas different than where the unemployed are; many new labor market entrants have a skills mismatch with what the market wants; and a large number of individuals are voluntarily unemployed, not willing to accept jobs at the prevailing wages. (Chaaban 2010: 7)

Supply and demand on the labor market do not match because demand for higher-education graduates comes mainly from the public sector whose growth is limited by budget constraints, while the private sector tends to demand lower-skilled workers. Since the public sector is the main potential employer for higher-education graduates, it shapes expectations and thus sets incentives for educational choices that do not correspond to private-sector needs (World Bank 2012b: 209).

Consequently, there is a skills mismatch on labor markets in core Arab economies as the education system has historically been built to respond to public-sector needs and is therefore not responsive to private-sector demands (Moghadam and Decker 2014: 94–96). Despite the fact that explicit or implicit public-sector job guarantees are not given anymore, the choice of educational tracks is still highly oriented towards public-sector needs because young people still look for the public sector for employment and many among them pursue degrees aimed towards a public-sector career. This skills mismatch notably among higher-education graduates helps explaining why unemployment among secondary school graduates is higher than among formally less educated youth (Rivlin 2009: 22; World Bank 2013: 25).

The skills mismatch in core Arab economies is related to a significant degree to the low quality of technical and vocational education and training (TVET) and the concomitant low reputation of TVET. In general, TVET systems in core Arab economies are not responsive to private-sector needs since there are no well-established links between education systems and the private sector (World Bank 2013: 23–25).

The skills mismatch results in a generally low educational quality in most Arab economies when compared internationally, although educational outcomes in Tunisia and Jordan as well as in Syria and Lebanon are more or less in line with other countries on similar income levels. Employers tend to regard lacking hard and soft skills of graduates as a constraint, but this is apparently more the case for TVET graduates than for university graduates (World Bank 2013: 168–175).

Amin et al. (2012: 62) explain the mismatch of qualifications supplied and demanded in core Arab economies as a "credentialist equilibrium" coupled with rising formal-education requirements by the public sector. Emphasis is put more on formal degrees as demanded for public-sector employment than on skills acquisition as demanded by the private sector. A lack of creativity-enhancing teaching and problem-solving methods in school education further add to the lack of soft skills (Amin et al. 2012: 62–70).

Hertog (2016: 16–31) confirms that firms in core Arab economies tend to be dissatisfied with the skills of graduates but at the same time do not offer in-house training. He concludes that a number of firms may "have made their peace with the low available skills levels, focusing on low-tech production and making no attempts to upgrade the skill levels of their workforce" (Hertog 2016: 16). Thus, the skills mismatch appears to be a steady state in the old Arab social contract. However, the skills mismatch is likely to cause fundamental structural deficiencies in terms of static and dynamic efficiency. The most visible outcome of these structural deficiencies is youth unemployment, but unseized opportunities for productivity growth may be another and equally worrying consequence of a lack of productivity-enhancing skills.

2.2.6   The Territorial Dimension: Spatial Economic Disparities

Spatially, the consequences of structural difficulties in core Arab economies are not spread evenly. Problems such as high youth unemployment tend to be significantly more severe in peripheral areas. Generally speaking, spatial inequalities are deep in core Arab economies and related in part to the relative neglect of lagging regions by central governments (Cammett 2014: 169–170). It is probably no coincidence that popular discontent was first and most vehemently voiced in peripheral regions in Tunisia in 2010 and 2011, eventually building up to the Tunisian revolution (Benner 2017; Cammett 2014: 170).

The World Bank (2011) gives an overview on spatial disparities across the Arab world as well as in Iran. An analysis of secondary statistical data reveals that in core Arab countries, economic and human development indicators differ sharply between urban and rural regions. For example, in Egypt, Jordan, Morocco, and Tunisia, poverty rates are significantly higher in rural regions than in urban ones (World Bank 2011: 297–335).

In Tunisia, unemployment rates in lagging regions in the Center-West and Southern regions are significantly higher than in the relatively more prosperous regions on the coast (Benner 2014, 2017; Medinilla Aldana and El Fassi 2016). For example, in 2010, the unemployment rate among youth aged 15 to 29 years stood at 30.0% in the Tunis governorate (and lower in most surrounding suburban governorates) and 12.7% in Monastir compared to 49.4% in Tataouine, 52.8% in Gafsa, 35.4% in Tozeur, and 41.2% in Jendouba. In 2012, 56% of higher-education graduates were unemployed in the governorate of Tataouine, 50.2% in Sidi Bouzid, 49.9% in Gafsa, and 48.9% in Kebili compared to 10.5% in Ariana in the Tunis agglomeration, 16.7% in the Tunis governorate, or 21.6% in Sfax and Sousse. Among graduates of secondary education, unemployment rates reached up to 60.1% in Tataouine compared to only 4.6% in Monastir (Observatoire National de l'Emploi et des Qualifications 2013: 32, 34).

In Morocco, interregional disparities in unemployment are less severe but still significant. For instance, in 2013, the former Marrakech-Tensift-Al Haouz region featured a total unemployment rate of 5.8%, while in the Oriental region, unemployment stood at 16.2%. Differentiating for educational levels yields an even more diverse picture. Unemployment among higher-education graduates reached up to 29.7% in the Guelmim-Es-Semara region in contrast to 11.8% in the Casablanca agglomeration (Haut Commissariat du Plan 2015: 72–73).

The two examples of Tunisia and Morocco demonstrate that the structural problems caused by the breakup of the old Arab social contract are to a large degree a spatial phenomenon. While comparatively prosperous urban regions such as Tunis or Casablanca do witness the same fundamental problems, the lack of acceptable economic perspectives notably for marginalized groups such as youth is significantly more severe in peripheral, rural regions.

The combination of high and persistent youth unemployment, particularly among highly educated youth, and severe spatial disparities perceived to be a consequence of long-term neglect by national-level policy can act as a strong catalyst of political change. Even after the Tunisian revolution which was sparked in the peripheral region of Sidi Bouzid in 2010, major waves of unrest have flared up in lagging regions in core Arab economies. For example, protests expressing persistent public discontent with the weak economic prospects of peripheral regions took place in Kasserine in 2016 and Tataouine in 2017 (both in Tunisia) and in Morocco with the *hirak* protest movement in the Rif region around the city of Al-Hoceima in 2017. It is plausible to assume that a perception of neglect by national policy among parts of the local population was a major driver of these protests.

It is thus evident that the major challenge for core Arab economies is not just to achieve higher economic growth and to do so in a way that creates attractive formal-sector employment particularly for well-educated youth and women but to do so in a spatially inclusive way. This triple challenge is highly complex and will most likely require a policy focus on enabling and facilitating productive private-sector-led growth and entrepreneurship, as well as targeted regional policies.

2.3 Private-Sector Growth and Entrepreneurship: Towards a Socio-economic Perspective of Economic Reform

The previous section has shed light on the state-centered nature of the Arab social contract. A weak private sector was the outcome of the prevailing regulation regime in most core Arab economies. This configuration had effects on the way entrepreneurial dynamism could or could not unfold. In a wider social and economic sense, an entrepreneurial spirit and entrepreneurial dynamics are critical for a vibrant private sector to develop. Thus, the degree of freedom for entrepreneurial initiative to unfold is key to facilitating the emergence of a stronger private sector. As the OECD and IDRC (2013: 26, 36) stress, high growth entrepreneurship is important not only because of its employment effects but also because of the competitive pressure it puts on established firms. In a state-centered regulation system such as the old Arab social contract, this Schumpeterian creative destruction process can be expected to be hampered, even if at times and as a response to economic reform entrepreneurial dynamics might flourish. The World Bank (2009: 3) argues that newcomers entering markets drive economic growth in transition countries and that the same holds true for MENA economies upon changes in the policy framework. Despite these windows of opportunity for entrepreneurial activity, the firm density in the MENA region is lower than in other world regions (World Bank 2009: 101). Low exit rates as well as comparatively old firms and managers add to a picture of weak entrepreneurial dynamism and creative destruction (World Bank 2009: 97–101).

Consistent with its state-centered nature, the old Arab social contract did not accord private-sector initiative and entrepreneurship a significant role as a driver of industrialization and economic development. The private sector and entrepreneurial initiative were more or less regarded with skepticism or even distrust. The remainder of this book departs from the hypothesis that the overreliance on government as a driver of economic development and the lack of private-sector development was the major flaw of the old Arab social contract and a critical factor contributing to the structural problems prevalent in core Arab economies such as high (youth) unemployment, weak industrialization, and serious spatial disparities.

When searching for solutions to the major structural deficiencies in core Arab economies, it is logical to accord private-sector dynamics and entrepreneurial dynamism a greater role. In so doing, instead of suggesting isolated policy interventions to promote entrepreneurial activity, considering the institutional environment of an economy is necessary (Dhillon and Salehi-Isfahani 2009: 246), basically calling for a broader perspective on socio-economic regulation and the role of creative destruction and entrepreneurship in a regulation system. Such a regulation perspective may suggest facilitating the emergence of an entrepreneurial ecosystem built on entrepreneurial attitudes (Amin et al. 2012: 135–136; Isenberg 2010). Regarding the Arab social contract, such a perspective includes on one of its major institutional features, the role of public-sector employment and related expectations and aspirations, and looks at ways to reorient both economic policy and institutions towards "getting young students to see entrepreneurship as a viable choice" (Amin et al. 2012: 135).

Yet, the Arab social contract should not be seen as a monolithic regulation regime that did not allow for attempts of readjustment over time. In view of its inherent lack of sustainability and efficiency, attempts to make readjust some its elements indeed occurred. For instance, *infitah* policies pursued by Egypt and Tunisia included some degree of liberalizing and opening up the economies to a more export-oriented growth model. IMF-/World Bank-sponsored structural adjustment programs typically assisted these reform efforts. However, not all reforms planned under structural adjustment programs were implemented, probably due to geostrategic interests by Western countries in maintaining regime stability in core Arab economies (Moore 2010: 83–84).

Rivlin (2009: 294–295) suggests that the rational choice of (pre-revolutionary) regimes in Arab countries not to undertake fundamental structural reforms can be described as a "low-level equilibrium" (Rivlin 2009: 294) which is inherent to the old Arab social contract. This low-level equilibrium is by definition static but can be shattered by fundamental movements calling for change including, for instance, political pressure due to high youth unemployment (Rivlin 2009: 295). This is precisely what happened during the 2010/2011 revolutions and protests which can be understood as a visible end to the old Arab social contract and the previously prevailing politico-economic "Arab equilibrium" (Rivlin 2009: 6). As the term equilibrium implies, a system that loses its equilibrium is in motion and can either stay so or gravitate towards a new equilibrium. How precisely such a new equilibrium of socio-economic regulation in core Arab economies could look like is not at all sure. The next chapter attempts to sketch how a new, higher-level, more efficient, and sustainable equilibrium could look like and how policy could contribute to the movement towards such a new equilibrium and draws on a wide perspective of socio-economic regulation.

References

Altenburg T (2011) Can industrial policy work under neopatrimonial rule? UNU-WIDER Working Paper No. 2011/41. UNU World Institute for Development Economics Research, Helsinki. http://www.wider.unu.edu/publications/workingpapers/2011/en_GB/wp2011-041/_files/86080661855076371/default/wp2011-041.pdf. (20.08.2012)

Amin M, Assaad R, Al-Baharna N, Derviş K, Desai RM, Dhillon NS, Galal A, Ghanem H, Graham C, Kaufmann D, Kharas H, Page J, Salehi-Isfahani D, Sierra K, Yousef TM (2012) After the spring: economic transformations in the Arab world. Oxford University Press, Oxford

Benner M (2014) Decentralised regional development policy in Tunisia: a new beginning after the "Arab Spring"? In: International Reports 06/2014, pp 31–50. http://www.kas.de/wf/doc/kas_38099-544-2-30.pdf?140618133239. (21.06.2014)

Benner M (2015) Europa und der Maghreb: Von der Nachbarschaft zur Wirtschaftspartnerschaft. (Europe and the Maghreb: from neighborhood to economic partnership). In: Neuss B, Nötzold A (eds) The Southern Mediterranean: challenges to the european foreign and security policy. Nomos, Baden-Baden, pp 57–82

Benner M (2017) The legacy of Sidi Bouzid: overcoming spatial inequalities in Tunisia. In: Krížek D, Záhorík J (eds) Beyond the 'Arab Spring' in North Africa: macro and micro perspectives. Lexington, Lanham, pp 47–65

Cammett M (2007) Business-government relations and industrial change: the politics of upgrading in Morocco and Tunisia. World Dev 35(11):1889–1903

Cammett M (2014) The political economy of development in the Middle East. In: Lust E (ed) The Middle East, 13th edn. CQ Press, Thousand Oaks, pp 161–208

Chaaban J (2010) Job creation in the Arab economies: navigating through difficult waters. Arab Human Development Report Research Paper. United Nations Development Programme Regional Bureau for Arab States, New York. http://www.arab-hdr.org/publications/other/ahdrps/paper03-en.pdf. (21.05.2014)

Desai RM, Olofsgård A, Yousef TM (2009) The logic of authoritarian bargains. Econ Polit 21(1):93–125

Dhillon N, Salehi-Isfahani D (2009) Looking ahead: making markets and institutions work for young people. In: Dhillon N, Yousef T (eds) Generation in waiting: the unfulfilled promise of young people in the Middle East. Brookings, Washington, DC, pp 240–251

Dhillon N, Yousef T (2009) Introduction. In: Dhillon N, Yousef T (eds) Generation in waiting: the unfulfilled promise of young people in the Middle East. Brookings, Washington, DC, pp 1–10

Ghali S, Rezgui S (2015) Structural transformation and industrial policy in selected Southern Mediterranean countries: Tunisia. In: Forum Euroméditerranéan des Instituts de Sciences Économiques (ed) Structural transformation and industrial policy: a comparative analysis of Egypt, Morocco, Tunisia and Turkey and case studies. European Investment Bank, Luxembourg, pp 39–68. http://www.femise.org/wp-content/uploads/2015/06/femip_study_structural_transformation_and_industrial_policy_en1.pdf. (10.06.2015)

Gray M (2011) A theory of "Late Rentierism" in the Arab States of the Gulf. CIRS Occasional Paper No. 7. Georgetown University School of Foreign Service in Qatar Center for International and Regional Studies, Doha. http://www12.georgetown.edu/sfs/qatar/cirs/MatthewGrayOccasionalPaper.pdf. (28.03.2014)

Haut Commissariat du Plan (ed) (2015) Activité, Emploi et Chômage 2013: Résultats détaillés, (Activity, employment, and unemployment 2013: detailed results). http://www.hcp.ma/file/169010/. (12.10.2017)

Hazboun W (2008) Beaches, ruins, resorts: the politics of tourism in the Arab world. University of Minnesota Press, Minneapolis

Hertog S (2016) Is there an Arab variety of capitalism? Economic Research Forum Working Paper No. 1068. https://erf.org.eg/wp-content/uploads/2016/12/1068.pdf. (02.03.2017)

Isenberg DJ (2010) How to start an entrepreneurial revolution. Harv Bus Rev 88(6):40–50

Jamal A, Khatib L (2014) Actors, public opinion, and participation. In: Lust E (ed) The Middle East, 13th edn. CQ Press, Thousand Oaks, pp 246–286

Mahdavy H (1970) The pattern and problems of economic development in rentier states: the case of Iran. In: Cook MA (ed) Studies in the economic history of the Middle East. Oxford University Press, Oxford, pp 428–467

Medinilla Aldana A, El Fassi S (2016) Tackling regional inequalities in Tunisia. ECDPM Briefing Note No. 84. http://ecdpm.org/wp-content/uploads/BN-84-Tackling-regional-inequalities-Tunisia-ECDPM-2016.pdf. (24.06.2016)

Moghadam VN, Decker T (2014) Social change in the Middle East. In: Lust E (ed) The Middle East, 13th edn. CQ Press, Thousand Oaks, pp 73–106

Moore PW (2010) Political economy. In: Angrist MP (ed) Politics and society in the contemporary Middle East. Lynne Rienner, Boulder, pp 69–90

Noland M, Pack H (2007) The Arab economies in a changing world. Peterson Institute for International Economics, Washington, DC

Observatoire National de l'Emploi et des Qualifications (ed) (2013) Rapport Annuel sur: Le Marché du Travail en Tunisie: Novembre 2013, (Annual report on the labor market in Tunisia: November 2013). http://www.emploi.gov.tn/uploads/tx_elypublication/Rapport_annuel_decembre_2013.pdf. (11.10.2017)

OECD (ed) (2014) Women in business 2014: accelerating entrepreneurship in the Middle East and North Africa region. Organisation for Economic Co-operation and Development, Paris

OECD, European Commission (2015) The Missing Entrepreneurs 2015: policies for self-employment and entrepreneurship. Organisation for Economic Co-operation and Development, Paris

OECD, IDRC (2013) New entrepreneurs and high performance enterprises in the Middle East and North Africa. Organisation for Economic Cooperation and Development, Paris

Richards A, Waterbury J (2008) A political economy of the Middle East, 3rd edn. Westview Press, Boulder

Rijkers B, Freund C, Nucifora A (2014) All in the family: state capture in Tunisia. Policy Research Working Paper No. 6810. The World Bank, Washington, DC. http://www-wds.worldbank.org/external/default/WDSContentServer/IW3P/IB/2014/03/25/000158349_20140325092905/Rendered/PDF/WPS6810.pdf. (28.03.2014)

Rivlin P (2009) Arab economies in the twenty-first century. Cambridge University Press, New York

Salem P (2014) Lebanon. In: Lust E (ed) The Middle East, 13th edn. CQ Press, Thousand Oaks, pp 609–630

World Bank (ed) (2007) Youth – an undervalued asset: towards a new agenda in the Middle East and North Africa: progress, challenges and way forward. The World Bank, Washington, DC. https://openknowledge.worldbank.org/bitstream/handle/10986/19614/433720REPLACEM10 Box327363B01PUBLIC1.pdf?sequence=1&isAllowed=y. (03.10.2017)

World Bank (ed) (2009) From privilege to competition: unlocking private-led growth in the Middle East and North Africa. The World Bank, Washington, DC. http://siteresources.worldbank.org/ INTMENA/Resources/Privilege_complete_final.pdf. (08.12.2013)

World Bank (ed) (2011) Poor places, thriving people: how the Middle East and North Africa can rise above spatial disparities. The World Bank, Washington, DC. https://openknowledge. worldbank.org/bitstream/handle/10986/2255/589970PUB0ID181UBLIC109780821383216. pdf?sequence=1. (19.02.2014)

World Bank (ed) (2012a) Enabling economic miracles. The World Bank, Washington, DC. http://siteresources.worldbank.org/INTMENA/Resources/WEBVERSIONREPORT.pdf. (08.12.2013)

World Bank (ed) (2012b) World development report 2013: jobs. The World Bank, Washington, DC

World Bank (ed) (2013) Jobs for shared prosperity: time for action in the Middle East and North Africa. The World Bank, Washington, DC. http://www-wds.worldbank.org/external/default/ WDSContentServer/WDSP/IB/2013/04/12/000445729_20130412114115/Rendered/PDF/724 690v40Full00Prosperity0full0book.pdf. (09.11.2013)

World Bank (ed) (2014a) Jobs or privileges: unleashing the employment potential of the Middle East and North Africa. The World Bank, Washington, DC. http://www-wds.worldbank.org/ external/default/WDSContentServer/WDSP/IB/2014/07/16/000333037_20140716151958/ Rendered/PDF/888790MNA0Box382141B00PUBLIC0.pdf. (10.10.2014)

World Bank (ed) (2014b) MENA quarterly economic brief: growth slowdown heightens the need for reforms. The World Bank, Washington, DC. http://www.worldbank.org/content/dam/ Worldbank/document/MNA/QEBissue2January2014FINAL.pdf. (20.02.2014)

World Bank (ed) (2014c) MENA quarterly economic brief: predictions, perceptions and economic reality. The World Bank, Washington, DC. http://www-wds.worldbank.org/external/default/ WDSContentServer/WDSP/IB/2014/08/06/000470435_20140806105353/Rendered/PDF/898 440REVISED00ue030JULY020140FINAL.pdf. (09.08.2014)

World Bank (ed) (2014d) The unfinished revolution: bringing opportunity, good jobs and greater wealth to all Tunisians. The World Bank, Washington, DC. http://www-wds.worldbank.org/ external/default/WDSContentServer/WDSP/IB/2014/09/16/000456286_20140916144712/ Rendered/PDF/861790DPR0P12800Box385314B00PUBLIC0.pdf. (27.09.2014)

World Bank (ed) (2015) MENA economic monitor: towards a new social contract. The World Bank, Washington, DC. http://www-wds.worldbank.org/external/default/WDSContentServer/ WDSP/IB/2015/04/09/000456286_20150409170931/Rendered/PDF/956500PUB0REVI0201 50391416B00OUO090.pdf. (16.04.2015)

Chapter 3
Socio-economic Regulation in Core Arab Economies: Institutional Contexts for Economic Reform

Abstract The chapter introduces theories dealing with socio-economic regulation and consolidates them into an integrated regulation framework. Further, the chapter focuses the framework on the context found in core Arab economies with their specific structural economic challenges.

Keywords Regulation school · National systems of innovation · Varieties of capitalism · Social systems of production · Inclusive and extractive institutions

The present chapter analyzes the relationship between economic action and socio-institutional context. While many approaches in economics as well as in economic geography and sociology use the term "institutions," understandings of what constitutes institutions and what does not vary. The arguments pursued in this book draw on the definition of institutions offered by Bathelt and Glückler (2014: 346) who regard institutions as "ongoing and relatively stable patterns of social practice based on mutual expectations that owe their existence to either purposeful constitution or unintentional emergence." Institutions can thus be understood "as patterned interactions which are neither fully determined by organizations nor by rules" (Glückler and Bathelt 2017: 123). In this definition, organizations are not understood as institutions but as "collective actors" (Bathelt and Glückler 2014: 346). Laws, regulations, or other formalized rules, summarized by Glückler and Lenz (2016) under the term "prescriptive rules," are not institutions either although "institutions develop in relation to rules, in response to them, or even against them" (Bathelt and Glückler 2014: 346). In this precise understanding, institutions are patterns of interaction defining "how the game is actually played differently in different contexts, but consistently across recurring situations" (Glückler and Lenz 2016: 261–262) with underlying expectations in interactions and possible sanctions for deviant behavior as their defining characteristics (Glückler and Lenz 2016: 262). Following Bathelt and Glückler (2014), Glückler and Lenz (2016: 261) emphasize that "practices are said to be institutionalized if they are widely accepted and enacted by actors in specific situations."

These definitions go beyond the traditional dichotomy of formal and informal institutions. Instead, they use the term "institutions" to capture a set of behavioral patterns in a society and economy and thereby establish a link between the economic action and social structures and practices. Economic action is thus conditioned by its institutional context (Glückler and Bathelt 2017) which includes prescriptive rules, institutions and organizations as components, and interactions between them. Such a socio-economic perspective is important for economic development because "institutional contexts may slow down or resist innovation processes or they may support and accelerate them" (Glückler and Bathelt 2017: 121). Glückler and Bathelt (2017: 130–131) emphasize that socio-economic regulation approaches and notably national innovation systems tend to focus on prescriptive rules and organizations while ignoring institutions as defined here as well as of processes and mechanisms of institutional change through upward and downward causation (Glückler and Lenz 2016). In the wider regulation perspective followed here, all components of the institutional context of an economy with their complex and bi-directional interactions causing institutional and organizational change and conditioning the effectiveness of policymaking are seen as critical parts of the system of socio-economic regulation.

In particular, entrepreneurship is a prominent driver of private-sector growth. Entrepreneurship is an important marker for the dynamism of an economy. Understood in a wider social and economic sense, an entrepreneurial spirit and entrepreneurial dynamics are central to building a vibrant private sector. Schumpeterian notions of creative destruction (Bathelt and Glückler 2012: 401–402) and the entrepreneurial struggle for new combinations (Bathelt and Glückler 2012: 344–345) underscore these arguments. Entrepreneurship is deeply rooted in the regulation system of an economy and its underlying institutions. As the OECD (2012b: 13) puts it, "values, beliefs and behaviours, embedded in the culture of a country and a place, influence [the] decision" of would-be entrepreneurs to start their own business, but the subsequent degree of success of entrepreneurial activities is equally conditioned by the institutional context in which they are situated. At the same time, entrepreneurship as a driver of innovation and structural change in a Schumpeterian sense affects regulation and can alter institutions. In a regulation context, entrepreneurship thus touches critical questions of agency by taking a role that can be understood with structuration theory and essentially through the insight that "structure is both medium and outcome of the reproduction of practices" (Giddens 1979: 5). When talking about regulation in economies, entrepreneurship is an essential mechanism of reproduction of institutional structures. The systemic role of entrepreneurship in linking structure and agency is captured by the term of "entrepreneurship ecosystem" (Isenberg 2010). Such an ecosystem includes, for instance, entrepreneurial attitudes, macro-level stability, and suitable degrees of regulation – all of which can be understood as part of the regulation framework of an economy. Ignoring the interconnected and systemic nature of entrepreneurship as an essential part of regulation in an economy can lead government to focus attention on isolated schemes of entrepreneurship promotion which might eventually generate unwanted results (Isenberg 2010).

Thus, the question of entrepreneurship cannot be isolated from wider regulation issues. This is why the present chapter uses the lens of entrepreneurship in discussing the role of economic, technological, and institutional innovation and change in regulation.

3.1 Theoretical Approaches of Regulation

Economic sociology and geography provide several approaches that address the fit between economic structure and socio-institutional context in national or regional economies. These approaches include the regulation school, national systems of innovation, varieties of capitalism including the variegated capitalism critique, and social systems of production. The newer theory of extractive and inclusive institutions developed in development economics complements the older approaches mentioned. Notwithstanding the common theme of socio-economic regulation, the theoretical perspectives offered by these approaches differ in critical aspects. This is why each of the five concepts is introduced in this section.

3.1.1 Regulation School

Since its emergence in the mid-1970s, the main interest of the regulation school was to explain the sequence of stable economic growth and structural crises in national economies. In contrast to earlier Marxist and Schumpeterian approaches such as long waves (Bathelt and Glückler 2012: 401–406), the regulation school rejected the idea of cyclical or deterministic regularities behind the sequence of stability and crisis. Instead, the regulation school combined the political and social framework of an economy with economic and technological developments (Bathelt 1994: 65).

One of the most prominent scholars of the regulation school, Boyer, describes regulation or, more precisely, the French term *régulation* which according to Bathelt (1994: 64) means coordination in a broader sense than only governmental regulation(s) – as dealing with "the process of fitting production and social demand in a given set of structures and institutions" (Boyer 1988: 68). The regulation school regards long-term economic and social development as a non-deterministic sequence of stable stages called formations and stages of crisis called formation crises or accumulation crises. Formations are stable if and when they combine economic and social structures such as technologies, production structures, consumption patterns, and coordination mechanisms in a consistent way. This socio-economic link is the regulation school's central tenet and can be summarized in a juxtaposition of two substructures, the growth structure or regime of accumulation and the coordination mechanism or mode of regulation (Bathelt 1994).

As illustrated in Fig. 3.1, the theoretical framework of the regulation school consists of three building blocks:

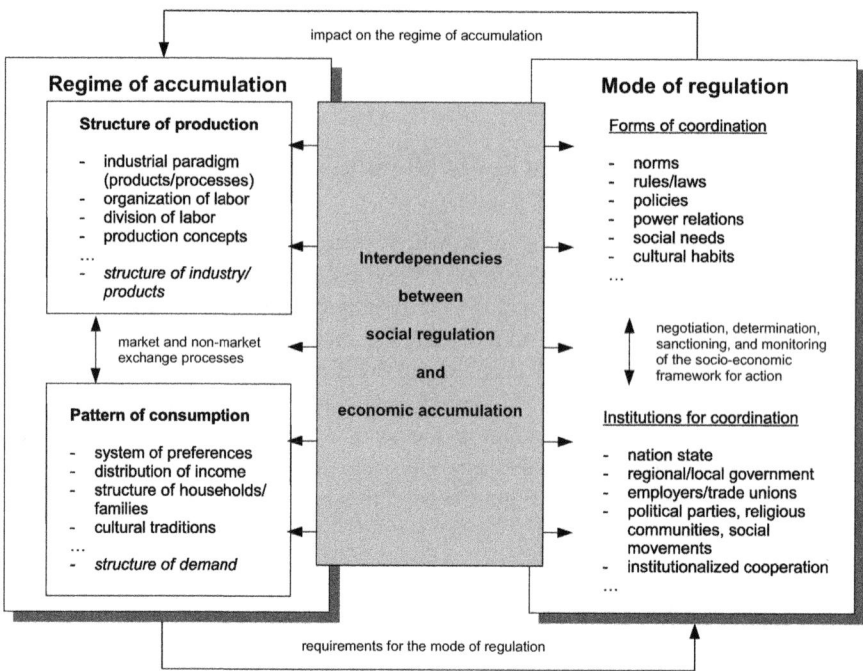

Fig. 3.1 Basic concept of socio-economic relations in regulation theory. (Source: Bathelt 1994: 66, own translation)

1. The *regime of accumulation* includes elements of the structure and functioning of an economy such as a particular pattern of productive organization constituted by elements such as firms' practices and routines; the prevailing time horizon for decisions on capital formation; the shares between various kinds of income accruing to employees, investors, or government; or the volume and composition of demand (Boyer 1988: 71). In essence, the regime of accumulation is shaped by the prevailing industrial paradigm which is in turn characterized by prevailing technologies. Such an industrial paradigm gives rise to a specific division of labor around dominant industrial sectors and a specific productive structure of the economy. Mirroring this productive structure is a pattern of consumption including, inter alia, consumer preferences, income distribution, household and family structures, and cultural traditions. The production structure is linked to the pattern of consumption through market or nonmarket relationships (Bathelt 1994: 67).

2. The *mode of regulation* includes elements of social structure such as prevailing norms, rules, laws, policies, power relations, social needs, and cultural habits. The mode of regulation defines the socio-institutional and political context for economic relations. Specific organizations and formal institutions shape, negotiate, organize, and supervise this socio-economic context. National states are still important agents in this regard, while regional and local government, political parties, employer associations, and trade unions and many other social and economic stakeholders are further relevant agents (Bathelt 1994: 68–69).

3. The regime of accumulation and the mode of regulation interact in many ways. While the mode of regulation shapes elements of the regime of accumulation, the regime of accumulation demands a mode of regulation consistent with its needs for a stable formation to emerge and to be maintained. Fundamental changes either in the regime of accumulation (e.g., through major technological changes), in the mode of regulation, or both endanger consistency and lead to a formation crisis. Formation or structural crises mean a breakup of the internal functioning of the regulation system and differ from cyclical crises that occur even under a stable formation. A formation crisis means that a formation "can no longer reproduce itself in the long run, at least on the same institutional and technological basis" (Boyer 1988: 76). During a formation crisis, the regulation system loses its equilibrium and will not gravitate to its previously stable state. Instead, agents are required to make long-term, strategic decisions leading to modifications in the regime of accumulation or in the mode of regulation. However, there is no deterministic solution to a formation crisis. Various new formations will be possible. Despite some degree of path dependence, a formation crisis opens up a window for opportunity for various courses of transition. Finding the eventual new formation requires negotiation and coordination between agents (Bathelt 1994: 66, 70–72; Boyer 1988: 75–77).

Since a stable formation goes along with a corresponding spatial structure, formation crises call into question the hitherto dominant spatial division of labor and therefore cause disorder in the spatial structure of an economy. At the same time, formation crises open up windows of locational opportunity (Storper and Walker 1989) since the negotiation of modifications in the regime of accumulation or the mode of regulation enables new forms of the spatial division of labor (Bathelt 1994: 72–74).

The regulation school stresses the importance of the institutional setup of an economy linked to credit relationships, the wage-labor nexus, prevailing types of competition, adhesion to the international regime, or prevalent forms of state intervention. In contrast to neoclassical models, the regulation school does not postulate one single process of reaching equilibrium but many different possible ones related to the various elements of the accumulation regime and the institutional setup. Therefore, the regulation school acknowledges the possibility of multiple equilibria in contrast to the absolute static equilibrium suggested by neoclassical models (Boyer 1988: 71–77).

Despite the important role technology plays, the regulation school does not follow the technological determinism inherent to the Schumpeterian theory of long waves (Boyer 1988: 67; Bathelt 1994: 64; Bathelt and Glückler 2012: 404–405). Rather, the regulation school stresses the importance of consistency between technology, institutions, and the other components of the formation (Boyer 1988: 83) as "the fate of any technological system cannot be disentangled from social (…) and economic determinants" (Boyer 1988: 89). Therefore, new modes of regulation cannot be predicted a priori because they are shaped by complex processes including, for example, social struggles and serendipity with uncertain outcomes (Boyer 1988: 91).

Bathelt (1994: 74–75) and Bathelt and Glückler (2012: 416–417) offer a critical appraisal of the regulation school by referring to the metatheoretical character of the approach; its determinism (although not purely technological); the mixture of macro-, meso-, and micro-level analysis; the vagueness of its understanding of institutions; and its disregard of secular socio-economic trends. Apart from this methodological critique, the regulation school has been used mainly to explain the crisis of Fordism and Keynesianism and to sketch presumable post-Fordist formations (e.g., Bathelt 1994: 75–86). Notwithstanding the relevance of the post-Fordism debate for industrialized countries in the latter half of the twentieth century, the strong focus of literature on this debate unnecessarily narrows the scope and applicability of the regulation school. The regulation school's strongest asset is the combination of economic and socio-institutional analysis in a unified theoretical framework. This combination makes the regulation school's perspective relevant for a much larger number of cases, many of them in developing or transition countries. The current economic, political, and socio-institutional transformation process in core Arab economies provides an example for such a case. The regulation school offers an approach to analyze such a transformational context and economic implications, while the aftermath of the "Arab Spring" provides an opportunity to extend the applicability of the regulation school to a wider context in development economics.

3.1.2 Social Systems of Production

The social systems of production (SSP) approach developed notably by Boyer and Hollingsworth (Boyer and Hollingsworth 1997a, b; Hollingsworth and Boyer 1997a, b) are closely related to the regulation school. In fact, the SSP approach might even be seen as a variant of the regulation school that focuses on specific questions of regulation under the post-Fordism debate.

The SSP approach develops a range of possible stable socio-economic arrangements in lieu of the neoclassical ideal type of an economy functioning along the lines of the perfect market. The SSP school challenges the neoclassical convergence thesis (Boyer and Hollingsworth 1997b: 51; Hollingsworth and Boyer 1997a: 1–2, 6) with the Polanyian "argument about the danger of the erosion of a society's cohesiveness when the market begins to dominate such fundamental social relations" (Boyer and Hollingsworth 1997a: 447). The SSP school emphasizes the importance of mechanisms of economic coordination other than market relationships (Boyer and Hollingsworth 1997a: 445). There is an inherent link between market dynamism and socio-institutional assets such as trust. However, "market activity – if not contained – will erode all kinds of traditional institutional arrangements (…) necessary in order to provide the trust on which transactions among economic actors depend" (Boyer and Hollingsworth 1997a: 447). This insight calls for striking a balance between the needs to achieve market dynamism and efficiency on the one hand and to contain the market's potentially destructive forces through social arrangements or constraints on the other hand (Boyer and Hollingsworth 1997a: 447).

Boyer and Hollingsworth (1997a) develop a framework for the socio-institutional embeddedness of firms. Intangible elements of what they call the "community" like trust, tacit, or collective knowledge, shared equipment, or mutual risk sharing influence characteristics of the firm and its capacity to innovate, which in turn is decisive for economic performance. Firm behavior is conditioned by governmental action aimed at securing the social arrangements necessary for markets to continue to function (Boyer and Hollingsworth 1997a: 447–449).

Similar to regulation theory, the SSP approach draws on the idea of stable configurations regulating economic action and socio-institutional context. Such a configuration includes various elements of the institutional context of an economy (Hollingsworth and Boyer 1997a: 2) and encompasses both firm-level and broader social elements such as labor relations, training arrangements, competitive relationships, buyer-supplier relationships, the configuration of capital markets, governmental action, or institutions such as societal ideas about justice (Hollingsworth and Boyer 1997b: 191).

Even if various SSPs coexist within an economy, one may be dominant (Hollingsworth and Boyer 1997b: 191). The elements of this socio-institutional context are interrelated and need to be coherent with one another since "an institutional logic in each society leads institutions to coalesce into a complex social configuration" (Hollingsworth and Boyer 1997a: 2). The SSP school attaches a similar role to technological change and structural crises as does the regulation school. Incremental technological change is managed within an existing socio-institutional framework, while radical technological change may require institutional changes and call into question an existing SSP (Hollingsworth and Boyer 1997a: 20–22).

The institutional arrangements of SSPs are "nested" across spatial scales, creating a complex web of multilevel interactions and calling for coordination between economic actors on all relevant spatial scales (Boyer and Hollingsworth 1997a).

Seen from the angle of the post-Fordism debate, possible forms of SSPs include customized production, diversified quality mass production, flexible diversified quality mass production, and adaptive production as possible post-Fordist techno-economic paradigms (Boyer and Hollingsworth 1997a: 456–458). Thus, the embeddedness of the SSP school in the post-Fordism debate is obvious. The narrow focus of the SSP school on the transition between Fordism and post-Fordist paradigms and on challenging the convergence hypothesis within the context of the post-Fordism debate restricts the approach's applicability to a specific historical and spatial context relevant primarily for industrialized countries. Further, the SSP school proposes modes of regulation below the macro-level and may be useful mainly in a sectoral perspective. The central role ascribed by the approach to governmental action in maintaining the social arrangements necessary to keep markets functioning raises questions of agency. For instance, what is the role of intermediary organizations such as chambers of commerce, business associations, or trade unions in an SSP? The SSP school does not address their action or the relevance of their interactions among each other and with both firms and government. Intermediary agents' highly relevant role in creating and brokering trust (Benner 2018) is not recognized by the SSP approach.

Despite the limited applicability of the SSP approach, its basic assumptions are relevant for wider questions of socio-economic regulation. In particular, the recognition of the Polanyian paradox of markets and their social or institutional preconditions as well as the resulting need to balance market forces and socio-institutional coordination mechanisms is an important insight for regulation in general which the SSP school shares with other regulation approaches introduced above.

3.1.3   National Systems of Innovation

The conglomerate of approaches known as national systems of innovation (or NIS for national innovation systems) emerged in the 1980s with a wide range of case studies analyzing particular NIS (e.g., Freeman 1988; Nelson 1988). These approaches dealt with the wider systemic context of economic development and specifically with the socio-institutional setting innovation takes place in. In a narrower focus than the regulation school, NIS approaches looked mainly at innovation as a driver of economic growth and development.

Another characteristic that the NIS approach shares with the regulation school is its rejection of technological determinism. This rejection is based on the insight that historically, industrialization was not a matter of mere invention but of new combinations of technology on the one hand and industrial or institutional organization on the other hand (Freeman 1988: 330). Institutional experimentation may be just as important in an NIS than technological innovation (Nelson 1988: 326).

While there are various differing interpretations of what constitutes an NIS, the common feature of NIS approaches is that they focus on systemic relationships instead of explaining innovation either on the demand side or the supply side only. NIS approaches look at interactions between agents in the system including those between users and producers, as well as nonmarket relationships. Thus, NIS approaches challenge to the formerly prevailing linear model of innovation while taking into account national specificities and variations. The latter point is the reason why NIS approaches analyze *national* systems of innovation. In an NIS, four important kinds of institutional aspects shape variations in the national context for learning and innovation: the time horizon of agents, the role of trust, the actual mix of instrumental rationality and other motivations, and the way authority is expressed which includes the actually prevailing relationship between trust and authority (Lundvall and Maskell 2000: 359–363).

Following Bathelt and Glückler (2012: 418) as well as Lundvall (1992a: 16–17), two schools of NIS approaches can be distinguished. The first one represented by Nelson (1988) tends to focus primarily on R&D producers, while the second one shaped in large part by Lundvall (1992a, b) analyzes interactions between enterprises within a value chain. Lundvall (1992a) considers learning an interactive and culturally embedded process. He characterizes an NIS as a social, dynamic, and self-reinforcing system with elements of cumulative causation. The focus is put on *national* systems of innovation because the national environment with its cultural norms and values defines the conditions for the transfer of tacit knowledge. This leads to the insight that "different systems may develop different modes of innovation while still following parallel growth paths" (Lundvall 1992a: 6). Given the importance of interactive learning (Lundvall 1992a: 9), NIS approaches shift the focus from individual forms of innovativeness and entrepreneurship to collective ones. Within an NIS, interactive learning takes place not only in R&D but also in routine activities in production and distribution. Therefore, an NIS is rooted in the national system of production. The institutional setup of an economy is important for innovation because under conditions of uncertainty, institutions provide the stability necessary for innovative activities. An NIS offers the socio-economic arena for innovative learning, searching, and exploring activities and can be divided into subsystems (Lundvall 1992a: 12). Innovation in an NIS is neither completely accidental nor completely predetermined by either economic structure or institutional setup. Both the economic structure and the institutional setup differ between nations and include national idiosyncrasies resulting from history, language, and culture. These idiosyncrasies include the internal organization of firms and their relationships with each other in terms of competition, networking, user-producer interactions, or clustering, the role of the public sector in education and R&D but also as a user of innovation, specifics of the financial sector, characteristics of the R&D sector such as resources and competencies, and the education and training system. Still, innovation does not occur exclusively within national borders. Instead, NIS have a certain degree of international openness (Lundvall 1992a).

In Lundvall's (1988) NIS approach, user-producer relationships play a major role in innovation because they are seen as a driver for interactive learning. Such user-producer interaction can be more efficient in a national context due to cultural, geographical, and social proximity likely to be bound to some degree by national borders. Furthermore, national governments play an important role in shaping the framework conditions for innovation. A specific NIS is the result of a historical and path-dependent process and therefore cannot easily be replicated elsewhere. Apart from the critical role of user-producer interfaces, links between industry, academia, and final users in a wider sense are relevant for driving innovation. Importantly, an NIS does not only represent the framework for narrowly defined technological innovation. The socio-institutional embeddedness (Granovetter 1985) of innovation means that organizational and institutional patterns prevalent in an economy can be important prerequisites for technological innovations to be exploited (Lundvall 1988).

The latter point calls for a systemic approach to innovation (Lundvall 1988: 366) and underscores the similarity between NIS and the regulation school. Despite coming from different scientific traditions and although the NIS school focuses more narrowly on innovation, both NIS and the regulation school argue for overcoming the strict technological determinism that characterized former approaches such as the theory of long waves. The two approaches call for integrating the analysis of economic action driving processes of economic growth including innovation into an analysis of the larger socio-institutional framework. Nonetheless, the NIS approach is marked by a certain vagueness. Basically, the approach draws on the following central tenets:

1. The critical role of innovation for processes of economic growth in economies which are becoming increasingly knowledge-based
2. The embeddedness of innovation in the wider socio-institutional context
3. The assumption that such a socio-institutional context is in several important aspects defined within the borders of a nation
4. The conclusion that innovation processes should be analyzed within a systemic national context that includes relationships and interactions between agents

Apart from the weak conceptualization of the exact nature of relationships between components of the system (with the exception of user-producer relationships), the NIS approach rests on assumptions that call for a further refinement. While the assumption of national embeddedness does make sense from a more formal institutional view (e.g., regarding legislation), the idea of a necessarily nationally delimited "culturally based system of interpretation" (Lundvall 1992a: 3–4) shared by agents within a national context (Lundvall 1992a: 3) appears essentialist and reductionist. This point becomes clear in a context such as the one studied here. In Arab countries defined by national borders often drawn artificially by colonial powers (Gasper 2014) but sharing cultural characteristics such as the same language, majority religion (Lee and Ben Shitrit 2014), political and social movements, ideas and ideologies (Gasper 2014; Lee and Ben Shitrit 2014), and an emerging cross-national media scene,[1] postulating a nationally defined cultural context becomes very questionable (Lynch 2014: 374–375).[2,3] While the formal institutional relevance of the national context remains a valid point, the cultural argument should be treated with utmost caution. The vague notion of "culture" bears the risk of becoming an analytical black box that escapes definition and lacks analytical rigor. Such a black box of a not further defined or refined "culture" could be used to explain everything and nothing at the same time while neglecting possibly more important and more complex elements of socio-institutional environments such as educational backgrounds or milieux. The latter point is particularly critical since socio-institutional indicators such as education or milieu affiliation are arguably

---

[1] The cross-country media scene in the Arab world can be seen, for instance, in the rise of satellite television channels such as Al Jazeera or Al Arabiyya (e.g., Lynch 2014: 378, 389), the popular casting show "Arab Idol," or the transnational appeal of Egyptian or Lebanese-produced television series or music.

[2] While the NIS approach has been adapted to subnational contexts by analyzing regional innovation systems (e.g., Bathelt and Glückler 2012: 421–423), a cross-national perspective on NIS and their elements (as might be interesting in the context of Arab countries) has not been figured yet prominently in the NIS literature.

[3] Historically, Rivlin (2009: 290) suggests that a sense of shared identity across Arab populations may be, at least in part, based on the common history during the Arab and Islamic empires under the Umayyad and Abbasid dynasties.

much more relevant for understanding both structures and agency than the vague ideas of a national "culture."[4]

3.1.4 Varieties of Capitalism

The varieties of capitalism (VoC) approach was developed first and foremost by Hall and Soskice (2001). The approach assumes "that many of the most important institutional structures (…) depend on the presence of regulatory regimes that are the preserve of the nation-state" (Hall and Soskice 2001: 4). In analyzing these structures, the VoC approach is agent-centered and specifically firm-centered, and it studies these agents' strategic interactions. The approach assumes that structures and interactions define the functioning of an economy which can differ from the workings of another economy, despite the economies considered being capitalist market economies and the differing configurations being stable over time and leading to successful growth trajectories. In this regard, the VoC approach is similar to what Lundvall (1992a: 6) suggest in the framework of different NIS. Bathelt and Glückler (2012: 425) stress this similarity in emphasizing the relational view on enterprises inherent to both approaches. The insight that capitalist market economies might work somewhat differently and that this difference be stable and potentially successful contrasts with the neoclassical assumption of convergence of all capitalist market economies towards a single model. In offering a different perspective and in empirically underscoring stable variations between capitalist market economies, the VoC approach looks at the specific mode of embeddedness of economic action in the socio-institutional context of an economy (Hall and Soskice 2001; Bathelt and Glückler 2012: 425–428).

Drawing on a literature of case studies focusing in industrialized countries, the VoC approach identifies two types of capitalist market economies (Hall and Soskice 2001):

- *Liberal market economies* (LMEs) such as the United States or the United Kingdom rely more heavily on pure market coordination and on formal contracts. Markets and hierarchies are the main coordination mechanisms. On markets and notably labor markets, competition tends to take precedence over collaboration. Capital markets are the main source for corporate finance, leading firm managers to align their corporate strategies with investors' interests, typically implying a more short-term perspective. Government plays a major role in securing the good functioning of markets which often includes policies directed towards deregulation and privatization.

---

[4] The critique brought forward here can be applied to the regulation school, too, as far as the regulation school refers to "cultural" aspects of nationally bounded regulation. However, unlike the NIS approach with its explicit focus on national systems of innovation, the regulation school is conceptually open to integrating socio-institutional framework conditions defined in a cross-national context.

- *Coordinated market economies* (CMEs) such as France, Germany, or Japan are more focused on other coordination mechanisms and particularly on relationships other than arm's-length market relationships. Intermediate institutional arrangements between markets and hierarchies, for example, networks in their many appearances, are often found. CMEs heavily draw on intermediate arrangements to reduce uncertainty in strategic interaction. These intermediate arrangements include associations, trade unions, ownership interlinkages, and legal frameworks inducing collaboration. An illustrative and often-cited example for such a collaborative arrangement is the organization of technical and vocational education and training (TVET) in Germany based on a partnership between government which provides vocational schools and a legislative framework, companies who hire apprentices, and public law chambers of commerce and industry who oversee the process and organize exams. In CMEs, agents such as employer associations, trade unions, or chambers provide capacities for sharing information, monitoring agents' behavior, and sanctioning defections in strategic interaction. These agents have an important role to play in finding solutions to new problems as well as reactions to exogenous shocks.

As the VoC approach follows a relational view centered on companies' behavior and strategic interactions with each other and with other agents in the economy, Hall and Soskice (2001) stress that the primary mechanism for coordination between economic action and socio-institutional context is the adaptation of firms to the coordination modes the national economy provides institutional support for. The precise shape of an eventual equilibrium is hence not predetermined but depends on informal institutions like shared strategic understandings and visions which are not only historically formed and path-dependent but also have to be reaffirmed periodically. While both markets and hierarchies are prevalent in CMEs and LMEs alike, a third type of coordination structure directed at strategic cooperation is what distinguishes these two stylized forms of capitalist market economies from one another. The establishment of collective institutions requires cooperation and coordination, and their establishment is in itself a strategic problem that often needs coordination by the government. The firm then adapts their strategies to the established collective coordination mechanisms. Therefore, firm strategy follows the structure of the political economy. However, this insight does not imply determinism as multiple possible ways of adaptation are possible (Hall and Soskice 2001).

Within a specific VoC, institutional complementarities emerge as "nations with a particular type of coordination in one sphere of the economy should tend to develop complementary practices in other spheres" (Hall and Soskice 2001: 18). These complementarities give rise to increasing returns (Hertog 2016: 3–4). Despite the attention and generally positive view on CMEs evident in much of the VoC literature, neither type is seen as strictly superior to the other. Overall, CMEs and LMEs seem to achieve similar outcomes in terms of well-being although innovative capacities of agents and the income and employment distribution tend to differ between CMEs and LMEs. Typically, LMEs exhibit higher levels of income inequality than CMEs (Hall and Soskice 2001).

Despite identifying two basic types of market economies, Hall and Soskice (2001: 33–35) emphasize that other types than CMEs and LMEs can be found and even within the two ideal types, much variation is possible. Remarkably, Hall and Soskice (2001: 21) hint at the possibility that Southern European nations may constitute a third type of capitalism termed "Mediterranean."[5] In contrast to absolute institutional advantage addressed by the NIS school, the VoC perspective focuses on comparative institutional advantage that can lead to an institutionally founded international division of labor (Hall and Soskice 2001: 38).

Another important feature of the VoC school is that instead of inducing private-sector agents to cooperate with the government, securing economic performance depends more on inducing them to cooperate with one another. This can be done in different ways. The choice of effective economic policies therefore depends on the particular VoC of an economy. The basic policy choices are market incentive policies and coordination policies, but the latter are confronted with information asymmetries that can be overcome through the intermediary role of organizations such as associations, chambers, or trade unions who build trust and social capital (Putnam 1995) and enter into implicit contracts with governments to implement coordination-oriented economic policies. To solve coordination problems and to share information, companies have to trust coordinating organizations; hence employer associations distant from government can fulfill coordination roles. However, for a credible government commitment, producer groups need to have structural influence in the political realm, e.g., through political parties. Such prerequisites for coordination-oriented policies are usually not given in LMEs to the same extent as in CMEs. Interestingly, in a VoC perspective "strong" governments may be counterproductive in securing coordination-oriented policies (Hall and Soskice 2001: 45–48; Wood 2001: 256–258).

According to Bathelt and Glückler (2012: 426–428), the VoC school can be criticized for its institutional determinism and for the difficulty to generalize from the wide range of firm behavior possible. Another element of the VoC school that warrants critical discussion is its national orientation. Similar to the NIS school, the VoC approach focuses on institutional variations on the national level. As was said above in relation to the NIS school, focusing on the national level renders the approach prone to the essentialist notion of national "culture" and its black-box character. Peck and Theodore (2007: 740) call the VoC school's nationally bounded approach "methodological nationalism." They detect "a tendency to reify national economic 'boundaries'" (Peck and Theodore 2007: 738) and stress the importance of what they call "(transnational) transformational processes" (Peck and Theodore 2007: 738).

More generally, Peck and Theodore (2007) offer a comprehensive critique of the VoC school. Their main argument is that idiosyncratic institutional analysis on the national level must be complemented by analysis of transnational transformative trends such as globalization, trade liberalization, and what they call "neoliberalization" (Peck and Theodore 2007: 756). Notwithstanding the vagueness of these

---

[5] Such a type might presumably exhibit some common features with Arab economies, notable in the Maghreb (Benner 2015).

tendencies,[6] the multilayered perspective that Peck and Theodore (2007) call "variegated capitalism" is definitely useful to complement the primarily nationally bounded VoC perspective. Peck and Theodore's (2007) critique of the nationally bounded perspective of the VoC approach calls for a consideration of transformative tendencies above the national level and eventually leads to the call for a wider, multi-scalar regulation framework. Such a perspective is particularly useful for understanding socio-economic regulation in core Arab economies by considering pan-Arab tendencies, EU *rapprochement* (notably in Maghreb countries), WTO membership, geopolitical interests, or the influence of international donors.

Peck and Theodore's (2007) call to consider transnational transformative forces relates to a further critique against the VoC approach. The VoC perspective is basically static and does not seem to pay sufficient attention to dynamic changes both from within and without national economies. Openness for transnational transformative processes and their path-dependent and embedded adaptation and absorption in a particular context, as suggested by Peck and Theodore (2007), is one way to render VoC perspective more dynamic. Yet, endogenously induced change in a VoC should not be ignored either. An integrated conceptual framework for socio-economic regulation should thus pay attention to transnational trends, endogenous dynamics, and the interrelationships between them.

3.1.5   Inclusive and Extractive Institutions

The fifth regulation approach introduced here is a significantly newer one with origins in a different academic tradition. The approach offers a theory of development elaborated in development economics. Still, similar to the other four regulation approaches stemming from economic sociology and geography, the fifth approach deals with the fit between long-term economic development and socio-institutional embeddedness.

Acemoğlu and Robinson (2012) propose a theoretical framework that centers on economic and political institutions. In both dimensions, institutions can be either inclusive or extractive, with inclusive institutions offering chances of economic participation to wide parts of a country's population and notably enabling newcomers to enter the entrepreneurial sphere and workers to use their skills in the best possible ways (Acemoğlu and Robinson 2012: 74–75). In contrast, extractive economic institutions are those "designed to extract incomes and wealth from one subset of society to benefit a different subset" (Acemoğlu and Robinson 2012: 76). Similarly, political institutions can be inclusive by giving a voice to wide parts of the population and to "a broad coalition or a plurality of groups" (Acemoğlu and Robinson

---

[6] Globalization is a highly vague term that calls for a rigid definition of what precisely it encompasses. The term "neoliberalization" (Peck and Theodore 2007: 756) is particularly fuzzy and lacks a commonly accepted definition, despite it being widely used in the public discourse and media.

2012: 80) or extractively by restricting political decision-making to a small group or even an individual only (Acemoğlu and Robinson 2012: 79–81).

Acemoğlu and Robinson (2012) argue that economic and political institutions are closely related. Equilibrium is about a socio-institutional fit, similar to the regulation and VoC schools. Extractive economic institutions are often shaped by extractive political institutions as to benefit the ruling political group economically, and they could not be maintained in an inclusive political system. Therefore, the framework leads to two stable socio-economic configurations: either a society with both inclusive economic and political institutions or one with both extractive economic and political ones (Acemoğlu and Robinson 2012: 81–83).

However, the case studies presented by Acemoğlu and Robinson (2012) suggest that the combination of both inclusive economic and political institutions is more conducive to long-term economic growth and development than the alternative one of extractive institutions. The authors conclude that "nations fail when they have extractive economic institutions, supported by extractive political institutions that impede and even block economic growth" (Acemoğlu and Robinson 2012: 83). In a reference to Schumpeterian creative destruction, Acemoğlu and Robinson (2012: 84–87) emphasize the role of new agents such as entrepreneurs in the process of structural change which often threatens established power structures and hence the ability of ruling elites to extract resources. Inclusive institutions facilitate creative destruction by entrepreneurs and thus the emergence of a new entrepreneurial and merchant class that competes for economic success with older, established economic agents and that will eventually claim political participation. This mechanism confirms the intricate link between inclusive economic and political institutions. In essence, Acemoğlu and Robinson (2012) extend the Schumpeterian notions of creative destruction and of the entrepreneur as an agent introducing new combinations (Bathelt and Glückler 2012: 344) from the techno-economic realm to the wider socio-institutional realm by creating a link between micro-level individual and relational economic action and meso- or macro-level institutional context (Acemoğlu and Robinson 2012).

The combined economic-political relevance of entrepreneurs and businessmen is similar to the argument of structural influence in the VoC school (Hall and Soskice 2001: 45–48; Wood 2001: 256–258). The theory of inclusive and extractive institutions focuses on developing nations (or industrialized nations during their historical periods of industrialization) instead of focusing on structural crises of industrialized nations that are in the focus of the other four regulation approaches that emerged under the influence of the post-Fordism debate. Still, much in Acemoğlu and Robinson's (2012) reasoning remains vague. In particular, their understanding of institutions is not precisely defined. A more precise and narrow understanding of institutions such as the one offered by Bathelt and Glückler (2014: 346) could add analytical rigor to the concept and lead to a deeper differentiation between formal and informal institutions and organizations and eventually to a better understanding of the relationships of inclusive or extractive structures and agency. Another open question is the exact delimitation of economic and political spheres. For example, where do institutions such as perceptions of justice or intermediary organizations such as trade unions and chambers of commerce belong? These organizations can be thought to belong both to the economic and political spheres. Despite having economic functions, they often unfold considerable political relevance and can become power bases of societal groups, either inclusively or extractively.

Despite these conceptual shortcomings, Acemoğlu and Robinson's (2012) theory does add an important idea to the other regulation approaches by stressing the critical economic and political role of entrepreneurs for long-term economic development. In a synthesis of regulation approaches, the notion of the entrepreneur as a Schumpeterian change agent both economically and politically and the distinction between inclusive and extractive institutional architectures are important elements. The next section turns to sketching the outlines of such a synthesis.

3.2   Towards a Synthesis of Regulation Approaches

The five approaches introduced in Sect. 3.1 exhibit a number of similarities but also differences and complementarities. The regulation school, SSP, NIS, and VoC share roots in related academic traditions such as economic sociology and geography, while the approach of inclusive and extractive institutions comes from development economics. Combining these five approaches can contribute to constructing a broader framework useful to analyze and explain regulation between economic action and socio-institutional context.

One of the most relevant weaknesses of the four regulation approaches used in economic sociology and geography is their strong orientation towards a particular historical and spatial setting. The regulation school and SSP are embedded in the post-Fordism debate and the quest for new techno-economic paradigms after the Fordism crisis. They focus on industrialized nations and their challenges related to structural change roughly between the 1970s and the 2000s. The VoC approach has a broader historical outlook, but VoC research so far is still mostly limited to industrialized countries,[7] with the United States, the United Kingdom, Japan, France, and Germany as the main cases studied. The theoretical foundations of the NIS approach equally tend to focus on industrialized countries and particularly the United States, Japan, and Northern European or Scandinavian countries.

Acemoğlu and Robinson's (2012) theory of inclusive and extractive institutions has a much wider historical and spatial scope. Consistent with its roots in development economics, the approach looks at long-term economic development of developing countries or of industrialized countries during their historical periods of industrialization. This wide scope makes the approach a valuable complement to the other four regulation approaches. With the possible exception of SSP and its highly specific tenets adapted to the quest for post-Fordist paradigms, there is nothing

---

[7] Hertog (2016: 4) briefly summarizes a few attempts to extend the VoC perspective to developing countries and applies the perspective to Arab economies. Apart from these attempts, the VoC school mostly focuses on industrialized countries.

inherent to the fundamental theoretical reasoning behind the regulation approaches used in economic sociology and geography that generally limits their applicability to other historical or spatial contexts. Coming up with a synthesis that adapts these regulation approaches to a different context, for example, today's industrializing or developing countries, and that adds the idea of inclusive and extractive institutions thus appears worthwhile.

While every regulation approach focuses on causes and effects of institutional advantages in economies and societies, there is some variation in what exactly is understood as institutional advantage. For example, VoC looks for comparative institutional advantage, while NIS turns to absolute institutional advantage (Hall and Soskice 2001: 38). The role of entrepreneurship as a central driver of economic action within socio-institutional contexts differs between the regulation approaches. Apart from Acemoğlu and Robinson (2012), there is no specific focus on entrepreneurship in the regulation approaches introduced. This is somewhat surprising since entrepreneurship is deeply rooted in absolute or comparative institutional advantages and can in turn cause them. Entrepreneurship therefore has to be a critical component of a synthesis of regulation approaches and can well be integrated as a driver of economic, technological, and institutional innovation and therefore structural change. On this account, too, the theory of inclusive and extractive institutions well complements the other regulation approaches.

Following these ideas, a framework for analyzing regulation in wider contexts of economic development and particularly for developing countries is suggested. Figure 3.2 illustrates this framework. It builds on the fundamental architecture of the regulation school as shown in Fig. 3.1. The regulation school's architecture with its building blocks, the regime of accumulation and the mode of regulation, appears well-suited to analyze economic action within socio-institutional contexts and provides the structural basis for a more comprehensive list of components for regulation enriched with ideas from other approaches. Ideas from NIS can be integrated by emphasizing more strongly the role that patterns of innovation and interaction play, for example, within the structure of production and notably in its role as a driver for structural change. Such an emphasis on innovation includes, for example, interactive learning in user-producer relationships. Placing innovation processes in the wider system of socio-economic regulation overcomes the black-box thinking about "culture" observable in the NIS approach, since the regulation school defines components of the socio-institutional setup of an economy more precisely. In addition, since many of these components are not necessarily nationally bounded, the framework proposed here allows for analyzing innovation processes along the tenets proposed by the NIS school but not necessarily within the confines of the nation-state.

The framework uses the precise definition of institutions proposed by Bathelt and Glückler (2014: 346) and distinguishes institutions from prescriptive rules (e.g., laws and regulations) that can eventually form the basis for institutions and organizations such as government agencies or intermediary organizations (e.g., chambers of commerce, trade unions, or trade associations).

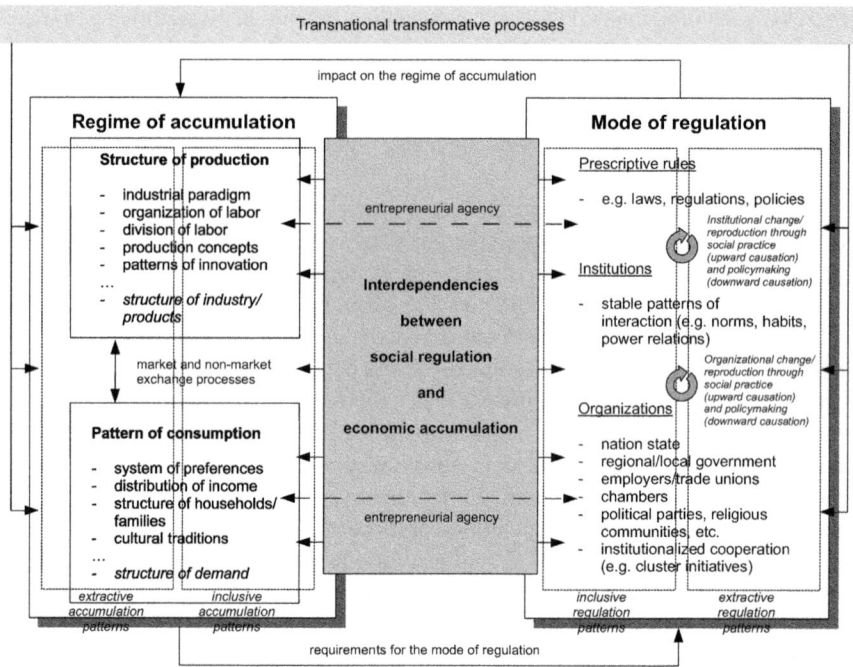

Fig. 3.2 Framework for a synthesis of regulation approaches. (Source: Own work based on Bathelt 1994: 66)

The reasoning behind the VoC approach fits well within this framework but is complemented by the framework's openness for dynamic change. In essence, each stable configuration between a particular regime of accumulation and a particular mode of regulation is equivalent to a certain VoC. The VoC perspective comes into play notably when looking at the mechanisms of negotiation, determination, sanctioning, and monitoring of the socio-economic framework for action within the mode of regulation. Such mechanisms that characterize a certain VoC have to be consistent with the regime of accumulation, thereby confirming the similarity between the architecture of the regulation school and the VoC approach.

The framework integrates some essential ideas brought forward by Acemoğlu and Robinson (2012), in particular by distinguishing between inclusive and extractive patterns of each component of accumulation and regulation. Complementing the framework with this idea allows for a more precise examination, of which "institutions" in a given economy and society have an inclusive or extractive character, and thus helps overcome the lack of rigor and the vague definition of "institutions" offered by Acemoğlu and Robinson (2012). Another idea adapted from Acemoğlu and Robinson (2012) is the critical role of entrepreneurial agency, which may even lead to the emergence of an economically and politically independent and confident entrepreneurial or merchant class, as a driver of both economic and institutional political change. Through this tenet, the Schumpeterian ideas of creative destruction

(Bathelt and Glückler 2012: 401–402) and his characterization of the entrepreneur as an agent introducing new combinations (Bathelt and Glückler 2012: 344) are part of the framework. As agents driving experimentation and creating new innovations, entrepreneurs play a prominent role particularly in patterns of innovation and thus stimulate and shape structural change. This important dynamic role of entrepreneurial agency unfolds best if and when it faces inclusive patterns of accumulation and regulation. This is why in Fig. 3.2, entrepreneurial agency is represented by arrows pointing in the directions of both the regime of accumulation and the mode of regulation but in both ways only to the sections of accumulation and regulation covered by inclusive patterns.

Transnational transformative processes, as argued by Peck and Theodore (2007), affect regulation in a national (or regional) economy. The arrows from the layer of transnational transformative processes and the various components of the regime of accumulation and the mode of regulation symbolize the manifold influences these processes can initiate. However, transnational transformative processes in and by themselves do not predetermine certain ways of changes in the various components of regulation. Rather, they will be met with internal dynamics of adaptation and change within a regulation regime that vary from one economy to the other. What the arrows from transnational transformative processes to elements of regulation stand for is therefore not any direct or deterministic change to regulation itself but rather a stimulus for dynamic processes internal to a particular regime of accumulation or mode of regulation and contingent on the extant elements of regulation and their systemic interrelationships with each other.

The framework builds on the regulation school, the NSI and VoC approaches including the variegated capitalism critique, and the theory of inclusive and extractive institutions. It does not directly include the SSP approach since this approach can be seen as a more specific elaboration of the regulation school that focuses on a peculiar historical context. However, this does not mean that the framework proposed here dismisses any ideas of the SSP school. Ideas such as nestedness across spatial levels, the relevance of internal firm structure, or the analysis of specific SSPs on the level of particular markets or sectors can indeed complement the framework when it is used in examining cases of regulation. Further, the SSP approach's basic tenet that markets do not function in a vacuum but are contained and maintained by institutional arrangements guaranteed by governmental action is inherent to the regulation perspective pursued here, calling into question pure free-market policy approaches.

The framework follows the distinction between organizations, prescriptive rules, and institutions as understood by Bathelt and Glückler (2014) and Glückler and Lenz (2016) but at the same time regards all of these three levels as components of the mode of regulation. When using the framework to examine and describe regulation in an economy, attention is thus drawn to the distinction between these three levels of institutional context (Glückler and Bathelt 2017).

It is important to note that these levels of the mode of regulation are not independent exogenous variables. Rather, they affect each other. As Glückler and Lenz (2016: 262–263) argue, institutions are affected by social practices and thus subject to upward causation of institutional change and reproduction from the micro-level. At the same time, prescriptive rules affect institutions, leading to processes of downward causation of institutional change and reproduction (Glückler and Lenz 2016).

Similar processes are plausible between prescriptive rules and organizations, as well as between institutions and organizations. Lastly, social practices within and between organizations may induce processes of upward causation of organizational change and reproduction. These conduits work in two directions (represented as circular arrows in Fig. 3.2). While prescriptive rules and organizations have causative effects on institutional change, institutions may condition the performance and effectiveness of prescriptive rules and organizations (Glückler and Lenz 2016: 264–265). Similarly, organizations may condition the performance and effectiveness of prescriptive rules.

When it comes to institutional change or reproduction, Glückler and Lenz (2016) suggest a taxonomy of interactions between prescriptive rules and institutions. Given that policies are directed towards shaping rules (or, analogously, organizations), the effects of these interactions on the framework of regulation become clear. The following mechanisms of institutional (or organizational) change or reproduction can be characterized (Glückler and Lenz 2016: 264–270):

1. Rule-reinforcing institutions can be shaped by upward causation and are thus a matter of micro-level agency processes (Benner 2014, 2017c) such as innovation and entrepreneurship.
2. Institution-reinforcing rules are a case for downward causation and thus of explicit top-down policymaking. These policies can be expected to have a considerable chance of proving effective.
3. Rule-substituting institutions[8] are subject to upward causation and therefore to micro-level agency processes such as innovation and entrepreneurship and bridge gaps on the level of prescriptive rules (Lehmann and Benner 2015). Institutional change through rule-substituting institutions can thus correct policy failure or inaction but can lead to beneficial or harmful aggregate effects, depending on the kind of institution that develops.
4. Rule-circumventing institutions, too, are subject to upward causation and therefore to micro-level agency processes such as innovation and entrepreneurship. They can endanger legitimate policy goals pursued by prescriptive rules, but it may equally be that rule-circumventing institutions unfold beneficial effects in terms of static or dynamic efficiency by circumventing rigid prescriptive rules that cannot be explicitly overturned, for example, because of political sclerosis or inertia.
5. Institution-circumventing rules are a case for downward causation and thus by explicit policy and are directed towards correcting harmful institutions according

---

[8]The opposite case of institution-substituting rules is not considered here because of its unlikelihood and lack of empirical validity (Glückler and Lenz 2016: 268).

to policy goals. For example, they can aim at upgrading processes in industries or regions such as tourism destinations or urban quarters.[9]

6. Rule-competing institutions are the last case of upward causation and thus of micro-level agency. In this case, agents adapt their behavior to new rules without complying with the rules' goals.

7. Institution-competing rules relate to downward causation policymaking but tend to exhibit low effectiveness in terms of their long-term effects.

It goes without saying that the framework cannot capture all possible elements of regulation in a complex economy and society. It can only be seen as a simplified and stylized model that can serve as a lens for analyzing regulation patterns and crises and that can draw attention to possible ways of overcoming structural crises through suitable institution-sensitive policies (Benner 2017b; Glückler and Lenz 2016). This is precisely what the next sections attempt to do in relation to socio-economic regulation in Arab economies in the context of the current economic and political transformations going on in the Arab world. The next section relates to the structural difficulties introduced in Chap. 2 and relates them to aspects of socio-economic regulation including historical developments and institutions.

3.3 Socio-economic Regulation in Core Arab Economies

Socio-economic regulation in core Arab economies is characterized by specific economic and socio-institutional configurations. While economic action and socio-institutional contexts certainly differ in each individual Arab country, some common features shared at least to some degree by most Arab economies can be identified. While the oil-producing Gulf states (and, in some respect, Algeria and Libya) exhibit economic and political conditions that differ significantly from those found in resource-poor, labor-abundant Arab economies, some historically grown ways of regulation may still be shared true between these groups of countries. This section and the following one put the emphasis on resource-poor, labor-abundant core Arab economies whose context is further detailed in the cases of Tunisia and Jordan.

The political and social transformations commonly termed "Arab Spring" can be seen as a symptom of a formation crisis with deeper economic roots. While economic reasons should not be seen as the only reason for the popular uprisings that occurred after 2010 in Tunisia, Egypt, and other countries across the Arab world, symptoms of a regulation crisis such as persistent high youth unemployment certainly represented major motivating factors for youth who took to the streets and

---

[9] The designation of business improvement districts including the concomitant funding arrangements is a good example for institution-circumventing rules because they are meant to counter institutionally based trading-down processes in urban quarters. Public law tourism associations promoting or upgrading tourist destinations through obligatory membership fees (e.g., in Austria) follow a similar logic.

formulated a wide range of political, social, and economic demands (Cammett 2014: 161; 170–171; Moghadam and Decker 2014: 73–74).

Assuming that these transformations and their underlying economic and social causes are intricately related to the breakdown of a formerly dominant mode of regulation, the next sub-section characterizes the old Arab social contract as this prior mode of socio-economic regulation along the lines of the framework developed in Sect. 3.2. Thereafter, the role of entrepreneurship as a major dynamic element of the regulation framework is discussed in the context of the old Arab social contract. This leads to the elaboration of possible future pathways for socio-economic regulation after the collapse of the old Arab social contract in Sect. 3.4.

3.3.1   The Arab Social Contract as a Mode of Regulation

The specifics of the interplay between the social and economic spheres of Arab countries, including their institutional landscape, and specifically the socio-economic configuration understood as the Arab social contract, can be conceptualized as a particular mode of regulation. The regulation approaches introduced in Sect. 3.1 and the integrated regulation framework proposed in Sect. 3.2 can help analyze and understand how socio-economic regulation tends to work in core Arab economies, although in a stylized way since a detailed analysis of socio-economic regulation in an economy needs to take into account the idiosyncratic features of a specific (national, regional, or even local) economy in question. The present section elaborates some stylized facts of socio-economic regulation in middle-income, resource-poor, and labor-abundant core Arab economies (including notably Morocco, Tunisia, Egypt, Jordan, and prewar Syria) and inserts these stylized facts into the proposed regulation framework.

Hertog (2016) argues that low- and middle-income Arab economies represent a particular variety of capitalism characterized by "a stretched, overcommitted and interventionist state; deep insider-outsider divides in private sectors and labor markets resulting from lopsided state intervention; and low levels of cooperation and trust between state, business and workers" and a resulting "equilibrium of low skills and low productivity" (Hertog 2016: 2). Richards and Waterbury (2008: 180–209) confirm the impression of interventionist states in most core Arab economies, both in republics that experimented with Arab socialism such as Egypt and Tunisia and in conservative monarchies such as Morocco and Jordan.[10] The state was seen as the driver of industrialization, and the private sector was seen as either weak or subject to outright distrust, enriched with ideological and anti-colonialist sentiments (Richards and Waterbury 2008: 181). Amin et al. (2012: 3–4) confirm that support

---

[10] State interventionism was a widespread tendency over much of the MENA region, at least for some decades during the twentieth century. Richards and Waterbury (2008: 180–209) cite examples not only from Arab economies but also from Iran, Turkey, and Israel, with Lebanon apparently being the exception.

for the idea of interventionist government seen not just as a regulator and redistributor but also as a producer persists (Amin et al. 2012: 4).

In detail, Hertog (2016) emphasizes the role of market segmentation in the Arab VoC through (i) the dependence of the a large part of the private sector on government support and protection; (ii) strong labor market regulation and a strong role of government as employer, creating a coalition of labor market insiders; (iii) the widespread distribution of resources by government to a comparatively broad middle class, again creating coalitions of insiders mirrored by the exclusion of outsiders not being part of these coalitions due to weak formal social security systems; (iv) vested interests of insiders resisting reform and change; and (v) low cooperation and trust due to government overstretch and broken promises, leading to what can be called a low-productivity equilibrium (World Bank 2013), a low-level equilibrium (Rivlin 2009: 294), or, more precisely, a low-investment, low-skills equilibrium (Hertog 2016: 4–6).

These features of the Arab VoC have to be understood historically. Starting with Arab nationalism in the newly independent states during the 1950s and 1960s and concomitant distributive needs and the necessity of state-building, the public sector expanded through rent distribution and extensive social commitments. Critically, these commitments included public employment guarantees for higher-education graduates, public housing, and supply-side subsidies[11] (Amin et al. 2012: 86–89; Hertog 2016: 7), thereby implicitly establishing the Arab social contract. In the 1970s, fiscal difficulties compelled Arab states to scale back their commitments, but the dominance of the state with high rates of government employment, bureaucracy, and subsidies persisted (Hertog 2016: 7). However, the former guarantees of public employment could not be maintained anymore, making coveted government jobs scarce and their allocation often intransparent (Hertog 2016: 8). Despite the breakdown of the public employment promise, large parts of the populations including young people still hold aspirations to attain a government job:

> Despite waiting lists that stretch up to 13 years, large percentages of Arab populations prefer government jobs to employment in the private sector. (Amin et al. 2012: 43)

At the same time, the Arab VoC exhibits a high degree of segmentation in the private sector, mainly due to uneven government intervention and rent-seeking by politically well-connected businesspeople at the expense of outsiders (Hertog 2016: 11). Despite its exclusiveness, the system was for a long time marked by a considerable persistence due to a coalition of regimes and cronies interested in blocking change (World Bank 2009: 172). Since the mixture of partial liberalization and protection from competition benefited established and well-connected businesspeople (World Bank 2009: 183), outsiders capable of driving structural change as entrepreneurial newcomers according to Acemoğlu and Robinson's (2012) theory find it hard to compete with the established and well-connected business elite of insiders. Inclusiveness towards new entrepreneurial agents under the old Arab

---

[11] For instance, Amin et al. (2012: 87) state that in Egypt food subsidies account for 2% of GDP, while fuel and electricity subsidies account for 6% of GDP.

social contract seems to be limited. Independent entrepreneurial activity was largely confined to small-scale trading, while regimes tended to prefer politically less daunting foreign investors and tried to pursue FDI-based strategies (Noland and Pack 2007: 249–250). Tunisia's special investment regime for offshore activities can serve as an illustrative example underscoring this claim. In the terminology of Acemoğlu and Robinson (2012), under the old Arab social contract, the dominant approach of regimes towards entrepreneurship was one of establishing and maintaining extractive economic institutions, although to degrees varying between countries. Partial liberalization in the latter decades of the twentieth century did not fundamentally change the role of the well-established business elite or ease the constraints for independent newcomer entrepreneurship. To benefit from liberalization, entrepreneurs needed ties to the public sector, notably for attaining the licenses required to enter newly opened sectors. In some instances, former officials or SOE managers started a business career to benefit from their ties and knowledge (World Bank 2009: 185).

The political and economic clout of an established, politically well-connected business elite precludes opportunities for economic development. Egypt offers an interesting case because "politically connected firms accounted for only 11 percent of total employment, but 60 percent of total net profits" (World Bank 2014a: 72), implying rents afforded by political connectedness. In part, these rents may stem from favorable enforcement of prescriptive rules as well as from the protection of connected firms from international competition (World Bank 2014a: 75, 78). The cost of rent-seeking by the politically well-connected business elite is considerable. In Egypt, sectors politically connected enterprises engage in witness lower competition, lower rates of firm entry, lower employment growth, and a concentration of unconnected firms in small-scale niches with lower productivity and higher degrees of informality (World Bank 2014a: 71, 79–83).

Furthermore, the well-established and politically connected business elite tends to dominate business organizations such as associations or chambers of commerce which under the Arab social contract are often not inclusive and lack political independence (World Bank 2009: 185). In many cases, intermediary organizations in core Arab economies tended to be controlled by government or dominated by large enterprises (World Bank 2009: 187–188). Hertog (2016: 13) confirms this impression, suggesting a low degree of effective organized advocacy for independent business. Business interests tend to be articulated primarily on an individual basis in the form of favoritism and rent-seeking by the politically well-connected established business elite at the expense of outsiders or newcomers (Hertog 2016: 12–13; Rijkers et al. 2014). It is therefore no surprise that the policy advocacy agenda of business associations in Arab economies tends to focus on furthering vested interests by calling for subsidies or other incentives (World Bank 2009: 188). Yet, the emergence of new business associations representing newcomers or young entrepreneurs is observable (World Bank 2009: 187–191). Similar to business organizations, trade unions in core Arab economies tend to be weak, segmented, and close to government with the partial exception of the Tunisian trade union federation UGTT (Hertog 2016: 14–15). The weakness and lacking inclusiveness of business associations as well as trade unions mean that agents advocating reform such as entrepreneurial newcomers, young people, or women do not enjoy sufficient voice to change policy agendas (Amin et al. 2012: 43–44). In the words of Acemoğlu and Robinson (2012), the old Arab social contract is marked by the absence of an inclusive, broad coalition powerful enough to push for change.

The regime of supply-side subsidies for energy and food is another core feature of the old Arab social contract, although fiscal constraints have forced the Arab government to reduce subsidies in recent years (Hertog 2016: 9–10). Together, the subsidy system and inflated public employment can be considered as non-inclusive "crypto-welfare policies" (Hertog 2016: 10). These policies cover more than those directly employed in the public sector, generating much wider webs of dependence through family relations (World Bank 2013: 8). Crypto-welfare policies are an essential part of the authoritarian bargain critical to the old Arab social contract (Amin et al. 2012: 32–40).

According to Hertog (2016), labor market segmentation in resource-poor and labor-abundant core Arab countries is high even in comparison to other developing world regions. Labor markets in core Arab economies are characterized by the dominance of public sector employment in formal employment, comparatively low mobility within the labor market, high degrees of inflexibility and rigidity, generous public-sector employment conditions, and, consequently, high de facto reservation wages leading to the waithood phenomenon. The consequence is that the major non-oil Arab economies have significantly shares of public-sector employment significantly higher than the global average, with only Morocco as an exception. These facts are underpinned by institutions including preferences and attitudes in favor of public employment. In almost all Arab countries,[12] the vast majority of school and university graduates desire public-sector jobs, with more than 70% of tertiary education graduates in Tunisia aspiring for government employment and more than 50% in Jordan[13] (Hertog 2016: 8–9, 25).

The skills mismatch prevailing in labor markets (see Sect. 2.2.5) seems to be based – at least to some extent – on institutional features of regulation in Arab economies. A lack of coordination between educational systems and the private sector as well as limited incentives for on-the-job training makes bridging skills mismatches difficult (World Bank 2013: 176). Accordingly, educational systems in Arab economies tend to be supply-driven and skewed towards the needs of the public sector, even though the explicit public-sector job guarantees to high school or university graduated valid in former times are no longer given (World Bank 2013: 181–182). Institutionally, high educational aspirations prevail, and tertiary education tends to be regarded as the educational path of choice, as is evident from the impression that "parents and students alike perceive 'good jobs' as those requiring a university degree (…). In the words of a secondary student from Jordan, 'It is simply not prestigious if you hold less than a bachelor's degree'" (World Bank 2013: 181).

---

[12] Lebanon is the major exception (Hertog 2016: 25).

[13] Interestingly, the desire to attain government jobs increases with educational attainment in Tunisia, while it decreases significantly in Jordan (Hertog 2016: 25).

The flip side of the coin is that TVET suffers from a fairly low reputation and tends to be perceived as a "punishment for failure" (Amin et al. 2012: 68) to enroll in university because of lower scores in important and competitive university entry exams (World Bank 2013: 182–184). Thus, TVET is seen as a second-best solution to an academic education at most (Amin et al. 2012: 68; World Bank 2013: 24). Consequently, apart from Tunisia, demand and enrolment for TVET significantly declined during the 2000s (World Bank 2013: 185–186). Driven by both the low reputation of TVET and the pursuit of academic tracks geared towards the needs of the public sector such as humanities, the skills mismatch contributes to the low-productivity equilibrium prevailing under the old Arab social contract (Hertog 2016; World Bank 2013: 7, 25).

Labor market segmentation in low-income Arab economies is exacerbated by the rigidity of labor laws with high levels of legal protection for public and formal private-sector employment and low or absent protection for informal-sector jobs. Restrictions of layoffs in Arab economies include requirements of third-party notification or even approval (World Bank 2013: 148). Coverage of formal social security systems in core Arab economies is limited, with marginal groups such as the poor, the young, or the unemployed being particularly exposed to risks (World Bank 2013: 152–153). Unemployment insurance schemes tend to be weak or non-existing in Arab economies with the exception of Jordan and Bahrain which introduced more comprehensive systems in recent years (World Bank 2013: 159–160). Thus, while there is intense labor market regulation in most core Arab economies, the large group of outsiders such as the unemployed or those working in the large informal sector by definition do not benefit from government regulation. Crypto-welfare policies such as public employment or subsidies do not address these outsiders' welfare needs (Hertog 2016: 13–16).

On the level of institutions, low trust creates disincentives for cooperation, driven by favoritism and exclusion. Mainly due to this lack of cooperation and trust, Hertog situates the stylized Arab VoC somewhere between the classical types of CME and LME. Relationships are typically situated somewhere between market-based and coordinated and often steered informally. However, organizations such as associations or trade unions play a significantly weaker role than in CMEs (Hertog 2016: 17).

Rivlin (2009) proposes a concept similar to Hertog's (2016) Arab VoC which he calls the "Arab equilibrium." In essence, what these authors describe is the socioeconomic regulation regime of the old Arab social contract. Historically, this regulation regime can be seen to have followed what Bobek (1959, 1974) describes as a system of relationships between farmers and landowners which he termed "rent capitalism." This system found in various places in the Middle East is essentially characterized by a split between productive agricultural labor and urban landlords who extract rents without reinvesting capital, thus preventing increases in productivity (Bobek 1959, 1974). Rent capitalism with its structures of urban-rural land ownership patterns was characterized by the lack of productive investments and the reliance of the landed elite on their rural land possessions (World Bank 2009: 129–149). Land ownership is one of the traditional factors underpinning the system of regulation in core Arab economies. Land allocation in Arab economies tends to involve a strong role of government and a traditional and well-established landowning (or today, real-estate development) elite (Bobek 1974; World Bank 2009: 129–149). However, the old Arab social contract refers to wider aspects of socio-economic regulation beyond land ownership and extended rent extraction to wider parts of the economy.

It is plausible to assume that during the 1950s and 1960s and due to the challenges of independence and nation building, land reform, industrialization, import substitution policies, as well as the prevailing ideologies of Arab nationalism and socialism, a regulation crisis led to the emergence of the old Arab social contract or Arab VoC as described above. Another regulation crisis became apparent in the 1980s in the wake of structural adjustment programs (Richards and Waterbury 2008: 218–226) and in the context of demographic challenges (see Chap. 2). One might argue that this long-lasting regulation crises eventually led to the events commonly known as the "Arab Spring" in the 2010s, but discontent built up over a long time (Amin et al. 2012; Richards and Waterbury 2008).

Beyond the purely economic sphere, socio-institutional framework conditions in Arab societies include the role of religion. Following Weberian reasoning, one might assume that in societies in which religion plays major role both in public and private life, religious attitudes will have a decisive influence on the conditions for economic growth. However, the argument is not as straightforward as Weberian thought suggests. The influence of Islam on economic growth and development is a hotly debated issue. Rivlin (2009: 50–54) provides an overview on the literature discussing the impact of Islam on economic growth and development. The arguments summarized by Rivlin suggest that while some elements of Islam can be shown to contradict the tenets of modern capitalism, the evidence on Islam's economic impact is inconclusive. This is not least because religion is endogenous to development processes. Even if religion in and by itself does not pose an obstacle to economic growth, constraining factors could be found in political realities such as regimes using religion or particular interpretations of religion as a means to legitimize and maintain power. The historically founded idea of the identity of state and religion in Islam could be another politico-religious concept conditioning economic development (Rivlin 2009: 50–54; 290–291).

Noland and Pack (2007: 139–144; 300–301), too, review the literature and by attempting to econometrically isolate the effect of religion on economic growth conclude that the evidence does not suggest that Islam in and by itself is an obstacle to economic development. Basedau et al. (2017) present an extensive literature review on empirical evidence of dimensions of religion in general (disaggregated into religious identity, religious practice, religious actors and organization, and religious ideas) on economic and social development outcomes. They conclude that while the empirical evidence on the effect of dimensions of religion is mixed and unclear (often due to methodological fuzziness), common hypotheses such as an alleged positive effect of Protestantism on economic development and an alleged negative effect of Islam are not supported (Basedau et al. 2017).

On a more general level, the different development paths taken by various majority Muslim societies suggest that religion does not predetermine the course of economic development. For example, comparing countries such as Malaysia, Turkey, Iran, Sudan, and Yemen with their Muslim majorities but extremely diverging economic development paths calls for a rejection of simplistic and monocausal explanations on the economic role of Islam. The fact that reforms in economically relevant policy areas have occurred in recent centuries shows that religion does not predetermine processes of economic development but that policy matters (Rivlin 2009: 52).

In sum, the evidence on the role of Islam in economic development and thus its role as a possible factor of socio-economic regulation are inconclusive. It appears that religion in and by itself can be seen neither as a promoter of long-term economic growth nor as an obstacle to it. Rather, religious beliefs and interpretations can indirectly affect the institutional framework conditions of an economy, but this relationship is a complex one. Religion or, more precisely, interpretations of religious prescriptions probably exert some influence on the level of institutions, but exactly how and to which degree they do so is a matter of each individual case and will most likely differ between countries and even between regions, sectors, and social *milieux*. This is why in the regulation framework developed here, religion is not accorded the status of an independent element of socio-economic regulation because doing so would create an analytical black box (just as would be the case for "culture"). The more precise approach chosen here is to identify institutions such as attitudes or preferences that condition socio-economic regulation which may or may not be affected by religious ideas or interpretations. On the level of organizations, religious authorities or entities can indeed play a role in socio-economic regulation and, through their agency and religious interpretations, affect institutions such as commonly accepted attitudes.

The nestedness of institutions in a complex multilevel system or web of interactions across spatial levels proposed by Boyer and Hollingsworth (1997a) implies that an analysis of regulation in Arab economies cannot be complete without considering external or overarching layers. For example, the modes of coordination known from France with its public-sector-centered approach (Hall and Soskice 2001: 35) might be relevant for Tunisia. Policy transfer from France – as is visible, for example, in Tunisian cluster policy which follows the French *pôles de compétitivité* model and wording – and post-colonial legacies such as French-inspired traditions in the education system but also general policymaking attitudes such as prevailing attitudes towards government and public-sector involvement in the economy arguably affect regulation in a French-speaking Maghreb country such as Tunisia. Interactions with the Tunisian diaspora in France and education of elites in French schools or universities can be expected to underscore these complex interactions and their effect on regulation. British legacies may exert an analogous influence in other Arab economies, although probably to a somewhat lesser degree.

Moreover, for some Arab economies – most notably Morocco and Tunisia – regulation is affected by EU *rapprochement*. Morocco's and Tunisia's relationship with the EU strongly intensified within the framework of the EU's Mediterranean neighborhood policy called "Barcelona process" since 1995 and the signature of bilateral association agreements. Basically, this process and related EU-assisted large-scale programs of institutional alignment and competitive upgrading for the private sector arguably contributed to de facto integration into EU structures and policies in technical and economic areas (Benner 2015; Ghali and Rezgui 2015: 40).

While other Arab economies did go as far in EU *rapprochement* yet – with Algeria following Morocco's and Tunisia's steps but trailing them (Benner 2015) – the EU neighborhood policy of the Barcelona process, including the Union for the Mediterranean as a EU-Mediterranean dialogue forum, is relevant for most Arab economies including Egypt, Jordan, Lebanon, the Palestinian Authority, and theoretically Libya and Syria. This context suggests that regulation in Arab economies will be, to a larger or lesser extent, affected by some regulation patterns known from Europe. In the case of (Mediterranean) Arab economies, this influence is a major element of what Peck and Theodore (2007) call transnational transformative processes, although others such WTO membership play a role, too. When examining regulation in a particular core Arab economy, it is necessary to carefully consider the degree and shape of transnational institutional alignment and policy transfer and to identify the particular forms of adaptation and possible modification occurring under the specific regulation patterns prevailing in a specific core Arab economy.

Taking together the considerations presented above, socio-economic regulation in Arab economies under the old Arab social contract can be conceptualized in a stylized way through the regulation framework proposed (Fig. 3.2) as follows.[14] Figure 3.3 illustrates the points elaborated in the subsequent discussion by summarizing the major findings on socio-economic regulation patterns prevailing in core Arab economies.

Salient features of socio-economic regulation prevailing in most core Arab economies under the old Arab social contract, as represented in Fig. 3.3, include the following ones:

- As part of to the regime of accumulation, the *structure of production* in labor-abundant core Arab economies is characterized by the high degree of labor market segmentation between formal and informal sectors and along age, gender, regions, and between public and private sectors, high levels of youth as well as female unemployment,[15] low female labor-force participation, inflated public sectors, a strong role of SOEs in production, low innovative dynamics, crowding out of private investment by large public sectors, and the orientation of educa-

---

[14] The following discussion offers a stylized characterization of socioeconomic regulation in core Arab economies without considering in detail the variation between core Arab economies. While variation can be extensive between countries, the discussion focuses on generally observable common features shared by most Arab economies (excluding special cases such as present-day Syria, Libya, or Yemen). To account for specifics of regulation in a particular economy, a detailed refinement will be necessary, as is attempted here for the cases of Tunisia and Jordan in Chap. 4.

[15] High youth unemployment does not only complicate the transition from education to work but also the transition to forming an own household since in Arab economies the prospects for marriage and founding an own family is related to employment (Amin et al. 2012: 57), underscoring the wider socio-institutional effects of a salient economic phenomenon such as unemployment and its wider implications for socioeconomic regulation. The common expectation for young people to be gainfully employed before marrying can well be understood as an institution.

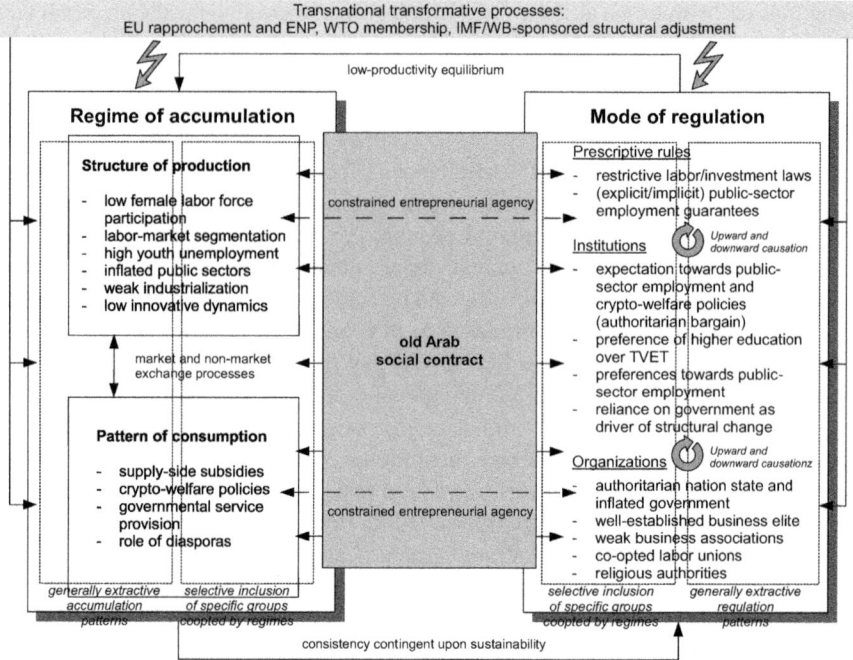

Fig. 3.3 Stylized regulation framework under the old Arab social contract. (Source: Own work based on Bathelt 1994: 66)

tional systems towards the employment needs of the public sector. Implicit in these characteristics is the skills mismatch between labor market supply and demand. Weak industrialization, evident in the comparatively low share of manufacturing in GDP and the higher shares of the agricultural and service sectors relative to other middle-income countries in comparable stages of development (Amin et al. 2012: 112–117) are further characteristics of the structure of production in core Arab economies. As part of the large and diverse service sector, tourism plays a major role in countries such as Tunisia and Jordan (Hazboun 2008), Egypt, Morocco, or some Gulf states.

- The *pattern of consumption* is characterized by the prevalence of supply-side subsidies, notably on fuel and foodstuffs; the effects of crypto-welfare policies (including inflated public-sector employment); the effect of public service provision by governments; the role of diasporas such as the Moroccan or Tunisian diasporas in France, the Netherlands, Spain, or Italy; and the effect of their remittances (Richards and Waterbury 2008: 389–390; 397–400; Maghraoui and Zerhouni 2014: 667; Benner 2015).

- Within the *mode of regulation*, relevant prescriptive rules include restrictive labor laws[16] and investment laws including, for instance, authorization require-

---

[16] When it comes to restrictive labor laws, one might expect a range of rule-circumventing institutions to deal with stringent regulations. One interesting example for a rule-circumventing institution

ments for investments in defined "strategic" sectors or polarized investment regimes with privileged offshoring or export processing zones, as well as formerly explicit or implicit guarantees for public-sector employment to university graduates. Institutions critical to the old Arab social contract include widely held expectations and aspirations towards public-sector employment and towards the maintenance of crypto-welfare policies including, for example, supply-side subsidies. These expectations and aspirations are a critical component of the authoritarian bargain (Amin et al. 2012: 18, 32–40; Desai et al. 2009: 93). Further institutions include prevailing preferences for public-sector employment among jobseekers and their families (Amin et al. 2012: 19, 43) as well as a continued reliance on state intervention in economic development and a general distrust towards the private sector (Richards and Waterbury 2008: 180–181). Parents' willingness to support their children during waithood while queuing for prestigious public-sector jobs is another institution under the mode of regulation, since "societal norms encourage parents to support their children well into their twenties rather than having them accept low-status employment" (Amin et al. 2012: 59). Organizations characteristic of the old Arab social contract include an authoritarian nation-state, inflated government and SOEs, a well-established and politically well-connected business elite either as an informal group or dominating non-inclusive business associations, and co-opted labor unions. Following Acemoğlu and Robinson (2012: 79–81), these organizations are the exact opposite of what an inclusive broad coalition would look like. Religious authorities may play a role in defining attitudes relevant for the socio-economic sphere of society, e.g., towards women's participation in the labor market, fertility (Richards and Waterbury 2008: 78), or legitimate financial instruments. Mechanisms of upward and downward causation between prescriptive rules, institutions, and organizations are apparent, for instance, in the design and implementation of the crypto-welfare policy of public-sector employment which was so central to the authoritarian bargain in the old Arab social contract. Prescriptive rules such as previously explicit public-sector employment guarantees shaped institutions such as citizens' expectations, aspirations, and educational/employment preferences, while together they led to inflated public sectors. In this regard, downward causation works through institution-reinforcing rules such as public-sector employment guarantees, while citizens' expectations, aspirations, and preferences formed rule-reinforcing institutions.

- Cutting through the regime of accumulation and the mode of regulation, *entrepreneurial agency* is constrained for a number of reasons. Entrepreneurial dynamism tends to be weak. Aspirations towards public-sector employment constrain entrepreneurial attitudes among jobseekers and notably among young university graduates. Educational systems are geared towards the needs demanded by the public sector instead of the private sector. The extractive nature of much of the

on a highly regulated labor market is the one cited by the World Bank (2009: 32) quoting a Syrian businessman's approach in countering legal constraints to dismissing workers by requiring employees to sign an undated resignation letter upon recruitment.

regime of accumulation and the mode of regulation severely limits the growth perspectives for entrepreneurial ventures, and the extractive political nature of the authoritarian bargain inherent to the old Arab social contract does not encourage the rise of a confident and independent new entrepreneurial class. The economic clout and political connectedness of the well-established business elite, its rent-seeking behavior, and resulting phenomena of state capture are all symptoms of the extractive politico-economic setup of regulation under the old Arab social contract which render successful independent and innovative entrepreneurship difficult. The constrained nature of entrepreneurship and, by extension, Schumpeterian creative destruction is thus an outcome of the dominance of selected insider groups and the generally extractive design of economic and political rules, institutions, and organizations that, according to Acemoğlu and Robinson's (2012) understanding, preclude the emergence of broad coalitions and the emergence of economic and political newcomers.

- The resulting system of regulation under the old Arab social contract is characterized by a low-productivity equilibrium and hence some degree of consistency, as the interplay between rule-reinforcing institutions and institution-reinforcing rules, for instance, between former public-sector employment guarantees and citizens' expectations, jobseekers' aspirations, and students' educational preferences, demonstrates. While the equilibrium is marked by low productivity and thus dissatisfying economic results expressed by structural deficiencies such as those explained in Chap. 2, it still was by definition stable as long as the general conditions of the old Arab social contract held. However, the system of regulation under the old Arab social contract was consistent and stable only as long as the model could be sustained fiscally and demographically. Coming under fiscal and demographic pressure due to the ever-increasing size of inflated public sectors and the youth bulge, the system of regulation of the old Arab social contract lost its internal consistency and hence its stability. *Transnational transformative processes* certainly contributed to the exposure of the growing inconsistencies under the old Arab social contract. In particular, structural adjustment sponsored by the IMF and the World Bank (Richards and Waterbury 2008: 218–226) contradicted entrenched features of the regime of accumulation and the mode of regulation such as crypto-welfare policies and notably supply-side subsidies. Thus, structural adjustment put additional political and societal pressure on an increasingly unsustainable system of socio-economic regulation, arguably exposing or even exacerbating structural deficiencies in socio-economic regulation. As will be discussed in Sect. 3.4, the sustainability deficit of the old Arab social contract and structural adjustment inserted new institutional configurations into the regulation regime such as institution-circumventing rules or even institution-competing rules, severely calling into question the prior internal consistency of the old regulation regime. The so-called "Arab Spring" may be seen as the culmination of public discontent with the not-so-latent cracks in a regulation system that lost its internal consistency.

The present sub-section has characterized the old Arab social contract in a stylized way and conceptualized it as a regulation regime. The sub-section thus addressed the first research question proposed (How does regulation between economic action and institutional context work in Arab economies, notably in relation to drivers of private-sector growth such as entrepreneurship?). The role and constraints of entrepreneurship and innovation as drivers of Schumpeterian creative destruction under the old Arab social contract merit a closer discussion, specifically if promoting a stronger role for entrepreneurship and innovation is regarded as a pathway to a higher-productivity equilibrium. Indeed, development policy in Arab economies increasingly focuses on promoting entrepreneurship and innovation, but as Isenberg (2010) observed, isolated schemes are questionable since entrepreneurship is a systemic driver of creative destruction operating within a complex regulation regime. The next sub-section therefore focuses on the role of entrepreneurship and innovation under the old Arab social contract.

3.3.2 Regulation in Arab Economies: What Role for Creative Destruction?

As was argued in Sub-section 3.3.1, the weak dynamism of the private sector and the low traction of Schumpeterian creative destruction in core Arab economies cannot be understood without having a look at the historically founded position of government in Arab economies. After independence, governments, not the private sector, were drivers of structural transformation in Arab economies. Creative destruction did not feature in this paradigm as an essential driver of structural change. Rather, on the institutional level, a wide acceptance and even expectation of a large, interventionist government emerged. The ideology of Arab socialism was abandoned sooner or later by most core Arab states that experimented with it (e.g., Tunisia in 1969), and conservative monarchical regimes such as Jordan or Morocco did not explicitly pursue Arab socialism in the first place. Still, the public sector was generally seen as the critical force for economic development, and the legacy of large public sectors and reliance on the government as the driving force in the economy, directing industrialization and solving structural problems, has survived and become an essential institutional reality in core Arab economies (Richards and Waterbury 2008: 179–181).

The strong role of government in core Arab economies is mirrored by a weak entrepreneurial middle class. Rivlin (2009: 55–59) describes that the weakness of the middle class in most Arab economies poses an obstacle to entrepreneurship and that hence challenges to political regimes from within the middle class used to be absent. Basically, in the terminology of Acemoğlu and Robinson (2012), the absence of a strong coalition calling for political and economic inclusiveness is critically related to weak entrepreneurship. Taking a historical perspective, Rivlin illustrates how a *bourgoise* mercantile class developed during the Abbasid era but failed to gain enough economic prominence to cause the development of capitalism because of too weak capital accumulation and government ownership of industries. Thus, the government was left to military rulers, while at the same time, inheritance laws prevented the rise of a landowning *bourgeoisie* that could have accumulated sufficient capital to set in motion the development of capitalism (Rivlin 2009: 87–89).

Rivlin's historical explanation of secular trends of deficient processes of Schumpeterian creative destruction in most Arab countries[17] is consistent with Bobeks' (1959; 1974) rent capitalism theory. Rent capitalism fits well with the absence of entrepreneurship in a Schumpeterian sense because neither the agricultural laborers not the urban landlords assumed it, the former ones due to the lack of reinvestable capital and the latter ones due to the lack of incentives. Rent capitalism might have been an obstacle to industrialization because of its role in preventing increases in productivity in the agricultural sector and thus making a shift of productive resources to the development of industry more difficult, an argument in line with Rostow's (1959) conditions for the takeoff of industrialization. In such a context, the lack of an independent entrepreneurial or merchant class enables the ascent of rent-seeking behavior by well-connected cronies – a phenomenon commonly known as crony capitalism – and the setup and maintenance of high barriers to entry against new entrepreneurs. In a regulation regime with highly extractive economic institutions that make the rise of a politically confident and economically powerful entrepreneurial class virtually impossible, thus reinforcing existing extractive political institutions, competition is limited, and Schumpeterian creative destruction is severely constrained.

Paradoxically, the gradual retreat of government from direct economic interference in the wake of partial liberalization did not create space for a more dynamic and entrepreneurial private sector. Although economic liberalization since the early 1970s in both Egypt and Tunisia led to an emergent private sector, entrepreneurship remained undynamic and lacking in terms of productivity and growth (Adly and Khatib 2014: 172). The space left by the receding public sector was filled by a privileged, politically well-connected business elite. Even under liberalization, crony capitalism posed constraints to entrepreneurship due to the dominance of the well-established and politically well-connected business elite and resulting power and information asymmetries, leading "to the transferring of once state-held assets and market shares into the hands of a few cronies that were tightly-connected to the incumbent regimes" (Adly and Khatib 2014: 173). The dominance of business associations and informal political advocacy channels by the well-established business elite further complicated conditions for entrepreneurial newcomers who had no political voice (Amin et al. 2012: 38; Adly and Khatib 2014: 174; World Bank 2009: 12–13).

Consequently, Arab economies tend to feature low levels of enterprise creation (OECD and IDRC 2013: 14). Hertog (2016: 12, 28) summarizes evidence of comparatively low entrepreneurial dynamism and Schumpeterian creative destruction in

---

[17]Rivlin (2009: 55–59) lists some exceptional cases featuring strong merchant middle classes in Arab economies, the most important being Lebanon.

core Arab economies, and resulting weaknesses in investment and productivity. Amin et al. (2012: 107) state weak competition and low entrepreneurial dynamism in Arab economies, leading to a slow pace of creative destruction. The World Bank (2009) confirms this result by suggesting a lack of dynamism and creative destruction. These insights are consistent with what Adly and Khatib (2014: 40) call "capitalism without entrepreneurship." While the two countries surveyed by Adly and Khatib (2014), Tunisia and Egypt, had some success in liberalizing and unleashing the private sector, the expanded private sector consists mostly of underproductive family-owned MSMEs and lacks dynamic efficiency. Interestingly, Adly and Khatib (2014) show that the bigger SMEs become, the more vulnerable they are to corruption and distortion, effectively incentivizing them to remain small (Adly and Khatib 2014).

Entrepreneurship in Egypt and Tunisia (and probably in other core Arab economies) is marked by a sense of muddling under conditions of sub-optimality (Adly and Khatib 2014: 167). Entrepreneurs in Egypt and Tunisia use social capital (Putnam 1995) to counter deficiencies in the formal environment by relying on family and friends for funding and a secure resource endowment (Adly and Khatib 2014: 178). Traditional values including family values support entrepreneurship not just through funding but more generally through a supportive attitude (OECD and IDRC 2013: 107–108). The finding that entrepreneurs use social capital to overcome deficiencies in the entrepreneurship ecosystem suggests the prevalence of rule-substituting or rule-circumventing institutions that may play an important role in a regulation regime marked by considerable deficiencies in terms of prescriptive rules and organizations. Further, barriers to entry for entrepreneurial newcomers are high in Arab economies, not necessarily because of strict formal rules but because of their arbitrary implementation (World Bank 2009: 97). In the framework of the regulation perspective pursued here, constraints towards entrepreneurship, entrepreneurial innovation, and related Schumpeterian creative destruction are thus not so much a matter of strict prescriptive rules but institutions in terms of arbitrary implementation.

Following the taxonomy of interactions between rules and institutions proposed by Glückler and Lenz (2016), in terms of entrepreneurship, innovation, and Schumpeterian creative destruction, the regulation system prevalent in the old Arab social contract exhibits the following features:

- Rule-reinforcing institutions such as expectations towards public-sector employment and other crypto-welfare policies, as well as widely held preferences among university graduates and jobseekers towards public-sector employment, are consistent with prescriptive rules such as formerly explicit or implicit public employment guarantees, restrictive labor laws, and generous public-sector employment conditions. These prescriptive rules function as institution-reinforcing rules, and the rule-reinforcing institutions mentioned are likely to constrain entrepreneurship by preventing the emergence of a strong entrepreneurial attitude.
- The reliance of entrepreneurs on social capital (Putnam 1995) based on family and friends to overcome formal barriers to entrepreneurship is a case of rule-substituting or even rule-circumventing institutions. Social capital enables them

to pursue their entrepreneurial activity by compensating a non-supportive environment of prescriptive rules or non-supportive ways of rule implementation with supportive relational capital. Yet, it is likely that this compensation mechanism will work only to a certain point, probably constraining the growth of entrepreneurial ventures.

• Arbitrary implementation of prescriptive rules may follow rule-circumventing or even rule-competing institutions caused by the agency of formal or informal organizations such as the well-connected business elite or through formal business organizations dominated by the business elite and authoritarian nation-states. Hence, institutions of arbitrary rule implementation represent a case of upward causation.

In such a regulation regime, consistency is assured under a low-productivity equilibrium as long as the regulation regime is stable, a condition which is confronted with severe long-term fiscal constraints. As long as the regulation regime is stable, the prevailing low-productivity equilibrium is marked by low entrepreneurial dynamism, low levels of innovative activity, weak competition, and a lack of vibrant Schumpeterian creative destruction. These features underscore the inefficiency of the regulation regime not just in terms of static efficiency but also, and probably even more importantly, in terms of dynamic efficiency.

The present sub-section has shed light on the conditions the regulation regime of the old Arab social contract offered for entrepreneurial dynamism and innovation. It has thus refined the answers to the first research question (How does regulation between economic action and institutional context work in Arab economies, notably in relation to drivers of private-sector growth such as entrepreneurship?), in terms of entrepreneurship and innovation and their role as drivers of private-sector growth through Schumpeterian creative destruction. Consistent with the wider perspective of socio-economic regulation pursued here, the sub-section highlighted the nexus between Schumpeterian creative destruction and political change through the importance, or absence, of an economically dynamic and politically confident independent entrepreneurial class.

The next sub-section turns to research questions two to four by dealing with the possibilities to come up with a new, consistent, and sustainable regulation regime or what could be termed a new Arab social contract, with a more prominent role of Schumpeterian creative destruction.

3.4   Alternatives for Socio-economic Regulation: Pathways Towards a New Arab Social Contract

The regulation regime under the old Arab social contract was consistent and stable as long as its major features could be sustained. However, the sustainability of the regulation regime came under increasing pressure since the late 1970s. The structural economic problems of Arab economies presented in Chap. 2 can be understood as the symptoms of these underlying pressures. Formerly explicit and subsequently implicit public employment guarantees for secondary or tertiary education graduates led to inflated public sectors that could no longer be fiscally sustained. Other crypto-welfare policies such as extensive subsidy schemes for food, fuel, and energy put additional pressure on public budgets (Amin et al. 2012: 86–89). Public infrastructure investment was getting more difficult to sustain. Demographic trends such as the youth bulge exacerbated the problem of youth unemployment. The weakness of the formal private sector left the young unemployed effectively with the alternative options of either waiting for future opportunities to attain a public-sector job or entering the informal sector. Structural adjustment programs sponsored by the IMF and the World Bank were designed to correct macro-level imbalances through reforms and austerity programs. Yet, the outcomes of reforms were generally disappointing. While structural adjustment helped countries in severe balance of payment or fiscal crises regain some degree of macroeconomic stability, it did not lead to significant decreases in unemployment or rises in living standards (Richards and Waterbury 2008: 218–261).

A socio-economic regulation perspective provides a plausible explanation for the mixed outcomes of structural adjustment. With the basic tenets of the regulation regime under the Arab social contract still in place, structural adjustment focused on fiscal imbalances did neither attempt nor achieve a readjustment of the socio-economic framework. Factual constraints towards entrepreneurship, innovation, and Schumpeterian creative destruction (see Sub-section 3.3.2) were not addressed. More generally, the institutional context in core Arab economies did not see significant modifications. In particular, structural adjustment did not change rule-circumventing or rule-competing institutions such as the arbitrary implementation of prescriptive rules. Even if structural adjustment led to the modification of prescriptive rules, giving in theory more freedom to private-sector development and entrepreneurship, the institutionally founded arbitrary implementation of these prescriptive rules did not improve the situation for independent entrepreneurs. While public employment guarantees were given up over time (a modification of prescriptive rules), institutions such as citizens' expectations and preferences for public-sector employment remained in place.

It is plausible to assume that changes in prescriptive rules brought about by structural adjustment combined with essentially unchanged institutions deepened the fissures in the regulation regime. As public employment guarantees and other crypto-welfare policies and thus the promises made by regimes to citizens under the authoritarian bargain were not fulfilled anymore while institutions such as citizens' educational and employment preferences remained unchanged, the old Arab social contract lost its internal consistency. Rule-reinforcing institutions such as jobseekers' preferences for public-sector employment and citizens' expectations towards the upkeep of crypto-welfare policies such as supply-side subsidies arguably turned into rule-competing institutions without avenues for upward causation through micro-level agency. New policies such as investment laws designed to promote private investment, entrepreneurship support policies, or policies implementing conditionalities related to IMF- and World Bank-sponsored structural adjustment programs established new prescriptive rules that were did not fit with prevailing institutions such as citizens' expectations and preferences. Therefore, these policies tended to put in place institution-competing rules in the case of "hard" policies such as the cutback in crypto-welfare policies or institution-circumventing rules in the case of "softer" policies such as entrepreneurship promotion. It is fair to assume that these new prescriptive rules did not radically change existing institutions. This lack of consistency became increasingly evident through structural problems such as high and persistent youth unemployment or deficiencies in governmental service provision. Amin et al. (2012) highlight results of opinion polls in core Arab economies including Egypt and Tunisia which show significant decreases in citizens' perceptions of their own well-being and in their satisfaction with governmental service provision during the late 2000s. In a regulation perspective, this hike in popular dissatisfaction is probably the logical outcome of an inefficient regulation regime with strong internal inconsistencies and of an authoritarian bargain that has become one-sided. In retrospect, the revolutions of 2010/2011 which led to the overthrow of the Ben Ali and Mubarak regimes can be regarded as the political side of a regulation crisis whose economic side has been evident since the late 1970s. Evolutionary reform movements marked by public protests and careful reactions by incumbent regimes as witnessed in Morocco and Jordan were much less radical than the revolutionary upheavals in Tunisia and Egypt.[18] Yet, the point of departure was the same: populations implicitly demanded a correction of the old Arab social contract through political accountability and citizens' participation in political decision-making, as well as effective solutions to structural economic problems such as high youth unemployment, interregional disparities, and deficiencies in public service provision.

While the revolutions or evolutions since 2010 were the culmination of a regulation crisis that has become more acute for years or even decades before, a new, consistent, and sustainable regulation regime will take years to unfold. Difficult processes of political and economic transformation in Tunisia and continued waves of demonstration in peripheral regions in the Center-West and South of Tunisia in 2016 and 2017 and in the Rif region of Morocco in 2017 underscore the complexity of painful and long-term regulation adjustment in a volatile political context and among widespread expectations of quick fixes. Yet, one might argue that the current period provides a window of opportunity for solving the long-standing regulation crisis in core Arab economies. The fact that Tunisia, Egypt, and Jordan are currently undergoing a new and painful process of IMF- and World Bank-sponsored structural adjustment which include, inter alia, cutbacks of crypto-welfare policies such as subsidies again underlines the inconsistency and unsustainability of the previously prevailing Arab social contract. At the same time, reforms could contribute to the development of an internally and externally more consistent and sustainable regulation regime, provided they are politically well managed and combined with the setup of sustainable and need-based social safety nets.

---

[18] Libya, Yemen, and Syria where initial revolutionary upheavals eventually turned into civil wars are not dealt with here.

While it is advisable to use historical analogies carefully, the current transformative political and economic context in core Arab economies may share some characteristics with the upheavals in Eastern Europe in the early 1990s. This is why considering how a new, consistent, and sustainable regulation regime for core Arab economies might look like, and which political and economic processes of transformation could facilitate the adjustment towards such a new regulation regime, is important. The remainder of the present section focuses on these questions and presents stylized arguments on what a more consistent and sustainable regulation regime in core Arab economies could consist of. While each country will develop its own new regulation regime, such a "new Arab social contract" could depart in several critical aspects from the previous regulation regime but at the same time draw on some of the specificities most core Arab economies share. The result could be a common regulation framework across core Arab economies that will most likely look different from the one-size-fits-all, "Washington Consensus"-type image of how an efficient economy is supposed to function (Williamson 1990; Richards and Waterbury 2008: 229–230). In essence, the new regulation regime proposed here attempts to offer a context-specific, institution-sensitive, and path-dependent approach (Bathelt and Glückler 2012: 48; 2014; Benner 2017b; Glückler and Lenz 2016) to structural economic reform in core Arab economies.

Considering the critical role of crypto-welfare policies and particularly of fiscally unsustainable and macroeconomically inefficient public-sector employment in the inconsistency of the old Arab social contract, it seems logical that a new Arab social contract will have to be based more on dynamic and efficient private sector that includes promoting entrepreneurships and SMEs (OECD and IDRC 2013: 13). To achieve private-sector-led growth, entrepreneurship, innovation, and concomitant Schumpeterian creative destruction will have to play a more prominent role in any new growth model for core Arab economies.

Such a new regulation regime or new Arab social contract could look like the one sketched in Fig. 3.4. The regulation regime depicted there in a stylized manner is an idealized and normative one. Essentially, Fig. 3.4 proposes hypothetical answers to the question of how a regulation regime in core Arab economies that gives a greater role to private-sector-led growth, entrepreneurship, innovation, and Schumpeterian creative destruction could look like, given the structural conditions found in core Arab economies. Figure 3.4 represents neither the only possible outcome of the current regulation crisis in core Arab economies, nor does it predict that the proposed regulation regime will be the result of the current political and economic transformation in the Arab world. Aspects related to the transition from the old regulation regime to any new one will be discussed below. The stylized regulation regime depicted focuses on some possible common answers across core Arab economies, but any new Arab social contract will most likely look somewhat different in each country. What Fig. 3.4 does attempt is to provide an impetus for discussing possible modifications of elements of the regulation regime in core Arab economies including institutional and organizational change, and the role policy can play in facilitating or even initiating these changes. In particular, the regulation regime sketched in Fig. 3.4 is meant to draw attention to a comprehensive policy agenda adapted to

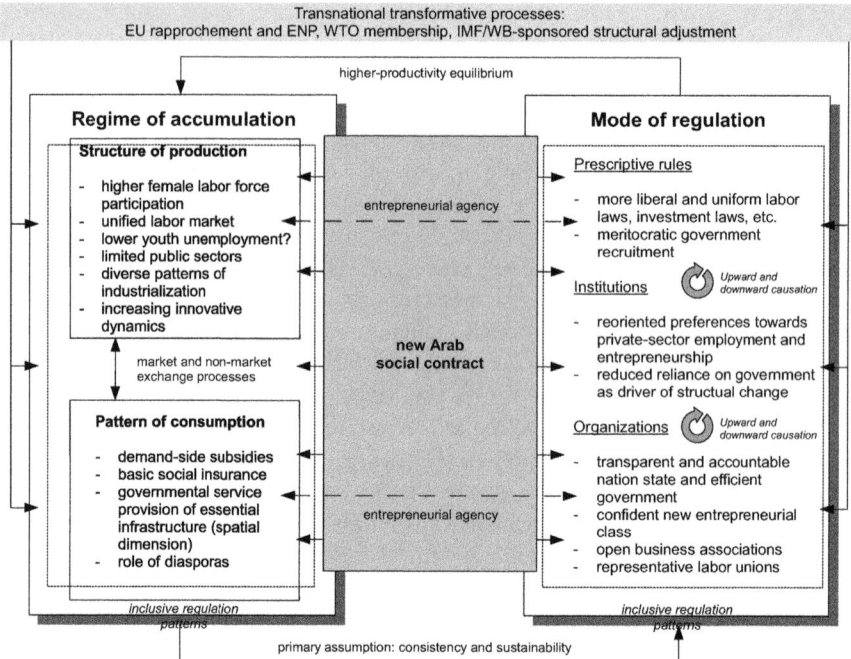

Fig. 3.4 Stylized regulation framework under a new Arab social contract. (Source: Own work based on Bathelt 1994: 66)

institutional context. Such a comprehensive, institution-sensitive approach (Benner 2017b; Glückler and Lenz 2016) would be the opposite of a piecemeal approach that tries to insert isolated policy measures into a regulation regime not suitable to absorb these measures because of institutional inconsistencies. A comprehensive and institution-sensitive policy approach requires looking at the levels of prescriptive rules *and* institutions as not to overlook institutional realities that condition the effectiveness of policies shaping prescriptive rules (Glückler and Lenz 2016: 272).

Stylized features of regulation under a new, sustainable, and internally and externally consistent Arab social contract as proposed in Fig. 3.4 and policy options directed towards reforming the regulation regime in a comprehensive and institution-sensitive approach include the following ones.

As part of a new regime of accumulation, the *structure of production* might include higher female labor-force participation which could be promoted, for instance, through policies to allow women to better balance job and family duties such as day care. Overcoming labor market segmentation is an important goal in reforming the regulation regime that would require policies described below under the mode of regulation because these policies require changes in prescriptive rules related to the labor market. The same holds true for the goal of limiting the size of public sectors, allowing for less crowding out of private-sector investments and recruitment. Increased innovative dynamics are another objective of a new regime of accumulation intrinsically linked to stronger entrepreneurial agency. Policies to promote entrepreneurship include multidisciplinary entrepreneurship education in schools and universities; incubation and acceleration services; training, coaching, and mentoring schemes to entrepreneurs; specific programs to support youth and women entrepreneurship and possibly senior citizen entrepreneurship; and policies to enhance innovation such as university-industry technology transfer schemes, science parks, cluster policies, or innovation vouchers. However, all of these measures' chances of success will most likely be limited if implemented in isolation. As the NIS approach emphasizes, innovation is a socially and institutionally embedded process that does not lend itself to engineering thinking. Higher levels of innovation are not simply the necessary outcome of isolated schemes of innovation support but may be path-dependent, contextual, and contingent (Bathelt and Glückler 2012: 48; 2014) outcomes of complex, interrelated, and relational social processes. This is why policies to promote entrepreneurship and innovation have to be an integral part of a comprehensive and institution-sensitive agenda to renew core Arab economies' regulation system such as the agenda proposed here and will have to include the long-term shaping of attitudes underlying an entrepreneurial ecosystem (Isenberg 2010; Amin et al. 2012: 135–136).

As for industrialization, it is hard to foresee significant growth of manufacturing sectors across the board in core Arab economies. Amin et al. (2012: 119–124) see three different industrialization challenges in Arab economies. For labor-abundant, resource-poor countries, entering global value chains is the main pathway towards industrial development, while for resource-poor middle-income countries, moving up the value chain through skills upgrading is the key challenge. Lastly, oil-exporting countries will have to diversify. Amin et al. (2012: 119) call these three pathways towards industrialization "break in, move up, and diversify." For instance, Tunisia will have to "move up" value chains towards more sophisticated tasks, products, or services through skills and knowledge policies such as entrepreneurship promotion and innovation policies as well as FDI attraction in more skills- and knowledge-intense sectors. Egypt and Morocco have to "break in" industrial development with a focus on provoking an export push in lower-value agro-industrial and trade-related areas through policy interventions such as export processing zones (EPZs) and FDI attraction. Algeria and the GCC countries will have to diversify into niche markets through skills and knowledge policies (Amin et al. (2012: 119–124).

As a relative forerunner in industrial development within the Arab world, Tunisia is a particularly interesting case. While Tunisia has achieved some relative success in industrialization (Cammett 2014: 164; Amin et al. (2012: 113; Diop and Ghali 2012; Ghali and Rezgui 2015), imitating the industrialization trajectories of the successful industrializers of the twentieth century, the East Asian NIEs (World Bank 1993), will be difficult because of the changes that have occurred in the global environment, including the rise of China and India, WTO membership, and a rising sentiment of protectionism notably in the United States and Europe. While for larger Arab economies such as Egypt, Morocco, or Saudi Arabia, growing the manufacturing sector in labor-intensive industries will be a necessity (Richards and Waterbury 2008: 67–68), pathways towards industrialization and underlying structural change in other countries may be more diverse. For example, Richards and Waterbury (2008: 68) classify both Tunisia and Jordan (as well as Israel) as "watch-makers," referring to their scarce natural resource base and the need to focus on human capital and skills development under an export-led strategy (Richards and Waterbury 2008: 68). For these countries, evolving into knowledge-based econo-mies will most likely be the way forward, calling for a broad menu of innovation policies (Amin et al. (2012: 23; M'Henni and Deniozos 2012; Smadi and Tsipouri 2012). Other countries such as Lebanon or smaller Gulf states might well establish themselves as trade, services, and tourism hubs and pursue industrial policies to promote these sectors accordingly. Generally, sectors such as ICT, logistics, educa-tion, and tourism seem promising fields to promote through industrial policy in core Arab economies (Amin et al. (2012: 24). In particular, tourism will remain an important service sector for countries such as Morocco, Tunisia, Egypt, Oman, and the United Arab Emirates, calling for the continuation of tourism policies but prob-ably with different goals in terms of target markets and differentiation. For instance, differentiating its tourism offer will be a continuing challenge and necessity for Tunisia (Hazboun 2008).

There is yet another reason for expecting diverse patterns of structural change and industrialization across core Arab economies. Given that university education in Arab countries tends to be directed towards traditional public-sector employment needs (World Bank 2013: 25; Moghadam and Decker 2014: 94–96), it focuses to a certain extent on social sciences and humanities. While a comparison of shares of students enrolled in science and technology fields and in social sciences and human-ities in various Arab countries suggests a diverse picture, with some Arab econo-mies having similar or higher shares of graduates in engineering, manufacturing, and construction fields than some industrialized countries (UNESCO Institute for Statistics 2015: 138–145), Achy (2010: 16) confirms that Maghreb countries in 2007 had rather low shares of students enrolled in engineering when compared to other emerging economies. Tunisia had the highest share (10.7%) among Maghreb countries but still lagged competitors such as Poland, Turkey, Indonesia, Romania, or Bulgaria (Achy 2010: 16). One might be tempted to call for a stronger focus on natural or medical sciences and engineering because at first sight, these disciplines appear more prone to entrepreneurship (Achy 2010: 26). However, it would be worthwhile to identify possible economic development trajectories that draw on the knowledge assets available in a society. For example, policies to stimulate entrepre-neurship among university graduates often turn their attention to natural and medi-cal sciences and engineering. A knowledge base in social sciences and humanities might, using this traditional lens, appear less conducive to entrepreneurship. However, a regulation perspective considers not only "hard" matters of technologi-cal and scientific possibilities but also "soft" factors such as the social acceptance of innovations or technologies. Theoretically there is no reason why a strong knowl-edge base in social sciences or humanities should not open up equally beneficial economic development trajectories than technological knowledge bases. Instead, a broader perspective towards differentiated knowledge bases and employing plat-form policies (Asheim et al. 2011) would be useful for policy to identify a wider range of possible trajectories that include using knowledge in social sciences or humanities as a base for entrepreneurship and innovation.[19] For example, the commercialization of technology requires the development of markets which, according to the SSP school, are social structures and conditioned by social acceptability, ethics, norms, and values which may constrain or enable the use of new technologies or innovations. Business knowledge such as marketing skills and broader social science or humanities skills will often be at least as relevant to successful commercialization of new technologies as technological knowledge.[20] In life sciences, ethical questions frame the adoption of medical technologies and therapies in societies. Cultural and creative industries are acknowledged as a promising field of economic development (Benner 2017a; European Commission 2010). The use of technology and innovation in tourism (e.g., tour guide apps) is another example for a trajectory where an innovation's competitiveness arguably rests more on "soft" knowledge on customer preferences than on "hard" knowledge on technological possibilities. As these examples demonstrate, knowledge bases in social sciences and humanities can create paths for economic development just as technologically oriented knowledge bases can. Indeed, the importance of multi-disciplinarity in entrepreneurship is recognized (OECD 2012b: 59). Assuming that some Arab economies might have comparative advantages in socially and culturally relevant knowledge bases, entrepreneurship and innovation policies could focus on trajectories emanating from these knowledge bases.

Reforming education is another aspect linked to industrialization. Considering the reputational deficits (Achy 2010: 18; Amin et al. 2012: 68; World Bank 2013: 24) and weak private-sector involvement in TVET systems in Arab countries, one might argue that efforts to build strong TVET systems modeled after European systems such as those known from Germany or Austria and their dual apprenticeship schemes (e.g., World Bank 2013: 179) do not correspond to basic factors of regulation in core Arab economies. High educational aspirations of youth and their families in Arab countries – including notably aspirations towards tertiary education – are an institutionally anchored fact. Instead transplanting elements of TVET systems from other countries to a regulation context marked by very different institutional patterns, looking for ways to better align university education with labor market needs appears more promising. For example, strengthening the role of entrepreneurial, managerial, or personal soft skills in university curricula or introducing dual-study programs combining paid employment in private-sector enterprises and academic education in universities (Lehmann and Benner 2015: 205) could reduce skills mismatches within the framework of existing organizational structures and given patterns of regulation. If TVET suffers from a rather low reputation and if students' and parents' aspirations are geared towards higher education in universities and other HEIs, a regulation perspective sensitive to institutional realities (such

---

[19] There are examples for policies promoting entrepreneurship and knowledge transfer in the humanities (e.g., OECD 2015a).

[20] For example, Felsenstein (1994: 107) finds evidence for the argument that "technical knowledge without business skill does not necessarily make for innovatively successful products or firms."

as aspirations and reputation) would probably advise policy not to invest in vocational schools but rather in building such dual-study programs in HEIs[21] since such programs can equip students with practical skills aligned with labor market needs and at the same time equip them with a high-prestige university degree.[22]

Ideally, the outcome of a reformed structure of production through a combination of policies such as the ones suggested here would be lower unemployment, notably among women and youth. Yet, the pathway towards this outcome is not straightforward. In the past, even in times of comparatively high growth, core Arab economies like Tunisia and Egypt barely managed to keep unemployment rates stable given the demographic situation in core Arab economies and notably the youth bulge (Richards and Waterbury 2008: 140). Even if in the best of cases, a new regulation regime such as the one proposed in Fig. 3.4 emerged and led to higher dynamism in terms of private-sector-led growth, entrepreneurial innovation, competition-induced efficiency gains, and Schumpeterian creative destruction, keeping youth unemployment roughly on current levels will be an ambitious goal. It thus appears fairly unlikely that unemployment levels will significantly fall until the effects of demographic change set in. In the meantime, establishing basic social security systems including unemployment benefits can only provide a partial reaction at best. To counter social pressure related to high and persistent youth unemployment, governments might have to promote the civil society to provide young unemployed at least with limited perspectives to employ their energy and creativity for social or cultural causes in the absence of sufficient employment opportunities.

As for the *pattern of consumption*, a new and sustainable regulation regime would include a reformed welfare system. Instead of the crypto-welfare policies prevailing under the old Arab social contract and supply-side subsidies for food and energy, a reformed welfare system would offer targeted, need-based, demand-side subsidies through cash transfers which are more efficient than supply-side subsidies. However, doing so is politically sensitive. Tunisia's "bread revolt" in 1983–1984 after cuts in government subsidies for bread (Hazboun 2008: 41–42) and riots in other Arab economies in the wake of cost-of-living raises (Richards and Waterbury 2008: 222) provide examples for the sensitivity of the issue, emphasizing the need to take a broader regulation perspective and to tackle long-term institutional change related to citizens' expectations and preferences. Without changing institutions, cutting subsidies can result in institution-competing rules, as it did in Tunisia in 1983. Further, the sensitivity of fuel and energy subsidies suggests that introducing need-based cash transfer will have to go hand in hand with subsidy cuts.

---

[21] Such a dual-study model was established at Al-Quds University in the West Bank and supported by German technical cooperation (Al-Quds University 2016). The author was involved in this project as a consultant. Another example for a scheme similar in its intention is the study model implemented by the German-Jordanian University that includes obligatory internships in Germany.

[22] In Tunisia, for example, the practically oriented higher educational entities called ISET (*Institut supérieur des études technologiques*) (Ben Miled-M'rabet n.d.; Erdle 2011: 29) may offer suitable conditions for setting up dual-study programs.

Basic social insurance including unemployment insurance would be another element of a reformed pattern of consumption. Moving from broad and inefficient supply-side subsidies to targeted demand-side transfers would free fiscal resources for the maintenance and provision of essential government services in the health, education, and transportation sectors. These services and the underlying infrastructure are particularly important for peripheral regions (World Bank 2011), underscoring the spatial nature of reforming the pattern of consumption. Further, the role of diasporas might be redefined. Apart from remittances, the role diasporas play in their economies of origin could include the transfer of skills and knowledge and possibly even entrepreneurial activity. For instance, returnees from Europe or North America could provide a potential for entrepreneurship and technology transfer.[23] Promoting deeper interaction of Arab countries with their diasporas abroad would require a more proactive and systematic diaspora policy, maybe following examples of East Asian NIEs in the 1970s and 1980s (Noland and Pack 2007: 259–260).

Within the *mode of regulation*, prescriptive rules under the new regulation regime suggested here would include somewhat more liberal and uniform labor laws and investment laws to alleviate the strong segmentation on the labor market and to create a legal landscape more conducive to competition with lower barriers to entry particularly for entrepreneurial newcomers. Instead of explicit or implicit public-sector employment guarantees for secondary or tertiary education graduates that were so characteristic of the old Arab social contract and its constituent authoritarian bargain, under a new regulation regime, government recruitment would have to be based on meritocratic criteria. On the level of institutions, consistency of the regulation regime would require that popular attitudes and preferences, notably towards public-sector employment and the role of government as the major driver of economic development, change into attitudes and preferences more directed towards private-sector employment and entrepreneurship as well as towards more trust in the private sector's capability and legitimacy in propelling economic development and structural change. In line with the argument that policies to counter the major structural problems prevalent in core Arab economies are less likely to succeed if they focus on isolated interventions without taking a wider look at the systemic interrelationships in the regulation regime, tackling widely held attitudes is an important yet challenging long-term policy goal. While entrepreneurship education in high schools and universities, business planning competitions, and incubation and acceleration schemes will not in and by themselves create a stronger entrepreneurial attitude, they can be parts of a wider policy to shape the public image of entrepreneurship and private-sector employment. Further elements could include the diffusion of good entrepreneurial practices and public awards for successful new entrepreneurs, building on the strong effect successful role models can have in shaping entrepreneurial attitudes (Isenberg 2010). In addition, changing attitudes will require ending the stigmatization of failure (Isenberg 2010). Modifying prescriptive

---

[23] Strictly speaking, entrepreneurial activity and knowledge or skills transfer by members of the diaspora would be part of the regime of accumulation and, if successful, strengthen innovative and entrepreneurial dynamism and thus Schumpeterian creative destruction.

rules such as bankruptcy laws which in some Arab countries consider bankruptcy a crime (Amin et al. 2012: 23–24) is important, but changing attitudes requires changing institutions through policies aiming at downward causation. Doing so is a contingent, contextual, and path-dependent process (Bathelt and Glückler 2012: 48; 2014) that can be approached with a broad set of policy measures over the long term. For instance, while successful role models are important, the usually much larger number of entrepreneurial failures is an important lever for entrepreneurship promotion largely ignored by policy. Learning from failure can be a powerful means of increasing future entrepreneurial ventures' chances for success and at the same time contribute to establishing an entrepreneurial culture of trial and error in repeated experimentation. Policy interventions that focus on learning from the experience of entrepreneurs who failed or interventions that even target failed entrepreneurs through second-chance mentoring or coaching schemes can thus be a part of the broad policy agenda required to tackle institutional change.

Finally, on the level of organizations, the regulation regime proposed here would ideally include a transparent and accountable nation-state with a smaller but more efficient administration. While difficult to achieve, a number of governance reforms on the administrative level will be necessary. Combating the arbitrary enforcement of rules on the level of institutions will be an important complement to organization- and rule-related administrative reform. If successful, the combination of regulation reforms suggested should over time lead to the gradual emergence of a confident new entrepreneurial class demanding administrative accountability and fairness (Acemoğlu and Robinson 2012) that should express its voice through more inclusive business associations. Representative labor unions might play a similar role for employees.

The regulation reforms suggested above would have to be consistent with *transnational transformative processes* such as IMF/World Bank-sponsored structural adjustment and EU *rapprochement*. Indeed, most of the reform measures included in the proposed regulation reform agenda have for years been advocated by international organizations such as the OECD (2012a, 2013, 2015b, 2018) or the World Bank (2009, 2011, 2013, 2014a, b, c, d, 2015). Yet, as was argued above, reforming prescriptive rules along classical "Washington Consensus" policies (Williamson 1990), even if combined with a "good governance" perspective (Richards and Waterbury 2008: 229–230), will not be sufficient to come up with a consistent and sustainable new regulation regime. For instance, sizing down the public sector will create friction in a regulation regime characterized by institutions that include reliance on government as the driver of economic development, distrust in the private sector, and aspirations of public employment. Without looking at institutions and designing appropriate long-term policies to tackle institutional change, not only will the regulation system remain unstable but also will reforms of prescriptive rules have a lower chance of success if they keep an institution-competing character.

EU *rapprochement* offers some opportunities to achieve greater inclusiveness in policymaking. For example, applying the concept of smart specialization with its inherent participatory method of prioritization and action planning or combining it with horizontal entrepreneurship policies in the concept of smart experimentation

(Benner 2014, 2017c) could be suitable for countries aligning their economies more closely with the EU while suffering intense interregional disparities. Morocco and Tunisia are probably the most apparent candidates for doing so. The smart specialization approach is a policy method applied under the umbrella of EU cohesion policy and focuses on diversification based on regional knowledge bases (Asheim et al. 2017), drawing on the notion of related variety (Asheim et al. 2011; Frenken et al. 2007). The approach includes a participatory public-private prioritization process embedded in the institutional context of a regional economy (Benner 2018). However, the process that is supposed to lead to the prioritization of activities towards diversification and supported through public funds under the framework of a smart specialization strategy is confronted with institutional and governance-related problems, particularly in economically weaker regions or countries. Challenges include a lack of trust among agents, lacking government capacities in coordinating public-private policymaking processes, established legacies of hierarchical policymaking, and weak intermediate organizations such as regional development agencies or chamber of commerce (Trippl et al. 2018). While these obstacles are generally difficult to overcome, paradoxically some of these aspects of (mostly regional-level) socio-economic regulation may improve due to upward causation of institutional change (Glückler und Lenz 2016) within the participatory prioritization process inherent to the smart specialization approach (Benner 2018).

For rural regions, a concept such as the EU's long-standing LEADER (*Liaison entre actions de développement de l'économie rurale*) or CLLD (community-led local development) methodologies to develop rural development policies in a process of broad stakeholder participation might be suitable to achieve higher consistency between prescriptive rules and institutions and in setting in motion mutually reinforcing cycles of upward and downward causation on the regional level (Benner 2017d, forthcoming).

If successful, reforming the regulation system could lead to more inclusiveness of economic institutions and, through the emergence of an independent entrepreneurial class and representative business associations and labor unions, to a certain degree of political inclusiveness. While Tunisia with its post-revolutionary democratic system offers an arena for political inclusiveness, other core Arab countries such Morocco or Jordan seem to pursue a more gradual, evolutionary opening which might eventually give more though still limited freedom to citizens to participate to a certain degree in political decision-making but at the same time keep the ultimate decision-making power centralized at the top echelons of the monarchy. Both ways could eventually come up with a reformed regulation regime with more economic inclusiveness and at least some degree of political inclusiveness on matters of economic policy.

More economic inclusiveness of the regulation regime, combined with modified institutions such as stronger entrepreneurial attitudes, could facilitate entrepreneurial agency and thus provide an opening for a more dynamic, innovative, and competition-driven economy marked by a higher degree of Schumpeterian creative destruction. If such a regulation regime is internally and externally consistent and sustainable – which is the primary assumption behind the definition of the elements of the new regulation regime proposed[24] – it could enable core Arab economies to reach a higher-productivity equilibrium than was the case under the old Arab social contract.

Moving towards such a new regulation regime requires policies directed towards institutional change. These policies, if successful, should lead to processes of downward causation. Establishing institution-circumventing rules will be important to change institutions such as citizens' expectations towards public-sector employment and other crypto-welfare policies. The policies towards changing attitudes and promoting a more entrepreneurial spirit mentioned above can be a part of such an effort but will require time. Current structural adjustment programs pursued in Tunisia, Jordan, and Egypt will have to be complemented by more efficient but sensible social policies such as the establishment of need-based cash transfers and basic social safety nets.

The current transformative context in most core Arab economies may provide a window of opportunity (Amin et al. 2012: 13) for pursuing policies designed to change institutions through downward causation and institution-circumventing rules. While such a process will in any way be difficult and painful, the processes of political reform (be they revolutionary or evolutionary) may facilitate concomitant economic reform. Changing institutions such as the persisting reliance on government as the driver of economic development may be somewhat easier in a context such as the one currently found in Tunisia, with a newly established political system with checks and balances and a flourishing civil society which demonstrates the effectiveness of private initiative at least politically, if not yet economically. In countries where political reforms were far more limited and evolutionary such as Jordan, institutional change towards more reliance on the private sector may be considerably more difficult but still possible. Downward causation of institutional change will require determination by policymakers to consistently advocate more reliance on private initiative. The economic necessities of limiting state interventionism in the current context of political and economic transformation and, in some cases, structural adjustment may create space for private entrepreneurialism to fill voids left by a receding state and eventually, if successful, contribute to a nascent culture of trust towards the private sector.

Amin et al. (2012: 16–17) stress that in contrast to the political and economic transformation in Eastern Europe in the 1990s, there is no coherent ideological vision for reform in the Arab world. While the previous state-led approach so prevalent under the old Arab social contract has not managed to solve the structural problems of Arab economies, a new comprehensive ideological paradigm generally appealing to populations is not in sight. However, this lack of an ideological vision

---

[24] Methodologically, in elaborating the new regulation regime proposed here, the approach was not to define a new regulation regime and then to claim its consistency and sustainability but to ask how elements of the regulation regime would have to look like to be consistent with each other and sustainable over the long term and then proposing elements of a new regulation regime and policy actions to facilitate the transition accordingly. This is why consistency and sustainability are the primary assumptions behind the new regulation regime suggested here. However, the proposed regulation regime is only a scenario, while other ones, too, are possible.

is not necessarily a problem because it may give rise to a pragmatic approach by younger generations eager to seize economic opportunities (Amin et al. 2012: 16). Hence, transitioning towards a new regulation regime might involve non-ideological, eclectic mixed economy solutions inspired by emerging economies such as Brazil or Turkey or successful CMEs such as Germany and in line with an evolving institutional context in core Arab economies (Amin et al. 2012: 16–17).

Such a mixture between a developmental state and private initiative may indeed lead to the formation of new, rule-circumventing institutions consistent with the necessities of scaling down the public sector and limiting the government's role to more efficient, effective, and catalytic interventions, to upward causation of corresponding policies establishing consistent prescriptive rules and eventually to a more internally and externally consistent and sustainable regulation regime. Eventually, coherent prescriptive rules and institutions centered around a more limited and catalytic nature of state intervention in the form of an effective developmental state and, at the same time, more dynamic private initiative may lead to the emergence and mutual reinforcement of rule-reinforcing institutions and institution-reinforcing rules.

The nexus between political transformation and economic reform is further underlined by the need for administrative reform designed to strengthen good governance and to reduce the institutionally entrenched arbitrariness of prescriptive rule implementation. This argument is consistent with the World Bank's (2009 15–16) claim that economic reforms will need to be accompanied by administrative reforms that signal commitment to even-handed implementation of reforms and thus shape private-sector expectations.

Provided that policies for institutional change through downward causation, notably through the establishment of institution-circumventing rules designed to change attitudes and preferences succeed, the internal and external consistency of a new regulation regime might lead to processes of cumulative and circular causation through both upward and downward causation. For instance, stronger entrepreneurial attitudes may strengthen organizational change through entrepreneurs' inclusion in more vocal and more representative business association and, through the political clout of a new and confident entrepreneurial class, shape policies and thus prescriptive rules through upward causation accordingly. Micro-level agency in processes such as entrepreneurship and innovation, both individually and relationally (Benner 2014, 2017c), and resulting dynamics of Schumpeterian creative destruction are likely to establish institutional patterns that exert pressure on policymakers to design prescriptive rules accordingly. For such a process to happen, private-sector entrepreneurs will probably need to gain structural influence in the political realm, e.g., in political parties (Hall and Soskice 2001: 47–48; Wood 2001: 257). Coalition governments may be conducive for entrepreneurs' political clout (Hall and Soskice 2001: 49–50), allowing for political representation of broad societal coalitions according to the argument suggested by Acemoğlu and Robinson (2012) and thus political inclusiveness. Again, the current transformational context in some core Arab economies could enable the emergence of such a coalition, presumably to the highest degree in a democratic system such as the new Tunisian one which is indeed characterized by multiparty democracy and coalition governments but maybe at least to some degree in countries subject to a limited and evolutionary (although sometimes partly retrogressive) political opening such as Jordan or Morocco. Eventually, these processes may establish a considerable degree of consistency between major prescriptive rules and institutions as their interactions may gradually assume the character of institution-reinforcing rules and rule-reinforcing institutions.

Even if past years witnessed much disappointment with the course of reform in core Arab economies, there is still reason for realistic optimism. Even if the ongoing transformative context and transnational transformative processes such as IMF- and World Bank-sponsored structural adjustment do not lead to the economic reform policies proposed, for example, because of political sclerosis or inertia, there may still be a chance for reforming the regulation regime through upward causation. Micro-level agency through entrepreneurship and innovation might lead to the formation of rule-substituting institutions such as stronger entrepreneurial attitudes and the emergence of a confident entrepreneurial class demanding policies to establish prescriptive rules accordingly. In the present regulation context marked by persistent preferences for public-sector employment and limited entrepreneurial dynamism, however, it is difficult to see what would trigger such a process. More likely, policies designed to promote entrepreneurial attitudes and innovation through downward causation are needed to kick off a process of cumulative causation of changing rules and institutions. However, this process is contingent and its outcome unpredictable. Firstly, it is unsure whether policies, even if well-designed, succeed in triggering institutional change. Secondly, even if they do, resulting new modes of regulation cannot be predicted because they are shaped by complex processes including social struggles and chance (Boyer 1988: 91).

The present section has attempted to propose answers to the second (Which new modes of regulation could help Arab countries in addressing structural economic and social difficulties by facilitating private-sector-led growth?), third (What role can entrepreneurship play in such new modes of regulation?), and fourth research question (Which implications does the current transitional context in Arab economies hold for regulation). The answers to the research questions proposed in Sects. 3.3 and 3.4 will be applied to the cases of Tunisia and Jordan in Chap. 4.

3.5 Regulation in Core Arab Economies: From Theory to Empirics

Drawing on the theoretical background on regulation approaches and their synthesis in Sects. 3.1 and 3.2, Sect. 3.3 proposed a stylized framework for regulation in Arab economies so far, while Sect. 3.4 took a dynamic perspective and discussed pathways towards the hypothetical scenario of a new, consistent, and sustainable regulation regime for core Arab economies. While these findings and propositions have the character of a scientific model and therefore are simplified representations of reality, empirical validation is necessary to develop them into a theory. As for the results of Sect. 3.3, empirical validation would turn the stylized regulation framework under the old Arab social contract into a positive theory, while empirical validation of the new regulation regime and policies to facilitate transition suggested in Sect. 3.4 would allow for deducting normative conclusions from the positive theory (Benner 2012: 5) if combined with politically set postulates or first principles.[25] While empirical validation of a positive theory is straightforward, attempts towards the empirical treatment of normative conclusions are more complex. The basic assumptions made in Sect. 3.4 that a new regulation regime would have to be internally and externally consistent as well as sustainable led to the definition of elements of the such a hypothetical new regulation regime and then to policies capable of facilitating the emergence of these new regulation elements. Empirically validating the axioms implicit in this reasoning (on one level, from assumptions to regulation elements and on another level, from regulation elements to policies) is beyond the scope of this book. What empirical validation can do is explore what kind of regulation elements and policies are perceived by agents as necessary or desirable and then analyze the consistency of these insights with the model proposed which departs from the assumed postulates that it be (i) internally and externally consistent, (ii) statically and dynamically more efficient, and (iii) economically sustainable. Empirical validation can assess whether transition to the model proposed is likely and finally elaborate conclusions on what would have to change to come to the regulation regime proposed or to modify the model to make its materialization more feasible and realistic.

The following chapters attempt to validate both the positive model and its normative conclusions. Chapter 4 will take a look at Tunisia and Jordan. While sharing a number of common features such as those identified in Chap. 2, core Arab economy countries differ from each other in several details of their regulation regime. For example, in a country such as Egypt where the military is a major economic factor (Masoud 2014: 457; World Bank 2014a: 58), the regulation regime proposed in Sect. 3.3 would have to be complemented with resulting country-specific implications. Still, bearing in mind that the model developed in Sects. 3.3 and 3.4 is highly stylized and designed to capture major features common to regulation in most core Arab economies, applying it and checking its validity in two smaller Arab economies that share some structural characteristics but at the same time exhibit considerable and important differences can indeed grant the model a higher degree of empirical relevance and thus validate it as a theory, thus adding validity to its normative conclusions.

Although featuring comparatively liberal long-term economic policies with more freedom for the private sector than in other core Arab economies, Tunisia and Jordan share the general pattern of structural deficits evident in most resource-poor and labor-abundant Arab economies, including the marked and persistent insider-

---

[25] For example, politically set normative first principles can refer to the desirability of a rise in living standards, income, employment, or other indicators of economic or human development.

outsider contrast that was so characteristic for the old Arab social contract (Hertog 2016: 18). Still, Tunisia and Jordan appear to have more efficient legal systems and less burdensome bureaucracy than other core Arab economies and arguably even vis-à-vis other international comparators (Noland and Pack 2007: 144–155). Due to these characteristics of both countries and their relative success in industrial and economic development so far but also due to their sharing the fundamental structural difficulties of most core Arab economies, these two case studies are meant to serve as an example of how to apply the regulation framework proposed in a specific context and to adapt it to the resulting particularities, notably on the national level but taking account of some important conclusions for regional development and considering some aspects of regional context.

References

Acemoğlu D, Robinson JA (2012) Why nations fail: the origins of power, prosperity and poverty. Profile Books, London

Achy L (2010) Trading high unemployment for bad jobs: employment challenges in the Maghreb. Carnegie Papers. Carnegie Endowment for International Peace, Washington, DC. http://carnegieendowment.org/files/labor_maghreb.pdf. (10.10.2013)

Adly A, Khatib L (2014) Reforming the entrepreneurship ecosystem in post-revolutionary Egypt and Tunisia. Center on Democracy, Development and the Rule of Law/Center for International Private Enterprise, Stanford/Washington, DC. http://cddrl.fsi.stanford.edu/sites/default/files/Reforming_the_Entrepreneurship_Ecosystem_in_Post-Revolutionary_Egypt_and_Tunisia-_Amr_Adly.pdf. (13.04.2015)

Al-Quds University (ed) (2016) Dual studies. http://www.ds.alquds.edu/en. (21.05.2017)

Amin M, Assaad R, Al-Baharna N, Derviş K, Desai RM, Dhillon NS, Galal A, Ghanem H, Graham C, Kaufmann D, Kharas H, Page J, Salehi-Isfahani D, Sierra K, Yousef TM (2012) After the spring: economic transformations in the Arab world. Oxford University Press, Oxford

Asheim B, Boschma R, Cooke P (2011) Constructing regional advantage: platform policies based on related variety and differentiated knowledge bases. Reg Stud 45(7):893–904

Asheim B, Grillitsch M, Trippl M (2017) Smart specialization as an innovation-driven strategy for economic diversification: examples from Scandinavian regions. In: Radosevic S, Curaj A, Gheorgiu R, Andreescu R, Wage I (eds) Advances in the theory and practice of smart specialization. Elsevier, London, pp 74–99

Basedau M, Gobien S, Prediger S (2017) The ambivalent role of religion for sustainable development: A review of the empirical evidence. GIGA Working Paper No. 297. https://www.giga-hamburg.de/de/system/files/publications/wp297_basedau-gobien-prediger.pdf. (08.02.2017)

Bathelt H (1994) Die Bedeutung der Regulationstheorie in der wirtschaftsgeographischen Forschung. (The significance of regulation approaches for economic geography). Geogr Z 82(2):63–90

Bathelt H, Glückler J (2012) Wirtschaftsgeographie: Ökonomische Beziehungen in räumlicher Perspektive. (Economic geography: economic relations in a spatial perspective), 3rd edn. UTB, Stuttgart

Bathelt H, Glückler J (2014) Institutional change in economic geography. Progr Hum Geogr 38(3):340–363

Ben Shitrit L (2014) Israel. In: Lust E (ed) The Middle East, 13th edn. CQ Press, Thousand Oaks, pp 537–563

Benner M (2012) Clusterpolitik: Wege zur Verknüpfung von Theorie und politischer Umsetzung. (Cluster policy: ways to link theory and political implementation). LIT, Münster

Benner M (2014) From smart specialisation to smart experimentation: building a new theoretical framework for regional policy of the European Union. Z Wirtsch (Ger J Econ Geogr) 58(1):33–49

Benner M (2015) Europa und der Maghreb: Von der Nachbarschaft zur Wirtschaftspartnerschaft. (Europe and the Maghreb: from neighborhood to economic partnership). In: Neuss B, Nötzold A (eds) The Southern Mediterranean: challenges to the european foreign and security policy. Nomos, Baden-Baden, pp 57–82

Benner M (2017a) Culture in local and regional development: a Mediterranean perspective on the culture/economy nexus. MPRA Paper No. 77787. https://mpra.ub.uni-muenchen.de/77787/1/MPRA_paper_77787.pdf. (08.04.2017)

Benner M (2017b) From clusters to smart specialization: tourism in institution-sensitive regional development policies. Economies 5(3):26. http://www.mdpi.com/2227-7099/5/3/26/pdf. (29.07.2017)

Benner M (2017c) Smart specialisation and cluster emergence: building blocks for evolutionary regional policies. In: Hassink R, Fornahl D (eds) The life cycle of clusters: a policy perspective. Edward Elgar, Camberley, pp 151–172

Benner M (2017d) The legacy of Sidi Bouzid: overcoming spatial inequalities in Tunisia. In: Křížek D, Záhořík J (eds) Beyond the 'Arab Spring' in North Africa: macro and micro perspectives. Lexington, Lanham, pp 47–65

Benner M (2018) Smart specialization and institutional context: towards a process of institutional discovery and change. Papers in Economic Geography and Innovation Studies 2018/03. http://www-sre.wu.ac.at/sre-disc/geo-disc-2018_03.pdf. (14.11.2018)

Benner M (forthcoming) Cluster policy in Tunisia: from institutional voids to smart specialization. In: Knedlik T, Wohlmuth K (eds) African Development perspectives yearbook 2018: science, technology and innovation policies for inclusive growth in Africa. In preparation

Bobek H (1959) Die Hauptstufen der Gesellschafts- und Wirtschaftsentfaltung in geographischer Sicht. (The main stages in the socio-economic evolution from a geographical point of view). Erde 90(3):259–298

Bobek H (1974) Zum Konzept des Rentenkapitalismus. (On the concept of rent capitalism). Tijdschr Econ Soc Geogr 65(2):73–78

Boyer R (1988) Technical change and the theory of "régulation". In: Dosi G, Freeman C, Nelson RR, Silverberg G, Soete LLG (eds) Technical change and economic theory. Pinter, London, New York, pp 67–94

Boyer R, Hollingsworth JR (1997a) From national embeddedness to spatial and institutional nestedness. In: Hollingsworth JR, Boyer R (eds) Contemporary capitalism: the embeddedness of institutions. Cambridge University Press, Cambridge, New York, Melbourne, pp 433–484

Boyer R, Hollingsworth JR (1997b) The variety of institutional arrangements and their complementarity in modern economics. In: Hollingsworth JR, Boyer R (eds) Contemporary capitalism: the embeddedness of institutions. Cambridge University Press, Cambridge, New York, Melbourne, pp 49–54

Cammett M (2014) The political economy of development in the Middle East. In: Lust E (ed) The Middle East, 13th edn. CQ Press, Thousand Oaks, pp 161–208

Desai RM, Olofsgård A, Yousef TM (2009) The logic of authoritarian bargains. Econ Polit 21(1):93–125

Diop N, Ghali S (2012) Are Jordan and Tunisia's exports becoming more technologically sophisticated? analysis using highly disaggregated export databases. The World Bank, Washington, DC. http://documents.worldbank.org/curated/en/716281468312890526/pdf/672480NWP00PUB07863B00FEBRUARY15NEW.pdf. (20.05.2017)

Erdle S (2011) Industrial policy in Tunisia. DIE Discussion Paper 1/2011. Deutsches Institut für Entwicklungspolitik, Bonn. http://www.die-gdi.de/CMSHomepage/openwebcms3.nsf/(ynDK_contentByKey)/ANES-8DEE7C/$FILE/DP%201.2011.pdf. (20.08.2012)

European Commission (ed) (2010) Green paper: unlocking the potential of cultural and creative industries. European Commission, Brussels. https://www.hhs.se/contentassets/3776a2d6d61c4 058ad564713cc554992/greenpaper_creative_industries_en.pdf. (20.03.2017)

Felsenstein D (1994) University-related science parks – 'seedbeds' or 'enclaves' of innovation? Technovation 14(2):93–110

Freeman C (1988) Japan: a new national system of innovation? In: Dosi G, Freeman C, Nelson RR, Silverberg G, Soete LLG (eds) Technical change and economic theory. Pinter, London, New York, pp 330–348

Frenken K, van Oort F, Verburg T (2007) Related variety, unrelated variety and regional economic growth. Reg Stud 41(5):S. 685–S. 697

Gasper M (2014) The making of the modern Middle East. In: Lust E (ed) The Middle East, 13th edn. CQ Press, Thousand Oaks, pp 1–72

Ghali S, Rezgui S (2015) Structural transformation and industrial policy in selected Southern Mediterranean countries: Tunisia. In: Forum Euroméditerranéen des Instituts de Sciences Économiques (ed) Structural transformation and industrial policy: a comparative analysis of Egypt, Morocco, Tunisia and Turkey and case studies. European Investment Bank, Luxembourg, pp 39–68. http://www.femise.org/wp-content/uploads/2015/06/femip_study_ structural_transformation_and_industrial_policy_en1.pdf. (10.06.2015)

Giddens A (1979) Central problems in social theory: action, structure, and contradiction in social analysis. University of California Press, Berkeley, Los Angeles

Glückler J, Bathelt H (2017) Institutional context and innovation. In: Bathelt H, Cohendet P, Henn S, Simon L (eds) The Elgar companion to innovation and knowledge creation. Elgar, Cheltenham, Northampton, pp 121–137

Glückler J, Lenz R (2016) How institutions moderate the effectiveness of regional policy: a framework and research agenda. Invest Reg – J Reg Res 36(2016):255–277

Granovetter M (1985) Economic action and social structure: the problem of embeddedness. Am J Sociol 91(3):481–510

Hall PA, Soskice D (2001) An introduction to varieties of capitalism. In: Hall PA, Soskice D (eds) Varieties of capitalism: the institutional foundations of comparative advantage. Oxford University Press, Oxford, New York, pp 1–68

Hazboun W (2008) Beaches, ruins, resorts: the politics of tourism in the Arab world. University of Minnesota Press, Minneapolis

Hertog S (2016) Is there an Arab variety of capitalism? Economic Research Forum Working Paper No. 1068. https://erf.org.eg/wp-content/uploads/2016/12/1068.pdf. (02.03.2017)

Hollingsworth JR, Boyer R (1997a) Coordination of economic actors and social systems of production. In: Hollingsworth JR, Boyer R (eds) Contemporary capitalism: the embeddedness of institutions. Cambridge University Press, Cambridge, New York, Melbourne, pp 1–47

Hollingsworth JR, Boyer R (1997b) How and why do social systems of production change? In: Hollingsworth JR, Boyer R (eds) Contemporary capitalism: the embeddedness of institutions. Cambridge University Press, Cambridge, New York, Melbourne, pp 189–195

Isenberg DJ (2010) How to start an entrepreneurial revolution. Harv Bus Rev 88(6):40–50

Lehmann T, Benner M (2015): Cluster policy in the light of institutional context – a comparative study of transition countries. Adm Sci 5(4):188–212. http://www.mdpi.com/2076-3387/5/4/188/pdf. (05.11.2015)

Lundvall B-Å (1988) Innovation as an interactive process: from user-producer interaction to the national system of innovation. In: Dosi G, Freeman C, Nelson RR, Silverberg G, Soete LLG (eds) Technical change and economic theory. Pinter, London, New York, pp 349–369

Lundvall B-Å (1992a) Introduction. In: Lundvall B-Å (ed) National systems of innovation: towards a theory of innovation and interactive learning. Pinter, London, pp 1–19

Lundvall B-Å (1992b) User-producer relationships, national systems of innovation and internationalisation. In: Lundvall B-Å (ed) National systems of innovation: towards a theory of innovation and interactive learning. Pinter, London, pp 45–67

Lundvall B-Å, Maskell P (2000) Nation states and economic development: From national systems of production to national systems of knowledge creation and learning. In: Clark GL, Feldman MP, Gertler MS (eds) The Oxford handbook of economic geography. Oxford University Press, Oxford, pp 353–372

Lynch M (2014) Regional international relations. In: Lust E (ed) The Middle East, 13th edn. CQ Press, Thousand Oaks, pp 367–395

M'Henni H, Deniozos D (2012) Erawatch country reports 2012. Tunisia. http://erawatch.jrc.ec.europa.eu/erawatch/export/sites/default/galleries/generic_files/file_0432.pdf. (26.08.2014)

Maghraoui D, Zerhouni S (2014) Morocco. In: Lust E (ed) The Middle East, 13th edn. CQ Press, Thousand Oaks, pp 660–687

Masoud T (2014) Egypt. In: Lust E (ed) The Middle East, 13th edn. CQ Press, Thousand Oaks, pp 448–477

Moghadam VN, Decker T (2014) Social change in the Middle East. In: Lust E (ed) The Middle East, 13th edn. CQ Press, Thousand Oaks, pp 73–106

Nelson RR (1988) Institutions supporting technical change in the United States. In: Dosi G, Freeman C, Nelson RR, Silverberg G, Soete LLG (eds) Technical change and economic theory. Pinter, London, New York, pp 312–329

Noland M, Pack H (2007) The Arab economies in a changing world. Peterson Institute for International Economics, Washington, DC

OECD (ed) (2012a) OECD investment policy reviews: Tunisia. Organisation for Economic Cooperation and Development, Paris

OECD (ed) (2012b) Promoting graduate entrepreneurship in Tunisian universities. OECD Local Economic and Employment Development (LEED) Working Papers 2012/18. Organisation for Economic Co-operation and Development, Paris

OECD (ed) (2013) OECD investment policy reviews: Jordan. Organisation for Economic Cooperation and Development, Paris

OECD (ed) (2015a) Lessons learned from the Lüneburg Innovation Incubator. Organisation for Economic Co-operation and Development, Paris

OECD (ed) (2015b) Tunisia: a reform agenda to support competitiveness and inclusive growth. Organisation for Economic Development and Cooperation, Paris. http://www.oecd.org/countries/tunisia/Tunisia-a-reform-agenda-to-support-competitiveness-and-inclusive-growth.pdf. (02.06.2015)

OECD (ed) (2018) OECD economic surveys: Tunisia: economic assessment. Organisation for Economic Development and Cooperation, Paris

OECD, IDRC (2013) New entrepreneurs and high performance enterprises in the Middle East and North Africa. Organisation for Economic Cooperation and Development, Paris

Peck J, Theodore N (2007) Variegated capitalism. Prog Hum Geogr 31(6):731–772

Putnam R (1995) Bowling alone: America's declining social capital. J Democr 6(1):65–78

Richards A, Waterbury J (2008) A political economy of the Middle East, 3rd edn. Westview Press, Boulder

Rijkers B, Freund C, Nucifora A (2014) All in the family: state capture in Tunisia. Policy Research Working Paper No. 6810. The World Bank, Washington, DC. http://www-wds.worldbank.org/external/default/WDSContentServer/IW3P/IB/2014/03/25/000158349_20140325092905/Rendered/PDF/WPS6810.pdf. (28.03.2014)

Rivlin P (2009) Arab economies in the twenty-first century. Cambridge University Press, New York

Rostow WW (1959) The stages of economic growth. Econ Hist Rev 12(1):1–16

Smadi R, Tsipouri L (2012) Erawatch country reports 2012: Jordan. http://erawatch.jrc.ec.europa.eu/erawatch/export/sites/default/galleries/generic_files/file_0454.pdf. (26.08.2014)

Storper M, Walker R (1989) The capitalist imperative: territory, technology, and industrial growth. Basil Blackwell, New York, Oxford

Trippl M, Zukauskaite E, Healy A (2018) Shaping smart specialisation: the role of place-specific factors in advanced, intermediate and less-developed European regions. Papers in

Economic Geography and Innovation Studies 2018/01. http://www-sre.wu.ac.at/sre-disc/geo-disc-2018_01.pdf. (14.11.2018)

UNESCO Institute for Statistics (ed) (2015) Global Education Digest 2012: opportunities lost: the impact of grade repetition and early school leaving. UNESCO Institute for Statistics, Montreal. http://www.uis.unesco.org/Education/GED%20Documents%20C/GED-2012-Complete-Web3.pdf. (13.02.2016)

Williamson J (1990) What Washington means by policy reform. In: Williamson J (ed) Latin American adjustment: how much has happened? Washington, Institute for International Economics

Wood S (2001) Business, government, and patterns of labor market policy in Britain and the Federal Republic of Germany. In: Hall PA, Soskice D (eds) Varieties of capitalism: the institutional foundations of comparative advantage. Oxford University Press, Oxford, New York, pp 247–274

World Bank (ed) (1993) The East Asian miracle: economic growth and public policy. Oxford University Press, New York

World Bank (ed) (2009) From privilege to competition: unlocking private-led growth in the Middle East and North Africa. The World Bank, Washington, DC. http://siteresources.worldbank.org/INTMENA/Resources/Privilege_complete_final.pdf. (08.12.2013)

World Bank (ed) (2011) Poor places, thriving people: how the Middle East and North Africa can rise above spatial disparities. The World Bank, Washington, DC. https://openknowledge.worldbank.org/bitstream/handle/10986/2255/589970PUB0ID181UBLIC109780821383216.pdf?sequence=1. (19.02.2014)

World Bank (ed) (2013) Jobs for shared prosperity: time for action in the Middle East and North Africa. The World Bank, Washington, DC. http://www-wds.worldbank.org/external/default/WDSContentServer/WDSP/IB/2013/04/12/000445729_20130412114115/Rendered/PDF/724690v40Full00Prosperity0full0book.pdf. (09.11.2013)

World Bank (ed) (2014a) Jobs or privileges: unleashing the employment potential of the Middle East and North Africa. The World Bank, Washington, DC. http://www-wds.worldbank.org/external/default/WDSContentServer/WDSP/IB/2014/07/16/000333037_20140716151958/Rendered/PDF/888790MNA0Box382141B00PUBLIC0.pdf. (10.10.2014)

World Bank (ed) (2014b) MENA quarterly economic brief: growth slowdown heightens the need for reforms. The World Bank, Washington, DC. http://www.worldbank.org/content/dam/Worldbank/document/MNA/QEBissue2January2014FINAL.pdf. (20.02.2014)

World Bank (ed) (2014c) MENA quarterly economic brief: predictions, perceptions and economic reality. The World Bank, Washington, DC. http://www-wds.worldbank.org/external/default/WDSContentServer/WDSP/IB/2014/08/06/000470435_20140806105353/Rendered/PDF/898440REVISED00ue030JULY020140FINAL.pdf. (09.08.2014)

World Bank (ed) (2014d) The unfinished revolution: bringing opportunity, good jobs and greater wealth to all Tunisians. The World Bank, Washington, DC. http://www-wds.worldbank.org/external/default/WDSContentServer/WDSP/IB/2014/09/16/000456286_20140916144712/Rendered/PDF/861790DPR0P12800Box385314B00PUBLIC0.pdf. (27.09.2014)

World Bank (ed) (2015) MENA economic monitor: towards a new social contract. The World Bank, Washington, DC. http://www-wds.worldbank.org/external/default/WDSContentServer/WDSP/IB/2015/04/09/000456286_20150409170931/Rendered/PDF/956500PUB0REVI020150391416B00OUO090.pdf. (16.04.2015)

Chapter 4
Case Studies

Abstract The case studies on Tunisia and Jordan introduce the specific structural economic challenges the countries are confronted with, present major economic policies pursued, and apply the integrated regulation framework to the countries.

Keywords Tunisia · Jordan · Case study

This chapter applies the consolidated regulation framework for core Arab economies developed in Chap. 3 to Tunisia and Jordan and refines it in view of the particular idiosyncrasies of regulation in these two countries. The case studies are based on a profound review of scientific literature on the Tunisian and Jordanian economies as well as on policy literature such as country-specific reports of international organizations and other international or national entities. To complete the picture and to add details on the particular questions addressed in the regulation framework proposed in Chap. 3, empirical research was conducted through qualitative, semi-standardized interviews with stakeholders relevant for socioeconomic regulation and with experts on particular aspects of regulation.

Following a deductive approach, the plausibility of the conceptual thoughts developed from theory and literature was tested during the expert and stakeholder interviews. These interviews were conducted for the purpose of triangulation. A comprehensive empirical test of theoretical arguments on all aspects of the regulation framework would by its very nature be highly complex and extensive and require a combination of quantitative and qualitative empirical data. Instead, the approach followed for the present chapter is a mixed methods approach that builds on theoretical reasoning developed from literature and based on the regulation framework elaborated conceptually in Chap. 3 and that performs a prima facie plausibility test through qualitative empirical triangulation.

A total of nine semi-standardized interviews were conducted per telephone or through Internet voice calls from 20 September 2018 to 17 December 2018. The interviews took between 21 and 77 min with an average duration of 42.22 min. One additional interviewee preferred to answer in writing, bringing the total number of interviewees to ten. Interviewees were either part of the policymaking community, experts, or stakeholders from the private sector from either Tunisia or Jordan. In

M. Benner, *A New Arab Social Contract?*, Economic Geography,
https://doi.org/10.1007/978-3-030-19270-9_4

order not to discourage interviewees from expressing their opinions on politically sensitive issues, it was decided not to take audio recordings. Instead, precise and comprehensive notes were taken. The interviews were guided by one detailed questionnaire per country, reflecting the major points of the regulation framework. Interviewees were assured anonymity.

The two case studies take a national perspective, but given the prevalence of spatial disparities and the importance of regional development in both countries, some focus was put on selected regions to highlight relevant aspects. In particular, the regions of Sfax (Tunisia) and Irbid (Jordan) were considered as exemplary arenas for policy interventions and recommendations.

Tunisia and Jordan offer interesting cases for applying and refining the regulation framework for core Arab economies proposed in Chap. 3. Among core Arab economies, Tunisia and Jordan exhibit a comparatively high degree of international economic integration with considerable levels of FDI and exports. Both share a highly educated workforce, skilled diasporas, and a young generation with a penchant for working with ICT. On the negative side, both countries have to cope with high unemployment levels among higher-education graduates significantly above average unemployment rates. To reduce unemployment, both countries would need economic growth rates of at least 6% annually, calling for growth-accelerating and inclusive structural reforms (Diop and Ghali 2012: 5–6).

Consistent with their status as "watchmaker" economies with a weak natural resource base but comparatively strong human capital base, both countries are left with virtually no alternative than to rely on knowledge and skills and to grow their economies through increasingly knowledge-intensive exports (Richards and Waterbury 2008: 68).

Apart from these similarities, both countries exhibit major differences. Political change since 2010/2011 took a revolutionary turn in Tunisia, while Jordan witnessed protests and, as a reaction, gradual political change but no upheaval of the political system. Tunisian economic policy experimented at times with the ideology of Arab socialism but has for decades embarked on a policy of considerable opening (*infitah*) to the world economy. Jordan's conservative monarchical system did not explicitly embark on socialist ideologies but left private entrepreneurial initiative a significant degree of freedom. Tunisia's economy is oriented towards the EU and the large Tunisian diaspora in European countries as well as the status of French as Tunisia's lingua franca in culture and economic affairs is underpinning the country's proximity to Europe. Jordan, in contrast, is embedded in the Middle East and its geopolitical realities including the Israeli-Palestinian conflict which have resulted, inter alia, in a large share of Jordanian citizens with Palestinian origins and high numbers of Syrian refugees in the country.

The next section addresses the Tunisian case. Then, the Jordanian case is introduced. The chapter concludes with a comparative summary of major insights drawn from both case studies.

4.1 Tunisia

The case study on Tunisia first presents a brief overview of structural economic challenges, both those confirming general trends in core Arab economies and those specific to the country. Then, policies pursued are examined by focusing on some relevant areas of structural policy. By applying the regulation framework developed in Chap. 3, the case study offers a stylized analysis of socioeconomic regulation in Tunisia during the Ben Ali era and implications for current regulation challenges in view of the institutional legacy left by the pre-revolutionary eras and closes by suggesting ways to achieve a more sustainable and efficient regulation regime in the context of the country's current transitional stage.

4.1.1 Tunisia's Economic Challenges

As a core Arab economy, Tunisia is confronted with the same fundamental economic challenges and structural difficulties found in other core Arab economies. Still, Tunisia is a special case because it has performed better than other Arab countries in long-term income convergence relative to OECD countries (Noland and Pack 2007: 39, 40–41, 43–44). Per capita income convergence appears to be based on a relatively vibrant business scene with a resulting comparatively efficient regulatory environment (Noland and Pack 2007: 238–241).[1] Remarkably, Tunisia exhibits a demographic situation similar to industrialized countries marked by a falling fertility rate and rising life expectancy (OECD 2015: 4). Tunisia's demographic change was not only rapid in recent decades, but in the period 2000–2005 the country witnessed the lowest fertility rate among MENA countries with 2.0 children per woman, lower than the rates found in the region's most industrialized countries Israel and Turkey (Richards and Waterbury 2008: 73).

Tunisia's old development model since independence was based on a strong authoritarian nation-state that limited civil liberties but assured stability and provided education, social services, and public infrastructure and a strategic approach to economic policy that mixed international openness for trade and investment with interventionism (OECD 2015: 2). This growth model delivered fairly impressive results on a range of human and social development indicators but brought with it fundamental structural problems in the economic sphere. To take one major economic indicator as a proxy for these structural problems, GDP growth in Tunisia fell behind that of comparable countries (World Bank 2014c: 24–26; 36–58).

In parallel with broad trends in the Arab world as described in Chap. 2, problems such as increasing unemployment among highly educated jobseekers or spatial

---

[1] In the broader picture, Morocco and Tunisia perform fairly well internationally when looking at the ease of starting a business, while Egypt (and pre-war Syria) exhibits a low performance comparable to India (Noland and Pack 2007: 242–243).

disparities increasingly came to plague the Tunisian economy (OECD 2015: 2). In particular, the labor market mismatch prevalent in core Arab economies (see Sect. 2.2.5) and the labor market dualism Hertog (2016) marks as one characteristic of the Arab VoC are evident in Tunisia (World Bank 2014c: 170–173). Specifically, the skills mismatch is observable in terms of jobseekers' qualifications. A shortage of workers with lower formal skills mirrors a shortage of jobs for workers with higher formal skills, meaning that not jobs per se are lacking but the right jobs corresponding to jobseekers' educational profile (World Bank 2014c: 171).

These realities lead to a particularly precarious situation of educated youth on the labor market since employment creation in Tunisia tends to happen in niches with lower value added and in the informal sector. These jobs are not attractive to higher-education graduates, exacerbating the skills mismatch and unemployment among university graduates (World Bank 2014c: 26).

In terms of regional development, the former growth model favored coastal regions which deepened spatial inequalities (OECD 2015: 8). A major component of this growth model was the integration in global value chains (GVCs) through gradual liberalization and international openness (International Monetary Fund 2016: 3–4) and notably a policy of export development that focused on a limited number of industries. These industries included the textiles and garments, leather and footwear, food and beverages, and electrical industries. Together, these industries account for the vast majority of manufacturing jobs. In 2016, electrical machines and apparatus made up 39.4% of Tunisia's total merchandise trade and textiles made up 26.5%, clearly highlighting the reliance of Tunisia's export on these two industries (OECD 2015: 71; OECD 2018: 8).

Export development promoted through tax incentives beginning in the early 1970s drove economic growth but resulted in an isolated offshore sector with low value added, notably in the textiles and garments industries (OECD 2015: 9). Tourism was another lead industry specifically promoted by the regime but, similar to the textiles and garments offshore sector, in low value-added market segments such as sun, sand, and beach-style package mass tourism (Hazboun 2008; OECD 2015: 9).

This growth model made Tunisian industry vulnerable to low-cost competition. High tariffs and slow trade liberalization put additional pressure on long-term industrial development, as did overstrict regulation and price controls in product markets; state monopolies in various important product markets, sometimes in connection with subsidies; as well as restrictions on FDI (OECD 2015: 9–11). Many market distortions seem to be caused by the Ben Ali regime's desire to protect cronies from the well-connected established business elite, or at least policies had this effect (OECD 2015: 11; Rijkers et al. 2014; World Bank 2014c: 115–123). In particular, barriers to market access and competition enabled the capture of rents by politically well-connected cronies. Prior to the revolution in 2010/2011, Tunisia was particularly marked by a high degree of state capture and crony capitalism. Two hundred and twenty firms owned by the Ben Ali clan that were confiscated after the revolution accounted for more than 20% of profits in the economy (OECD 2015: 8, 69; Rijkers et al. 2014; World Bank 2014c: 110–114).

Tunisia suffers from a deep labor market dualism between private and public sectors, the latter including SOEs. Government employment is associated with significantly above average wages, setting incentives in favor of public-sector employment and affecting reservation wages. For example, graduates' wages are roughly 35% higher in the public sector than in the private sector. In addition, family-related benefits are more generous in the public sector, creating an additional incentive particularly for women to seek public-sector jobs. Consistent with these incentives, Tunisia exhibits a high share of government employment in Tunisia. The flip side of the coin is a hitherto low level of entrepreneurship including women entrepreneurship. Apart from public-sector employment, crypto-welfare policies observable in Tunisia include subsidies which account for 7% of GDP (OECD 2015: 11–12, 30, 36, 51–52, 67).

Unemployment, in particular among economically disadvantaged groups such as youth and women, is the most visible symptom of the Tunisian economy's structural deficiencies. In the first quarter of 2014, the overall unemployment rate stood at 15.2%. While the unemployment rate was at 12.7% for men, it was 21.5% for women and 37.6% for youth. Unemployment was particularly high among university graduates, with the share of unemployment among graduates reaching roughly 40% among female university graduates and roughly 20% among male university graduates. Spatially, unemployment was particularly high in the Center-West and South regions. Furthermore, the Tunisian labor market is characterized by a much higher labor-force participation rate among males (70.3%) than among females (25.8%) and high levels of informality (OECD 2015: 28, 40; World Bank 2014c: 40–41).

Furthermore, skills demanded and offered seem to diverge, confirming the prevalence of a skills mismatch in Tunisia. At the same time, Tunisia's labor laws are among the most restrictive among MENA countries which, together with a high degree of informality, underscore the dualism on the labor market (International Monetary Fund 2016: 4, 11).

Tunisia is marked by strong interregional disparities, notably in terms of unemployment and poverty, and a lack of general convergence in terms of economic activity (World Bank 2014c: 282–283). Spatial disparities are particularly pronounced between more prosperous coastal regions (OECD 2018: 114–115; World Bank 2014c: 286–287) and peripheral regions in the interior of the country, as was evident in a considerable gap in poverty rates between the Tunis agglomeration on the one hand and the North West and Center-West regions on the other hand in 2010 (World Bank 2014c: 284). The structural problem of unemployment is most serious in the peripheral regions of the North West, the Center West, and the South (World Bank 2014c: 284). The OECD (2018: 115) stresses that "while unemployment in 2016 affected less than 10% of the population aged 15 to 64 years in Monastir and Sfax, it exceeded 25% in Gafsa and Tatouine" and with a stronger increase in the most affected regions (OECD 2018: 115). Between 2005 and 2011, Gafsa and Tataouine governorates not only had the highest unemployment rates but displayed the highest rates of increase in unemployment, while unemployment decreased in coastal regions of the country (World Bank 2013: 5, 54–55; 2014c: 39, 284).

Despite improvements in public services and infrastructure and a general decline of the poverty rate during the past two decades, the export-led development model pursued by Tunisian economic policy over the decades and the lack of interregional connectivity exacerbated the economic polarization of the country and benefitted coastal regions disproportionately (OECD 2018: 112). The polarization even increased during the 2000s, as is evident from the rise of the high share of private firms located in the North and East among all firms registered in the country (OECD 2015: 38). Accordingly, 85% of Tunisia's GDP is produced in the three coastal economic hubs of Tunis, Sousse, and Sfax, and these cities' agglomerations account for 92% of all industrial enterprises (World Bank 2014c: 282).

In terms of the country's human capital endowment, Erdle (2011) sees some disadvantages of the Tunisian higher-education system, including a focus on infrastructure investment and a neglect of investments in educational content, a lack of building skills demanded on the labor market, and the fact that "60 percent of [Tunisian universities', M.B.] students are still enrolled in liberal arts, social sciences, law, or economics" (Erdle 2011: 28–29). The latter tendency is confirmed by the World Bank (2014c: 175) and Achy (2010: 17) who contrasts the high share of students in the humanities and social sciences with a share of less than 25% of students in science and engineering. The specializations chosen by the majority of students seem less in demand on the Tunisian labor market since students in technical fields such as architecture, medicine, telecommunication and electricity, or engineering are employed below their qualification level much less often than students from other fields such as business, commerce, administration, humanities, or law (World Bank 2013: 174–176).[2]

Still, Tunisia has made some progress on becoming an increasingly knowledge-based economy, consistent with its status as a "watchmaker" economy whose only realistic option of long-term economic development is building on human capital and focusing on exports of skill-intensive manufacturing products or services (Richards and Waterbury 2008: 68). Rodríguez-Pose and Hardy (2014) assess Tunisia's way towards becoming a knowledge-based economy and highlight that gross domestic expenditure on research and development (GERD), commonly measured as a share of GDP, is typically low in emerging countries. However, Tunisia is a remarkable exception and additionally witnessed a high rise in GERD between 1999 and 2009. For instance, in 2007–2008 Tunisia featured a share of GERD in GDP of 1.03%, significantly above the levels founds in other Arab economies such as Morocco, Jordan, Qatar, Lebanon, Algeria, Egypt, Kuwait, Oman, Syria, and Bahrain and above the level found in Turkey (Mahroum et al. 2013: 38). Furthermore, Tunisia features exceptionally high numbers of researchers in R&D among comparable emerging countries. While Tunisia's GERD is largely dominated by public expenditure, during the early 2000s public expenditure as a share of GERD increased

---

[2] However, the conclusion drawn from these insights may not necessarily be to "reorient" students towards technical fields but better seizing the economic potential of business studies, social sciences, or humanities, e.g., through entrepreneurship or the commercialization of humanities in cultural and creative industries or in tourism.

significantly, due presumably to public incentives to private-sector innovation (Ben Abdessalem and El Elj 2011: 4; Rodríguez-Pose and Hardy 2014: 89–90).

When looking at Tunisia's growth performance within the global economy, it is important to note that the Tunisian economy heavily depends on the EU market with over three quarters of exports going to the EU, almost three quarters of FDI coming from the EU, and 90% of remittances originating from the diaspora in the EU, and France, Italy and Germany alone accounting for two thirds of the country's international trade (Achy 2010: 11; Erdle 2011: 40; World Bank 2014c: 311). International openness is inextricably linked to competitiveness and innovation. As the World Bank (2013: 93) demonstrates, Tunisia's trade integration has been driving total factor productivity (TFP) growth in the 1990s and early 2000s, but at the same time mentions that TFP growth in Tunisia remains lower than in comparable Asian countries such as South Korea or Malaysia. While productivity between 2000 and 2008 grew by 2% annually in Tunisia, the country's labor productivity performance is below that of competitors such as Turkey, Romania, Poland, or Asian NIEs (Achy 2010: 10). As Achy (2010: 11) suggests, the failure to reduce the (youth) unemployment rate in Tunisia may be related to its comparatively weak productivity growth. Instead of relying on higher competitiveness driven by increasing productivity, Tunisia "built its growth strategy around low-skilled sectors that rely on cheap labor" (Achy 2010: 11).

In this regard, cause and consequence appear to mix. While youth unemployment among higher-education graduates apparently hampers knowledge-intensive growth, precisely this slow pace of knowledge-intensive growth exacerbates the prospects of highly educated youth on the labor market. Over time, Tunisia witnessed a marked change in the profile of its labor supply. The share of jobseekers with postsecondary education rose from 20% to over 55% from 2000 to 2008, but labor demand has not kept pace, and the shift to a more knowledge-based economy has so far not generally succeeded, due not least to an unfavorable business environment that hampers entrepreneurship and private investment (Achy 2010: 11).

Summing up the challenges for the Tunisian economy in terms of the sources of its future competitiveness, Ghali and Rezgui (2015: 64) stress the necessity for the country to move beyond its dependence on low-cost labor and low value-added activities towards more technology- and skill-intensive activities (Ghali and Rezgui 2015: 64). How precisely to do so is visibly in the focus of the country's long-term economic policy, as will become evident in the following section.

4.1.2 Tunisia's Economic Policies: Past and Present

While core Arab economies' development trajectories are not all too different from that of comparable developing countries, among them Tunisia has performed comparatively well (Noland and Pack 2007: 181). Therefore, taking a closer look at Tunisia's economic policies since independence seems worthwhile.

Tunisia's economic policy has witnessed several phases mirroring general trends in core Arab economies such as import substitution and Arab socialism as well as later liberalization and opening up to the world economy through export development and FDI promotion, although with some noted differences. While the country's socialist phase in the 1960s was comparatively short-lived, Tunisia was an early mover in liberalization, and opening up to the world economy as its *infitah* policy was begun already in 1969 (Richards and Waterbury 2008: 195–196).

Still and despite Tunisia's role as front-runner in economic reform among Arab economies, Rivlin (2009) sees the country hitting a "glass ceiling" towards achieving higher economic growth and lowering its unemployment rate, something developing countries in other world regions succeeded to do (Rivlin 2009: 277). The next sub-sections introduce major streams of Tunisia's long-term structural policy and address their weaknesses that may help explain why the country's reform efforts have not yet effectively solved the structural difficulties of the Tunisian economy.

4.1.2.1 Industrial Policy

At the outset, colonial history explains the weak initial levels of industrialization in Tunisia. To promote the country's industrialization, a policy of import substitution was pursued until the 1980s after the private sector's reaction to encouragement right after independence was weak. Even during Tunisia's socialist phase in the 1960s, policy was not hostile towards the private sector despite the pursuit of a state-led growth model and the centralization of economic decision-making (Rivlin 2009: 277–278).

In its industrial policy since independence, Tunisia has often taken the role of policy pioneer in the Arab world. Major policy eras included major social reforms after independence during the 1950s, Arab socialism during the 1960s, *infitah* policies during the 1970s, and structural reform supported by the IMF and the World Bank, WTO membership, and participation in the EU's European Neighborhood Policy (ENP), Euro-Mediterranean Partnership (EMP), and Union for the Mediterranean (UfM) in recent decades. In the latter context, Tunisia was the first country to sign an association agreement (AA) with the EU (Altenburg 2011: 70; Erdle 2011: 3; Hazboun 2008: 74).

Tunisia's brief Arab socialist era is a particularly relevant episode, both in its own right and in view of the subsequent *infitah* era. During the 1960s, Tunisia embarked on a short socialist experiment orchestrated by planning and finance minister Ahmed Ben Salah. This period was marked by import substitution and state-led growth and saw a rapid increase in the number of SOEs and their share in national investment. The Salahist experiment ended in 1969 as abruptly as it had begun in 1961 because it could not be sustained for various structural reasons including difficulties in raising funds to fund import substitution industrialization. Under the following policy regime, Tunisia's industrial policy shifted towards a mixture between import substitution and export promotion, notably in the textile industry and tourism. This *infitah* policy was still marked by a leading role for the state in economic development but offered greater freedom for the private sector. The rationale behind this *infitah* policy was for Tunisian industrial policy to benefit from the country's strategic advantages such as its human capital and low-cost labor, political stability, and spatial and cultural proximity to Europe (Erdle 2011: 8–9).

New investment and trade legislation in the early 1970s and the creation of private-sector promotion agencies were part of the *infitah* policy that eventually resulted in the emergence of a private manufacturing sector (Erdle 2011: 9–10). Still, the public sector continued to grow, giving rise to an economy segmented into a large public sector including SOEs and strategic monopolies, a highly regulated and protected domestic industrial sector, an export- and investment-oriented offshore sector, and a residual private sector containing small firms (Erdle 2011: 10). Rivlin (2009: 282–283) similarly highlights the major dualism between a liberalized offshore export sector (mainly for the textiles and clothing industry) promoted through financial incentives and a separated and protected domestic economy still operating under conditions of import substitution (World Bank 2014c: 50, 138). The special regulatory regime governing the offshore sector allowed for industrial development in isolated pockets of the economy but with limited spillovers to other sectors that remained subject to a less encouraging business environment (World Bank 2014a: 63). The 1972 investment law was a milestone in Tunisian industrial policy. The law was designed to attract FDI in labor-intensive activities and paved the way to the country's integration in the international division of labor by taking over low-skill tasks (Ghali and Rezgui 2015: 40). The law laid the groundwork for a selective economic policy by stipulating incentives for the offshore sector but at the same time prescribing restrictions for the onshore sector such as authorization requirements (World Bank 2014a: 84). Hence, Tunisia's *infitah* policy was a compromise between state-led growth and private-sector-led growth as "on the one hand, the state encouraged private sector growth and foreign direct investment while, on the other hand, it tightly regulated market access and resource allocation" (Erdle 2011: 10). The state-led part of the *infitah* policy did contribute to short-term successes such as high economic growth and increasing living standards notably for the urban middle class but involved unsustainable measures such as expanding the public sector and accumulating deficits. It was arguably the fundamentally unsustainable character of Tunisia's industrial policy that forced the government to resort to IFI-sponsored structural adjustment in 1986 (Cammett 2007: 1892–1895; Erdle 2011: 10–11; Rivlin 2009: 278).

Structural adjustment and EU rapprochement were major externally induced drivers of trends in Tunisia's economic policy in recent years. Structural crises were arguably triggers for Tunisian policy to integrate into these transnational transformative processes. After high economic growth in the 1970s, structural crises in the early 1980s forced the Tunisian government to commit to a vast program of economic liberalization and private-sector promotion beginning in 1986 that was accompanied by structural adjustment assisted by the IMF and the World Bank (Rivlin 2009: 268–275). This reform package led to a liberalization more far-reaching than in any other Arab economy (Rivlin 2009: 272). Under pressure from IFIs, Tunisia adopted a more private-sector-led approach towards industrial policy which, however, resulted in the distribution of fiscal privileges, favoritism, rent-seeking, and state capture (Ghali and Rezgui 2015: 40–41).

Structural adjustment was aimed at macroeconomic stabilization but did not change the structural configuration of the Tunisian economy. For instance, privatization was very limited and excluded sectors defined as "strategic" including utilities as well as the mining, chemicals, and steel industries (Erdle 2011: 18). It was only under the Ben Ali regime that a reorientation of the Tunisian economy towards a more market-based paradigm and greater openness to trade and integration into global value chains occurred. The private sector was acknowledged as a driver of economic growth because it was supposed to fill the void left by the receding public sector, in part through innovation, productivity enhancement, and job creation (Erdle 2011: 18–19).

Part of the opening effort under Ben Ali's industrial policy was the regime of offshoring free zones and incentives for exporting companies such as tax and tariff exemptions, tax breaks, infrastructure, and social security incentives for employers (Erdle 2011: 24). While association and free trade with the EU posed considerable challenges for the still heavily protected domestic Tunisian economy, the rationale behind economic *rapprochement* was that the country's industrialization effort would benefit from locking in policy into durable market opening through the legal stability afforded by the AA, as well as from technical assistance offered by the EU and other donors (Erdle 2011: 13–14).

The *infitah* era saw the setup of various support agencies such as the *Agence pour la Promotion de l'Industrie* (API) offering technical assistance to firms and the *Fonds de Promotion et de Décentralisation Industrielles* offering finance, both created in 1973. In 2005, the *Fonds de Promotion des Exportations* (FOPRODEX) and the *Fonds d'Accès aux Marchés d'Exportation* (FAMEX) were established to support exporting firms. Further agencies include the national tourism promotion agency (ONTT), the foreign investment promotion agency (FIPA), the export promotion agency (CEPEX), the standardization agency (INNORPI), the research promotion agency (ANPR), and the promotion agency for the agricultural sector (APIA). Considerable efforts towards trade facilitation were made in Tunisia since the late 1980s including the setup of a one-stop window for firm creation and the simplification of trade documentation and processing (Cammett 2007: 1894–1895; Ghali and Rezgui 2015: 64).

Measures to prepare Tunisian industry for liberalization and integration into EU markets included the ambitious industrial upgrading scheme *Programme de mise à niveau* (PMN) setup in 1995. A major part of the perceived need to upgrade Tunisian industry was that the AA implemented by 2008 and the end of Multi Fibre Arrangement (MFA) in 2004 challenged Tunisian industry due to its heavy export dependence on textiles and clothing (and tourism) and on EU markets (Rivlin 2009: 281–282). As the main pillar of the Tunisian government's industrial upgrading effort, the PMN-assisted companies in upgrading their competitiveness supported the improvement of the business environment and the development of support infrastructure such as industrial zones and promoted certification, standardization, and innovation. The program was steered by the Tunisian government and supported by funding from the EU. Key decisions were taken by the government, but key stake-holders were included in decision-making processes. Despite its large scale, the PMN focused on larger firms and did not target traditional parts of the domestic economy such as small trades and crafts (Cammett 2007: 1895; Erdle 2011: 31–35; Ghali and Rezgui 2015: 54).

Altenburg (2011: 5) perceives a strong commitment in Tunisia to competitive upgrading of the economy in comparison to other developing countries, as is evident from policy support initiatives to strengthen firms' competitiveness and in the setup of support agencies. The Ben Ali regime's orientation in industrial policy was clearly outward-oriented and made the country a Southern Mediterranean pioneer in free trade with the EU (Altenburg 2011: 70). This policy was partly successful in the sense that the Tunisian economy "achieved sustained GDP growth rates of over five per cent per year since the early 1990s, clearly above the regional average, and created 500,000 jobs in the manufacturing industry" (Altenburg 2011: 70).

Despite these successes, Tunisian industry still exhibits a strong focus on activities with low value added (Erdle 2011: 41). According to Ghali and Rezgui (2015: 15, 45), a gradual transformation of the Tunisian manufacturing sector from textiles and garments towards electrical and mechanical equipment such as electrical wiring systems and other components for European automotive industries is ongoing, but both groups of industries are dominated by low value-added activities (Diop and Ghali 2012: 15; Ghali and Rezgui 2015: 45). Rivlin (2009: 283) confirms that while the textiles and electrical and mechanical equipment industries are relatively well-performing export sectors in Tunisia, they still have not driven widespread industrialization because they add little value added and mainly transform inputs into presumably labor-intensive exports. The World Bank (2014c: 223–224) sees the Tunisian economy's comparative advantages in textiles and garments, leather and footwear, electrical and mechanical engineering, chemical products, construction materials, and furniture. At the same time, these industries in which Tunisia has comparative advantages suffer from shallow integration in international value chains and overreliance on very few European markets, basically making the Tunisian economy an assembly subcontractor economy primarily for two European countries, France and Italy (World Bank 2014c: 311).

However, in line with the gradual trends towards higher value-added manufacturing Erdle (2011: 42) hints at, Diop and Ghali (2012: 13) see Tunisian exports moving slowly into higher value-added niches with higher technological content. Between 1005 and 2009, the share of low-technology products in Tunisia's exports declined from 56.7% to 38.3%, while products with higher technological content increased their shares correspondingly (Diop and Ghali 2012: 13). The growing technological sophistication of Tunisian exports seems to mirror the decreasing importance of the textiles and garments industries (Diop and Ghali 2012: 14; Hazboun 2008: 39–40). Still, Tunisia trails other emerging economies such as Turkey, Brazil, India, or Indonesia in terms of high-technology exports. In comparison with India and Indonesia, at the same time, Tunisia features a higher share of medium-high-technology exports, implying that the Tunisian economy is in an earlier stage of becoming a knowledge-based economy (Diop and Ghali 2012: 19).

Despite the changes in the country's industrial fabric, the Tunisian economy did not significantly change from its growth model from being highly dependent on governmental intervention and steering. The public sector remained the primary driver of economic development, and it kept "employing up to 40 percent of the national workforce, and accounting for well over 50 percent of GDP" (Erdle 2011: 41).

Another important aspect of Tunisia's industrial policy during the Ben Ali era was its highly restrictive approach to competition in protected sectors that were typically those regime cronies were active in (OECD 2015; Rijkers et al. 2014). In a sense, Ben Ali's industrial policy shifted the constraints to independent private-sector dynamism from official administrative, government-set barriers to private, oligarchic structures protected from competition by subtle administrative measures and presumably arbitrary policy implementation. When it comes to restrictions stipulated by the investment law, "64% of Ben Ali firms [were, M.B,] in sectors subject to authorization requirements and 64% in sectors subject to restrictions on FDI. For non-Ben-Ali firms the comparable numbers [were, M.B.] 45% and 36%, respectively" (Rijkers et al. 2014: 12–13).

Tunisia's halfway progress on becoming a knowledge-based economy, presumably its only choice towards continued economic development as one of the comparatively resource-poor and human capital-abundant "watchmaker" countries (Richards and Waterbury 2008: 68), is inextricably linked to the country's science, technology, and innovation policy but at the same time conditioned by the constraints to Schumpeterian creative destruction and entrepreneurship. While the wider context for Schumpeterian creative destruction including cronyism under the Ben Ali regime and the heavy weight of the public sector is addressed in a regulation perspective in Sects. 4.1.3 and 4.1.4, the next sub-section sheds light on the innovation policy approaches adopted by the Tunisian government in recent decades.

4.1.2.2   Science, Technology, and Innovation Policy

Tunisia's growth model centered on labor-intensive, low-cost, and low-skill manufacturing for export to European markets mainly in the textiles and garments industry, and tourism at a certain point reached its limits in an environment marked by increasing international competition. In particular, the model was not capable of reducing unemployment and absorbing increasingly well-educated youth entering the labor market in large numbers (Ghali and Rezgui 2015: 50).

The transformation of the country's industrial structure was accompanied by a marked shift in the formal skills profile of the labor force, as becomes clear from the "evolution of the national average of share of graduates of higher education from 1.6% in 1975 to 17.3% in 2011" (Ghali and Rezgui 2015: 45). With such an increase in formal qualifications by jobseekers, it is clear that the low-cost, low-skills export development model with its focus on labor-intensive industries with limited possibilities for productivity increases such as textiles, garments, and tourism could not provide adequate opportunities for young generations looking for employment on par with their formal education. As a result, it is not surprising that unemployment rates in Tunisia are higher for tertiary-educated jobseekers than for unskilled ones (Ghali and Regzui 2015: 56). From a policy perspective, the solution to this dilemma could only be to focus on knowledge-based growth.

Ghali and Rezgui (2015: 52–53) survey indicators to measure Tunisia's progress towards becoming a knowledge-based economy. On the one hand, the strong sectors in the Tunisian economy to a considerable extent remain dominated by low-skilled activities, implying a growing demand for workers with lower formal skills. At the same time, Tunisian education policy in recent years was fairly successful and led to high rates of school enrollment, increased public spending on education, and a significant rise in university enrollment. Tunisia's ratio of R&D spending to GDP is low compared to leading OECD countries but above the levels reached in Turkey and India, and it grew during the 2000s. Yet, the contribution of firms to R&D spending is significantly lower than in the EU or in Turkey, implying a rather weak state of R&D in Tunisian industry (Ghali and Rezgui 2015: 52–53).

While academic education greatly expanded during past decades, the economic role of universities seems constrained by their limited alignment with private-sector needs. Interviewees mentioned that Tunisia's university culture follows a French model striving for academic achievement such as publications but lacks practical focus. There are, however, regional initiatives to change this culture. For example, the new e-health cluster initiative in Sfax is now developing a new model for doctoral studies in medicine that includes practical tasks for hospital work.

In terms of innovation, Tunisia was ranked 74th among 127 countries in the 2017 Global Innovation Index. While rankings are a somewhat questionable approach to measuring the complex realities of inherently social and systemic processes such as innovation, it is still interesting to look at the details of Tunisia's result. While Tunisia scores comparatively better on human capital and particularly on its expenditure for education as well as on the number of graduates in sciences and engineering (3rd place internationally behind Oman and Iran and above Morocco)[3] as well as on knowledge creation through scientific and technical articles (M'Henni and Deniozos 2012: 20–21), Tunisia is ranked particularly low on the dimension of innovative linkages such as university-industry research collaboration or cluster development, as well as on knowledge absorption. What is particularly interesting is that Tunisia scores comparatively well on high-technology exports less re-exports as a share of total trade and on the share of creative goods exports[4] of total trade (Cornell, INSEAD and WIPO 2017: 300, 333).

Ben Miled-M'rabet (n.d.) maps the Tunisian NIS and lists a large number of organizations relevant for the innovation and entrepreneurship ecosystem in Tunisia

---

[3] It is interesting to note the contradiction with the often-expressed claim that too many students in Tunisia specialize in social sciences or humanities and too little in science and engineering (e.g., Achy 2010: 17; Hertog 2016; World Bank 2013: 25).

[4] The latter finding further confirms the argument brought forward in Sect. 3.4 that a knowledge base in humanities and social sciences can serve as a resource for entrepreneurship and innovation in a resource-poor and human capital-rich country such as Tunisia.

and its regions. The ecosystem includes the following types of entities (Ben Miled-M'rabet n.d.):

- Public universities and other higher-education entities (HEI)[5] and their research units and laboratories
- Public R&D centers for a large number of fields and technologies including, inter alia, biotechnology, energy technology, nuclear technology, maritime technology, or telecommunications
- Science and technology parks (*technopôles*) currently being set up under the *pôle de compétitivité* scheme with the Elgazala ICT technology park in the Tunis agglomeration as the first and most advanced one (Benner forthcoming; Rodríguez-Pose and Hardy 2014: 56–57)
- Regional incubators (*pépinières*) hosted by *technopôles*, HEIs such as the applied-science *Instituts supérieurs des études technologiques* (ISET) or engineering schools, or R&D centers (M'Henni and Deniozos 2012: 32)
- The national agency for the promotion of industry and innovation API (*Agence de Promotion de l'Industrie et de l'Innovation*) providing technical assistance to enterprises, managing incubators, and acting as Enterprise Europe Network (EEN) contact point
- Regional business centers (*centres d'affaires*) providing technical assistance to entrepreneurs in the stages prior to and during new business formation
- The national R&D promotion agency ANPR (*Agence Nationale de Promotion de la Recherche Scientifique*)
- The national standardization and intellectual property agency INNORPI (*Institut National de la Normalisation et de la Propriété Industrielle*)
- A number of funds administrating innovation grants to enterprises, as well as the PMN

A range of entrepreneurship support schemes exist in Tunisia and have become a vital part of the country's industrial and innovation policies. Most public HEIs offer some kind of entrepreneurship education, and many of them provide additional services such as advice. However, these schemes are usually not designed in a multidisciplinary way and are offered by individual faculties instead of crosscutting university institutes. Furthermore, university support activities for entrepreneurship rarely include incubation services, although there are exceptions such as the University of Sfax (OECD 2012b: 14, 20–21).

Business centers set up in the 24 Tunisian governorates provide support for entrepreneurship such as coaching, consulting, business planning support, microfinance, and networking support. However, interaction between universities and business centers is limited and refers mainly to marketing and raising awareness for business centers' offers among students and graduates, as well as offering seminars (OECD 2012b: 35).

---

[5] The commonly used abbreviation "HEI" for "higher education institution" is used here for the sake of consistency with the literature on innovation systems, although according to the perspective taken in this book, HEIs are not institutions but organizations.

Somewhat similar to business centers, incubators (*pépinières d'entreprise*) such as those funded by API offer services to entrepreneurs or startups such as expertise, space, or networking support (OECD 2012b: 35). As with business centers, incubators' interaction with HEIs is limited, although their mission is clearly linked to entrepreneurship among HEI graduates (OECD 2012b: 74).

Further, there are so-called entrepreneurship spaces (*espaces entreprendre*) offering training and business planning support in micro-entrepreneurship for young unemployed, supported by the national employment agency ANETI (OECD 2012b: 73–74).

Further schemes to promote innovation and entrepreneurship include funds providing financial support, one-stop shops, technical centers providing technical support to private-sector enterprises, industrial zones set up since 1973, and business planning training schemes (Erdle 2011: 25–26; M'Henni and Deniozos 2012: 13; OECD and IDRC 2013: 93).

One particularly prominent scheme to promote innovation in Tunisia since the early 2000s is the country's ambitious cluster policy with its *pôles de compétivitité*. The first *pôle* was the Elgazala technopark located in the Tunis agglomeration including two satellite sites in other parts of the Tunis agglomeration and regional ICT incubators called *cyberparcs* all over the country. Launched in 1999, this technology park was set up in the early 2000s to promote the upgrading of the ICT sector in the country. The park hosts an incubator, the *Centre d'Études et de Recherche des Télécommunications* (CERT) research center, HEIs in ICT-related disciplines, and national agencies regulating the telecommunications industry. Importantly, the technology park has managed to attract renowned international anchor tenants such as Microsoft, Ericsson, Huawei, or Alcatel-Lucent and is home to roughly 100 enterprises. A certain degree of collaboration between tenants is observable in the technology park (Aubert et al. 2013: 99–101; Benner 2017c, forthcoming; M'Henni et al. 2013).

Hence, Elgazala technopark is regarded as a relative success in promoting place-based innovation. Following the observation made by Rodríguez-Pose and Hardy (2014) that science and technology parks in development or emerging countries tend to be successful if and when they benefit either from strong research universities or from innovative multinational anchor tenants, Elgazala technopark is an example for the second case. Encouraged by the relative success of Elgazala technopark, the Tunisian government during the 2000s developed plans to extend the model to other sectors by launching the *pôles de compétitivité* program. In essence, these *pôles* draw on a combination of place-based clustering and sectoral networking. A *pôle's* backbone is a technology park similar to Elgazala technopark hosting companies, research centers or HEIs, and an incubator. *Pôles* in manufacturing-oriented industries include industrial or offshoring zones hosting manufacturing firms. To achieve sectoral networking beyond the technology parks and industrial zones, sectoral networks are organized which are open to enterprises in the wider region or in the whole country. These formalized networks are typically called "clusters." Including Elgazala, so far nine *pôles* were designated and set up, or are at least partially operational, with technology parks situated in Elgazala and its satellite sites (ICT industry), Bizerte (agrifood industries), Borj Cédria (renewable energies, environment and water, green biotechnology, materials), Gabès (environmental technologies), Gafsa (substances and phosphates), Monastir (textiles and garments industries), Sidi Thabet (medical biotechnology and pharmaceuticals), Sfax (ICT), and Sousse (mechanics, electronics, nanotechnology, and ICT). Two further *pôles* are planned for Jendouba (agriculture and forestry products) and Médenine (desert resources) and will be located in peripheral regions of the country. *Pôles* are usually set up as a public-private partnership with large firms or banks involved in running the *pôle* (Agence de Promotion de l'Industrie et de l'Innovation 2016, n.d.; Aubert et al. 2013: 99–101; Benner 2017c, forthcoming; Erdle 2011: 26–27; Lehmann and Benner 2015; M'Henni et al. 2013; M'Henni and Deniozos 2012: 33–34; Rodríguez-Pose and Hardy 2014: 56–57).

The success of the *pôles* program and its relevance for driving the Tunisian economy's move towards becoming a more knowledge-based economy cannot yet be judged. Elgazala technopark was viewed as a success by interviewees. The park's relative success was ascribed mainly due to its presence in the dynamic urban area of Tunis, the proximity of renowned university faculties, and the presence of large international anchor companies. The *pôles* in Sfax and Sousse might eventually replicate the model but need time and resources to do so. The prospects for success of other *pôles* were questioned in the interviews. The relevance of an anchor tenant strategy, as pursued in the Elgazala technopark, was underlined in the interviews. Since Tunisian companies are seen to be lacking the capacities to commercialize research available in universities, multinational enterprises investing in Tunisia and specifically in *pôles* adapting their technological solutions to the Tunisian context, developing prototypes, and mobilizing locally available research and knowledge were suggested as drivers of innovation during the interviews. In any case, replicating the relative success of Elgazala with its successful acquisition of technologically sophisticated multinational anchor tenants in other locations and sectors is a not an easy task for the other *pôles* (Ghali and Rezgui 2015: 51).

Given that the Elgazala *pôle* was set up as from 1999 on and that the other *pôles* are still in various stages of their establishment, it is probably too early to evaluate their success (Benner 2017c: 53–54; forthcoming). Seen from a spatial perspective, it is worth noting that the *pôles'* backbone technology parks are located primarily in the comparatively prosperous coastal areas of the country such as Bizerte, the Tunis agglomeration, Monastir, Sousse, and Sfax (Benner 2014a, 2017c, forthcoming; Lehmann and Benner 2015). While other technology parks like those set up or planned in Gabès, Gafsa, Jendouba, and Médenine are located in peripheral location, the *pôles* program follows the growth-oriented policy rationale of innovation policy much more than the spatial-equity rationale of regional policy. Given the large economic and social disparities between regions in Tunisia, the country's regional structural policy has come up with other schemes to enable lagging peripheral and rural regions to catch up with more prosperous urban ones. These schemes will be introduced in the next sub-section.

4.1.2.3 Regional Structural Policy

Considering Tunisia's enormous economic and social disparities between prosperous urban coastal regions such as Tunis, Nabeul/Hammamet, Sousse/Monastir, and Sfax on the one hand and peripheral regions such as Jendouba, Le Kef, Kasserine, Sidi Bouzid, Gafsa, Tozeur, or Tataouine on the other hand (Benner 2014a; Medinilla Aldana and El Fassi 2016; OECD 2018: 51–52; World Bank 2011), the relevance of regional policy in Tunisia is clear.

The Tunisian government's *pôle de compétitivité* scheme inspired by the comparatively successful experience of Elgazala technopark follows a growth-oriented logic. In the few cases where the backbone technoparks of *pôles* are located in peripheral regions, this growth logic is mixed with the equity-base rationale of traditional regional policies (Benner 2014a). The growth logic of the *pôles de compétitivité* as a measure of innovation policy is consistent with the spatial concentration of higher education and R&D in Tunisia since almost four-fifths of public HEIs and researchers are located in coastal regions with Tunis, Sousse, Monastir, and Sfax as the dominant university centers (M'Henni and Deniozos 2012: 14).

Nevertheless, as was the case with the designation of *pôles de compétitivité* in peripheral regions, Tunisian regional policy strives to decentralize the innovation system to some degree (M'Henni and Deniozos 2012: 14). However, the relationship between innovation policy and regional development in Tunisia is complex. In particular, spreading innovation infrastructure such as technology parks or incubators across the country is fraught with difficulties because a critical mass of innovative firms is not available everywhere (M'Henni and Deniozos 2012: 35). While it remains to be seen whether *pôles de compétivitité* whose technology parks are located in peripheral regions will unfold their full innovative and growth-related potential or not, unlocking endogenous growth potentials in peripheral regions arguably requires other tools.

One of those tools designed to facilitate the unfolding of endogenous growth potentials of peripheral regions in the center, West, and South of the country is the setup of *complexes industriels and technologiques* (CIT) located in towns and cities in Tunisia's peripheral governorates (Benner forthcoming). The architecture of the CITs follows that of the *pôles de compétitivité*, but their rationale focuses more on endogenous regional development than on technology transfer and technological innovation. The backbone of a CIT is an industrial zone, similar to the *pôles'* technology parks but without co-located universities. Instead, CITs may involve some degree of cooperation with technical centers or ISETs. A CIT is managed by a *société complexe industriel et technologique* (SCIT), a management company that offers services to tenants. Again similar to the *pôle* architecture, CITs set up regional networks called "clusters" to promote cooperation and networking among companies within the CIT's industrial zone and outside. Different from the *pôles* with their sectoral focus determined a priori in a top-down way, CITs have no predetermined sectoral focus but tend to specialize on a few sectors according to the profile of an industrial zone's eventual tenants and the regional economy (Benner 2017c, forth-coming; Ministère de l'Industrie, de l'Énergie et des Mines 2014).[6]

Apparently inspired by the *pôles de compétitivité* program, the CITs emphasize a newer orientation of Tunisian regional policy more focused on endogenous growth than older schemes supporting regional development in lagging, peripheral regions. This shift is well in line with international trends in regional development theory and policy. In the case of Tunisia, traditional regional policies focused on achieving interregional equity through spatial redistribution. One part of these traditional, redistributive regional policies was the designation of 140 regional development zones (*zones de développement régional* or ZDR) in lagging regions in the interior of the country. Firms located in these zones enjoyed tax exemptions or breaks (World Bank 2011: 253). Until 2007, the Tunisian government offered 25% invest-ment grants for companies deciding to locate in these zones. The results of this traditional, redistributive regional policy with its focus on the ZDR were mixed. The incentives given to firms locating in the ZDR led firms to locate on the eastern fringe of the area to be closer to the prosperous coastal regions instead of spreading across peripheral regions in the interior of the country. The Tunisian government reacted by readjusting the policy. It decided to differentiate incentives according to three classes of ZDR. Under this readjustment, the highest rates of grant support of up to 30% go to investments in priority development zones (*zones de développement pri-oritaires*) primarily located in the Western and Southern parts of the country (Benner 2014a; Medinilla Aldana and El Fassi 2016: 6; World Bank 2011: 253, 257–258).

Regional economic development in Tunisia in the past decades cannot be under-stood without taking a look at the broader trends in Tunisian industrial policy (see Sect. 4.1.2.1). In particular, Tunisia's offshore regime for export-oriented manufac-turing and notably for the textiles and garments industry provides a framework highly relevant for regional development. It is safe to assume that the upswing of coastal regions was critically related to the relative attractiveness of coastal regions for export-oriented manufacturing. Indeed, the designation of offshore areas located in coastal regions and related tax and bureaucratic advantages offered to export-oriented manufacturers increased the spatial polarization (OECD 2015: 41). In addition, the country's tourism policy that for a long time focused primarily on sun, sand, and beach package mass tourism (see Sect. 4.1.2.4) most likely contributed to the phenomenon the World Bank (2011: 101) calls "bipolar convergence," meaning that since the 1980s, regions in the central-eastern part of the country and particu-larly the governorates of Mahdia and Monastir managed to catch up with the pros-perous Tunis agglomeration but other lagging regions such the Center-West region did not (World Bank 2011: 101–102).

It is thus not surprising that Tunisian regional policy witnessed a partial turn towards approaches focusing on endogenous growth such as the *pôles de compé-titivité* or the CITs (Benner 2014a). Another attempt to facilitate the endogenous growth of regional economies is the establishment of industrial zones (Erdle 2011:

---

[6]The author was involved as a consultant in a project to support CITs and clusters in Tunisian regions funded by German technical cooperation.

26; World Bank 2009: 138–139). Tunisia has a comparatively well-developed system of public-private management of industrial zones. The system is based on a law from 1994 that stipulates the setup of tenants associations in industrial zones called *Groupement de Maintenance et de Gestion* (GMG) funded by tenants and whose task is to assure the management of the industrial zone. Here too, the Tunisian government-set special incentives for regional development in lagging regions as government funding for zones' investment expenditure was higher in the interior regions than in Tunis. Yet, the industrial zone program is confronted with major difficulties such as delays in setting up active GMGs and tenants' reluctance to fund the associations through fees (Erdle 2011: 26; World Bank 2009: 139).

Newer initiatives in Tunisian regional policy include the intended establishment of a regional development investment bank for funding youth and women projects (Mattes 2016: 6). Currently the Tunisian government is pursuing a plan for decentralization of political decision-making (OECD 2018: 52; 117; 121–124). The ongoing postrevolutionary decentralization process might eventually provide new opportunities for regional development policies designed in a more pronounced bottom-up manner but will most likely require strengthening competences and resources on the regional level (Benner 2014a; Medinilla Aldana and El Fassi 2016). There are indeed endogenous assets available in peripheral regions, as was highlighted in the interviews. Although industry, R&D, and entrepreneurship are concentrated in Tunisia's urban regions, rural areas have their own resources and assets, for instance, in agriculture or cultural heritage. For instance, one interviewee mentioned the production of essential oils as a promising industry in Tunisia's rural regions but stated that economic opportunities are often not seized because of a lack of knowledge about (international) market opportunities. Additionally, the country's entrepreneurship policy was said to focus on employment and income generation primarily but not on upgrading to internationally common levels of excellence, e.g., in terms of quality standards and norms. Furthermore, interventions (presumably often driven by international donors) often follow a youth or gender dimension, thus possibly creating societal cleavages. To counter the risk of societal cleavages, one interviewee suggested a territorial development perspective would be preferable because focusing interventions on the resources and assets of a territory could strengthen solidarity within the population instead of undermining it. Summing up, there appears to be a certain awareness for the role of endogenous regional development that could be seized with participatory approaches as described in Sect. 4.1.5.

4.1.2.4 Tourism Policy

Both industrial and regional policies in Tunisia are affected by the prominent role the tourism industry plays in the country's economic development. Tourism in Tunisia originally started as a French colonial project but after independence became a postcolonial national vision promoted by President Bourguiba. First investments in tourism occurred after 1959 by the parastatal *Société Hôtelière et Touristique* (SHTT) in hotels. Investments undertaken by SHTT were meant to serve as a model to mobilize private investment and thus entrepreneurial initiative to jump-start the creation of tourism supply. Tourism development followed the goal of spatial equity through investments not only in Monastir (a center of the Bourguiba regime) but also in Gafsa, Kairouan, and Kasserine. Yet, today the Tunisian tourism sector is spatially characterized by a strong degree of clustering in tourism zones. In recent decades, Tunisian tourism policy has come to focus on the development of integrated tourism complexes such as Port El Kantaoui and Yasmine Hammamet, but for a long time Tunisia's tourism development model retained its dependence on low-cost mass tourism in "a low-equilibrium trap where the product had to continue to undercut prices at other destinations" (Hazboun 2008: 30). Despite efforts towards creating more unique features of Tunisian tourism in the integrated tourism complexes, the Tunisian tourism sectors still offers a comparatively standardized product focused mainly on sun, sand, and beach mass tourism (Hazboun 2008).

Since the 1960s, Tunisian tourism policy followed a state-led strategy to attract standardized, Fordist mass tourism. Government-funded hotel investments served to demonstrate the viability of the mass package tourism business model and to mobilize private investment, combined with government incentives such as subsidies for hotel project feasibility studies or access to capital provided by state-owned banks. Private investment did kick in, leading to the emergence of large Tunisian hotel chains owned by established merchant families and assisted by the state-owned bank STB. Part of the strategy was the strong concentration of mass tourism in three regions, Nabeul/Hammamet, Sousse/Monastir, and Jerba which together accounted for almost three quarters of the country's hotel capacity in the early 1970s, arguably reinforced by the inflow of FDI by TNCs in mass tourism hotels (Hazboun 2008: 7–14).

According to the OECD (2015: 77), Tunisia took the third place on the African continent in terms of international tourist arrivals after South Africa and Morocco, welcoming 6 million visitors. Tourism contributes between 6.5% and 12% to the country's GDP and about 11% of employment in the active population (OECD 2015: 77; World Bank 2015: 6).[7] At the same time, tourism in Tunisia is concentrated in low value-added segments of the market, mirroring the long-standing orientation of the Tunisian manufacturing sector. The flip side of the coin is that "opportunities for cultural, sport and eco-related tourism activities remain largely unexploited," and "on average receipts per tourist arrival in Tunisia are low" (OECD 2015: 77). The insight that the Tunisian tourism sector captures little added-value compared to other Mediterranean destinations is confirmed by the World Bank (2014c: 207). The World Economic Forum (2017) presents data suggesting that average spending per international tourist in Tunisia stands at 257.70 USD which is fairly low compared to Morocco (575.10 USD), Egypt (663.60 USD), Turkey (674.20 USD), or Jordan (1080.80 USD).

---

[7]The estimates used in different sources vary significantly because of the difficulty of separating tourism-related activities from other economic activities and thus follow different methods of measurement.

Hazboun (2008: 43–45) puts the Tunisian tourism sector in the context of the post-Fordism debate. According to this narrative, in the 1980s and 1990s, the end of Keynesianism-Fordism affected tourism and gave rise to more flexible and individual forms of tourism instead of standardized Fordist mass tourism prevalent in the 1960s and 1970s. New and more differentiated preferences among European travelers called for more differentiation in the tourism offer, a trend that Tunisia still has not fully responded to. Hence, "the large, boxy hotel complexes that lined the Tunisian coast faced a challenge similar to the one faced by the Fordist manufacturing plants that dotted the American Midwest in the era of deindustrialization" (Hazboun 2008: 44–45). Responding with lower prices to its reputation as a low-cost destination for mass tourism, the Tunisian tourism sector entered a cycle of deteriorating quality (Hazboun 2008: 45). Therefore, the combination of lacking quality and a focus on low-cost, standardized mass tourism still appears to a considerable degree characteristic for the structure of production in Tunisia's tourism sector.

Apart from the past and present attempts to "re-territorialize" Tunisia's tourism product mainly through integrated tourism complexes (Hazboun 2008), further efforts towards differentiation and entry into attractive, higher value-added market niches (OECD 2015: 77) will probably be necessary. Furthermore, the new "Open Skies" agreement between Tunisia and the EU signed in late 2017 can be expected to unfold significant influence on the Tunisian tourism sector with consequences that are difficult to predict (Dahmani 2017).

4.1.3 Regulation in the Tunisian Economy

After the presentation of Tunisia's major structural economic challenges and policies in the previous sub-sections, the present sub-section characterizes the main features of how the old Arab social contract looked like in Tunisia under the Ben Ali regime.

A major aspect of socioeconomic regulation in Tunisia is the weakness of the private sector, a problem Tunisia shares with other Arab countries save Lebanon (Rivlin 2009: 277). Still, the Tunisian economy is, apart from its major problem of high unemployment, structurally strong but suffers from excessive government control with related distortions (Rivlin 2009: 285). Under the Ben Ali regime, reforms took place but in a selective and patrimonial manner, benefitting coalitions of regime supporters (Rivlin 2009: 286). This patrimonial approach gave way to rent-seeking and extended the dominance of the state to a "network of connections in the public-private sector" (Rivlin 2009: 286). Trusted and well-connected crony capitalists were favored, leaving no room for the development of an independent entrepreneurial class. Furthermore, the Tunisian business community was split between anti- and pro-liberalization factions (Rivlin 2009: 280–281) which presumably made it even more difficult for a confident and independent entrepreneurial class to emerge and to speak with one voice vis-à-vis the regime. The isolation of the offshore sector and the presence of politically connected firms particularly in the services sector led to entry barriers for entrepreneurial newcomers and undermined productivity (World Bank 2014a: 63).

Consistent with the constraints for an independent and confident entrepreneurial class to emerge, during the Ben Ali era upgrading support was aimed at individual firms, while collective action in the private sector was not encouraged. Business associations were co-opted by the regime and thus lacked independence (Cammett 2007: 1896–1898).

In general, while prescriptive rules are often rigid, major problems seem to be the arbitrary and discretionary implementation of administrative and regulatory procedures (World Bank 2014c: 145–156). This finding is well in line with general trends in Arab economies and explains part of the difficulties new and independent entrepreneurs are confronted with (World Bank 2009). Hence, obstacles for economic dynamism to increase are not only found on the level of prescriptive rules but also, and maybe more importantly, on the level of institutions that are much harder to change.

A highly regulated labor market in the formal sector is another characteristic of the regime prevalent in the Tunisian economy during the Ben Ali regime. Strict laws governing formal labor relations gave rise to rule-circumventing institutions such as firms entering the informal sector or employers and employees agreeing on informal arrangements (Achy 2010: 19). While flexibility on hiring is on par with international averages, the rigidity on layoffs on the Tunisian labor market is very high. The Global Innovation Index hints at the rigidity of Tunisia's formal labor market by ranking the country 89th among 126 countries on the ease of dismissing workers as measured in terms of the notice period and severance pay (Achy 2010: 19–20; Cornell, INSEAD and WIPO 2017: 323; Erdle 2011: 29–30; World Bank 2014c: 182–186).

As in other core Arab economies, vocational training appears to have a negative image and suffers from a low reputation (Achy 2010: 18; OECD 2018: 111). Widespread preferences for university education were confirmed in interviews, as was the skills mismatch on the labor market. TVET is seen not to respond to the demands of firms when it comes to skills relevant to day-to-day work. In part for this reason, TVET is perceived as a second-best educational choice only. Often, firms do not offer TVET graduates prospects for professional advancement as they do for university graduates. Maybe because of these disadvantageous prospects but also because TVET is seen as the educational track of choice for less performing students, TVET generally suffers from a bad reputation. This insight confirms the prevalence of a further set of problems on the institutional level of the Tunisian economy.

The negative image of technical and vocational training and education is likely to underscore the gravity of the labor market mismatch. Interviewees confirmed the skills mismatch in the Tunisian labor market. In particular, soft skills are lacking among higher-education graduates. The problem seems to be exacerbated by spatial disparities in the education system between prosperous coastal regions such as, the Tunis agglomeration and peripheral regions of the country.

Transnational transformative processes (Peck and Theodore 2007) affecting Tunisia include policy transfer from Europe and notably from France which is evident in the *pôles de compétitivité* scheme that uses the same name as the French cluster policy. In addition and probably more importantly, EU *rapprochement* and structural adjustment supported by the IMF and World Bank condition socioeconomic regulation in Tunisia in many ways. For instance, Tunisia is currently undergoing another wave of structural adjustment under IMF assistance and conditionality. Tunisia's ongoing *rapprochement* to the EU leads to a considerable degree of de-facto integration of the county in major parts of the EU's economic context. As the pioneer in the EU's Barcelona process of Euro-Mediterranean cooperation and integration, Tunisia has gone far in implementing the AA by aligning its economy and economic policy with EU standards. The subsequent *Programme de mise à niveau* (PMN) very well illustrates this point. Since Tunisia was the first country to sign an AA, the Tunisian government saw the need to prepare domestic firms for competition from the EU. Given that cost advantages waned, under these conditions Tunisian industry needed to strengthen its competitive and innovative capacities, a problem the PMN sought to address (Hazboun 2008: 74).

While policy alignment with EU policy standards created a policy anchor that may have been beneficial to some parts of Tunisian industry, and while the AA with its perspective of free trade gave Tunisian producers far-reaching access to EU markets, firms were confronted with an urgent need to upgrade their competitiveness and thus to accommodate or even drive the country's move towards becoming a more knowledge-based economy. This is an ongoing effort that will probably get a new impetus through the Deep and Comprehensive Free Trade Area (DCFTA) agreement currently being negotiated between the EU and Tunisia (European Commission 2017b; OECD 2012a: 127–128). This agreement, once completed, will cover a range of trade and economic policy areas, deepen the Tunisian economy's integration into the single market, and align trade-related prescriptive rules with EU standards (European Commission 2017b).

Based on the discussion of elements of socioeconomic regulation above, Fig. 4.1 gives a stylized overview on the major components of the Arab social contract in Benalist Tunisia within the terms of the regulation framework developed in Chap. 3. These components are marked by the following characteristics.

Within the regime of accumulation, the *structure of production* in Benalist Tunisia shares the general characteristics found in other labor-abundant core Arab economies such as a high degree of labor market segmentation between formal and informal sectors as well as along characteristics such as age, gender, regions, and between public and private sectors (OECD 2018: 95–102), high levels of youth and female unemployment, and particularly unemployment among higher-education graduates (OECD 2018: 98–100; World Bank 2013: 66; 2014c: 39), low female labor-force participation (OECD 2014: 41; 2018: 49; World Bank 2014c: 40–41), and an inflated public sector (Hertog 2016: 13, 29).

In particular, labor market segmentation in Tunisia is well documented by recent data. For instance, the employment rate among those aged 15 years and over for Tunisia in 2016 was only 39.8% compared to an average of 66.9% in OECD coun-

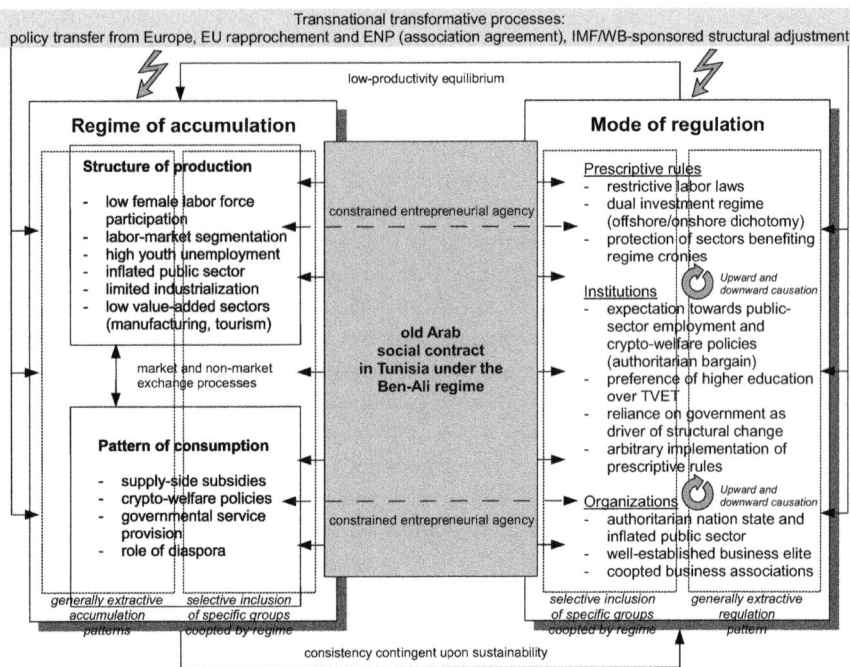

Fig. 4.1 Stylized regulation framework under the old Arab social contract in Tunisia under the Ben Ali regime. (Source: Own work based on Bathelt 1994: 66)

tries (for those aged 15–64). For men, Tunisia's employment rate stood at 59.8%, and for women, the rate stood at only 20.5%, compared to OECD averages of 74.7% and 59.3%, respectively. Tunisia's unemployment rate in 2016 was 15.5% compared to an OECD average of 6.3%. For youth aged 15–24, Tunisia witnessed an unemployment rate of 37.6% compared to an OECD average of 13.0% (OECD 2018: 8).

Interviewees confirmed that youth unemployment is a problem particularly among higher-education graduates and linked to expectations and preferences on the institutional level. Since university graduates expect to be hired for jobs on a par with their level of educational attainment, they often do not find adequate employment. These institutional patterns are anchored within the mode of regulation but shape phenomena shaping the structure of production through the profile of the workforce.

The labor market mismatch is very obvious in the Tunisian case (OECD 2018: 109–111). When it comes to industrialization, Tunisia is a relative success story among core Arab economies (Cammett 2014: 164; Amin et al. 2012: 113; Diop and Ghali 2012; Ghali and Rezgui 2015), but still and notably when compared to East Asian NIEs, industrialization in Tunisia remains limited and in a certain sense shallow. Although the country's economy is making some slow progress towards becoming more knowledge-based and innovation-driven, Tunisian manufacturing is still to a large extent dependent on low value-added subcontracting for European markets and notably for France and Italy. Somewhat similar to Tunisia's dominant manufacturing industries, textiles and garments and mechanical and electrical engineering, the tourism sector is marked by limited diversification, and a focus on low value-added mass package tourism aimed at European markets (Benner 2017a; Hazboun 2008).

As for the *pattern of consumption* under the old Arab social contract in Benalist Tunisia, the salient trends identified across core Arab economies in Sect. 3.3.1 generally apply. Untargeted supply-side subsidies exist for foodstuffs such as milk, sugar, and wheat as well as fuel (OECD 2018: 36–37; World Bank 2014c) as a part of the crypto-welfare policies typically found in core Arab economies that include public service provision by governments. Examples for the extent of public service provision and the activist role of government in Tunisia include the involvement of the state in providing water and sanitation, electricity, and public transport, the dominance of SOE in these and other service markets, or SOEs with monopoly status in importing, producing, or distributing agricultural commodities (World Bank 2014c: 89). Relations with the diaspora are important with the Tunisian communities in European countries such as France, and remittances in 2004 equaled more than 5% of Tunisia's GDP (Richards and Waterbury 2008: 389–390; 397–400; Benner 2015).

The *mode of regulation* under the old Arab social contract prevalent in Benalist Tunisia was marked by prescriptive rules such as restrictive labor laws underpinning labor market segmentation (e.g., OECD 2018: 47–49; 104–106) as well as an investment regime discriminating along an dichotomy between onshore and offshore sectors (OECD 2018: 70–73) including selective and often restrictive authorization requirements for investments in defined strategic sectors that had the effect of protecting the business interests of the established and well-connected business elite of regime cronies. Arbitrary implementation of prescriptive rules (World Bank 2014c: 145–156) is another institutional feature of the old Arab social contract in Benalist Tunisia. While guarantees for public-sector employment to university graduates were given less explicitly in Tunisia than in other core Arab economies such as Nasserist Egypt, public employment was still part of the Ben Ali regime's crypto-welfare policies. The institutional legacy left by the crypto-welfare policies during the pre-revolutionary era remains visible. Even in the postrevolutionary era, public protests against youth unemployment still may prompt the Tunisian government to resort to promises of public employment provision, as was the government's reaction to protests in the peripheral governorate of Tataouine in 2017 (Marzouk 2017). This pattern of governmental action is in line with institutions such as widely held expectations and aspirations towards public-sector employment and towards crypto-welfare policies such as supply-side subsidies. The public attitude towards subsidies became particularly obvious during the "bread revolt" that occurred in the early 1980s after subsidy cuts (Hazboun 2008: 41–42; Richards and Waterbury 2008: 222). Governmental reactions to calls for public employment via the creation of public employment can be understood as an institution-reinforcing rule that, through a process of cumulative and circular causation, reinforces aspirations and calls for public employment and thus shapes rule-reinforcing institutions. Among Arab economies, aspirations of tertiary-educated graduates towards public-sector employment are particularly strong in Tunisia (Hertog 2016: 25). In a 2010 survey, 46% of Tunisian youth expressed their willingness to work in the public sector, while only 15% were willing to work in the private sector (World Bank 2014b: 13). The high prominence of higher education and the institutionally based preference for academic education over TVET are very visible in Tunisia (Achy 2010: 18; OECD 2018: 111). As for the preferred model of economic development, it seems that institutions in the Tunisian regulation system during the Ben Ali era (and, presumably, even in the postrevolutionary era so far, as calls for public employment during protests in peripheral eras in recent years have demonstrated) included the public expectation that the state act as the main driver of economic progress. Organizations characteristic of Benalist Tunisia's old Arab social contract included an authoritarian nation-state, an inflated government and SOE sector, and a dominant well-established and politically well-connected business elite of regime cronies including members of the Ben Ali clan. Representation in business associations with UTICA (*Union Tunisienne de l'Industrie, du Commerce et de l'Artisanat*) at the pinnacle tended to lack political independence due to cooptation by the Ben Ali regime (Cammett 2007: 1898). Religious authorities, however, did not seem to play a major role in the mode of regulation in Benalist Tunisia. Mechanisms of upward and downward causation between prescriptive rules, institutions, and organizations in the case of Benalist Tunisia seem similar to those found in the stylized model for core Arab economies presented in Sect. 3.3.1. These mechanisms include, for instance, the design and implementation of the crypto-welfare policy of public-sector employment as a reaction to open or latent public discontent or as an approach to extend regime patronage to important societal groups. This policy of regime patronage through public employment provision may have shaped citizens' expectations, aspirations, and educational or employment preferences and led to an inflated government and SOE sector. The onshore/offshore sector dichotomy and the restrictive investment law with its authorization requirements and barriers to entry in sectors protected presumably for the sake of safeguarding regime cronies' business interests strengthened the role of the well-established and politically connected business elite, while a lack of political independence of business associations underpinned the lack of inclusiveness of the regulation regime towards independent economic agents.

Taking together the major elements of the regime of accumulation and the mode of regulation, the conditions for *entrepreneurial agency* in Benalist Tunisia seem similarly constrained as in the stylized model of regulation in core Arab economies introduced in Sect. 3.3.1. Even if Tunisian policy left somewhat more freedom for the private sector and even if Arab socialism in Tunisia lasted a shorter time than in other core Arab economies and left a weaker institutional legacy, independent entrepreneurial agency as a driver of Schumpeterian creative destruction still appears severely hampered by two major factors. The first factor is the model of state-led growth pursued since independence – as in other core Arab economies – with its elements so characteristic of the old Arab social contract such as crypto-welfare policies and inflated public sectors and the related crowding out of private investment as well as the adaptation of human capital to government needs and the skills mismatch. The second factor is specifically Tunisian although similar phenomena may be found in other core Arab economies. The economic dominance of the Ben Ali clan and barriers to competition and entrepreneurial market entry in protected sectors is arguably one of the most salient factors conditioning entrepreneurship in Benalist Tunisia and represents a specific form of crony capitalism and extractive configuration of the economy in favor of an established and politically well-connected business elite.

Transnational transformative processes conditioning socioeconomic regulation in Tunisia in the Ben Ali era and after include EU *rapprochement* through the AA the need to upgrade firms' competitiveness through schemes such as the PMN and IMF/World Bank-supported structural adjustment, as well as policy transfer from Europe.

As in other core Arab economies, structural deficiencies such as high (youth) unemployment and massive interregional economic and social disparities hint towards a low productivity equilibrium of the regulation system found in Benalist Tunisia. While the system in its low productivity equilibrium featured a certain degree of internal consistency, it exhibited the same lack of sustainability as the old Arab social contract in general. In the case of Tunisia, this lack of sustainability became visible and acute in the wake of transnational transformative processes such as IMF/World Bank-sponsored structural adjustment, as was demonstrated by the public reaction to the consequences of structural adjustment during the Tunisian "bread revolt" in 1983–1984 (Hazboun 2008: 41–42; Richards and Waterbury 2008: 222). While this event happened before the Ben Ali era, it is obvious that the friction between the need to achieve economic sustainability of the country's economic model and the internal consistency of the regulation system persisted and, through the persistence and exacerbation of structural deficiencies as symptoms of the system's underlying lack of sustainability, was a major driver of public discontent that led up to the Tunisian revolution in 2010/2011.

The regulation system's underlying unsustainability is visible in structural deficiencies such as high unemployment and intense spatial inequity, but the fundamental problems in terms of the Tunisian economy's dynamic efficiency are to a significant degree related to the role of Schumpeterian creative destruction. Hence, the next section takes a closer look at the state of entrepreneurship and innovation as drivers of Schumpeterian creative destruction as they played out under the old Arab social contract in Benalist Tunisia.

4.1.4   Entrepreneurship and Creative Destruction in the Tunisian Institutional Context

Entrepreneurship cannot be isolated from wider socio-economic realities. In particular, institutions such as widely held preferences for public employment condition and limit the propensity of young graduates to set up new businesses. Still, interviewees saw a change in attitudes. While the long-standing preferences of young people to work in the public sector as first choice and for large enterprises as a second choice still persist (notably in peripheral regions), an entrepreneurial spirit seems to gain ground particularly in the ICT sector, as does young people's willingness to work in the private sector, although the risk-taking culture still seems limited in international comparison. Long-term changes in government policy seem to play a role here, probably in line with international trends towards the encouragement of private-sector work and entrepreneurship. While previously, Tunisian university students were (at least implicitly) given the perspective of working at university, in administration, or in SOEs, today universities offer and emphasize entrepreneurship education and the government offers extensive entrepreneurship support. A more supportive ecosystem involving incubators or co-working spaces has emerged in recent years, but government support for entrepreneurship is still considered too weak. For instance, incubators were sometimes considered real estate only, and too little emphasis was placed on intangible support such as networking support. However, the awareness for the importance of intangible entrepreneurship support seems to grow but still suffers from a scarcity of skilled human resources for tasks such as networking support of cluster management. Further, interventions to engage the Tunisian diaspora of entrepreneurs and students in the EU were suggested during the interviews. While international donors have started to work on the latter subject, government agencies such as API could put a stronger focus on promoting cross-border entrepreneurship.

The trend towards entrepreneurship support became dominant in Tunisia in the wake of a growing belief among policymakers that promoting entrepreneurship is a necessary step towards confronting high youth unemployment and the demographic situation (OECD 2012b: 14). Indeed, in their survey comparing Egypt and Tunisia, Adly and Khatib (2014: 168) find some relative advantages in Tunisia's entrepreneurial ecosystem, including some of the support structures established during the Ben Ali era such as public banks supporting entrepreneurs, business centers, and incubators. Despite the prominence of entrepreneurship support, on a strategic level the goals of entrepreneurship support measures in Tunisia are not made explicit. In particular, possibly conflicting goals such as offering employment opportunities to the unemployed, enhancing employability, or building skills are often mixed. Hence, support structures were deficient due to their fragmentation and disintegration, a mixture and confusion of economic and political goals in support structures' mission (e.g., fighting youth unemployment of university graduates, raising the value of formal education) and work (e.g., requiring that supported ventures fall into the domain of the applicant's university degree), and the (mis-) use of entrepreneurship support as channels for patronage. Entrepreneurship promotion is subject to overlapping programs of different ministries such as the Ministry of Industry or the Ministry of Employment. A lack of support, incentives, and training for entrepreneurship teachers is another shortcoming of Tunisian entrepreneurship promotion. Cooperation between ministries and support agencies appears limited. HEIs and entrepreneurship support entities (e.g., incubators) tend to be disconnected from each other, and collaboration is not systematically organized but rather ad hoc and personalized. In some contrast to the high prominence accorded to entrepreneurship education in HEIs, entrepreneurship education in the TVET system is lacking, and TVET entities and startup support structures are not aligned (Adly and Khatib 2014: 168–170; OECD 2015: 34–36, 75).

The extensive landscape of entrepreneurship promotion schemes apparently designed to confront youth unemployment stands in a stark contrast with the constraints to independent entrepreneurship inherent to the wider regulation regime. It is likely that notwithstanding the deficiencies of entrepreneurship support in Tunisia listed above, even a well-designed and efficient entrepreneurship support landscape could not effectively have helped independent entrepreneurs overcome the fundamental barriers to entrepreneurship and competition built into the regulation regime under the old Arab social contract during the Ben Ali era. These built-in barriers in the regulation regime included notably the protection of cronies' business interests from competition. It is plausible to assume that during the Ben Ali era, fundamental incentives for entrepreneurship were heavily distorted by state capture and crony capitalism in favor of established and politically well-connected cronies. The economic dominance of the well-connected business elite and particularly of firms related to the Ben Ali clan suggests tight constraints to competition and market entry against independent entrepreneurial newcomers (OECD 2015: 11; Rijkers et al. 2014; World Bank 2014a).

Rijkers et al. (2014) demonstrate the extent of state capture and crony capitalism under the Ben Ali regime related to prescriptive rules limiting competition and protecting cronies' business interests. For example, "220 confiscated Ben Ali firms appropriated 21% of all net private sector profits and accounted for approximately 3% of private sector output" (Rijkers et al. 2014: 3). Sectors containing connected firms were more likely to be protected by authorization requirements and other restrictions. Looking at the success of firms connected to the Ben Ali clan in the pre-revolutionary era, the authors find a significantly higher market share of these firms than that of the average firm in Tunisia and relate this finding to high legal barriers to market entry. Interestingly, the setup of new firms connected to the Ben Ali clan was correlated with the introduction of new restrictions (Rijkers et al. 2014: 3–4, 12–13).

Even the ambitious *Programme de mise à niveau* illustrates the distorted incentives for entrepreneurship and independent firm growth. Paradoxically, while the PMN was designed to enhance the openness of the Tunisian economy in the wake of trade liberalization after the signature of the AA, upgrading Tunisian enterprises was promoted through a tightly monitored and filtered, state-managed process. The effect of this controlled opening was that upgrading support was directed not towards broad echelons of Tunisia's entrepreneurial scene but rather towards a limited number of businesses, presumably underpinning the dominance of a closed-off and well-connected business elite (Hazboun 2008: 74–75).

Ghali and Rezgui (2015: 60–63) provide a number of examples on the role of the established and politically well-connected business elite in the design and implementation of Tunisian economic policy before 2011. In particular, they highlight the prominent role of established businesspeople and family conglomerates as beneficiaries of the PMN (Ghali and Rezgui 2015: 61). Another example is the strong lobbying power of established entrepreneurs involved in the garment industry within the UTICA business federation (Ghali and Rezgui 2015: 62).

The impact of these constraints to independent entrepreneurship and firm growth is limited creative destruction in the Tunisian economy as evident in low rates of entry of new firms and limited firm growth. Further, severe restrictions in market access including for foreign investment, limited competition, supply-side subsidies, and price controls in many product markets further constrain processes of creative destruction and, thus, opportunities for independent and growth-oriented entrepreneurship (World Bank 2014c: 59–65, 82–94).

Correspondingly, in the Global Entrepreneurship Monitor's expert ratings of Tunisia's entrepreneurial ecosystem, some stylized facts on strengths and weaknesses related to entrepreneurship become apparent. While Tunisia is in line with the global average of countries surveyed on the dimensions of entrepreneurial finance, government policies, government entrepreneurship programs, and physical infrastructure, Tunisia ranks significantly above average on its internal market dynamics and its commercial and legal infrastructure. In contrast, Tunisia is below global average on cultural and social norms towards entrepreneurship, entrepreneurship education at school and post-school stages, R&D transfer, and internal market burdens or entry regulation (Kelley et al. 2016: 110).

These findings confirm the role of an established and politically well-connected business elite and concomitant systemic constraints to competition, to entrepreneurial initiative and innovation, as well as to Schumpeterian creative destruction in a wider sense, in pre-revolutionary Tunisia. Hence, one of the major features of the old Arab social contract as was identified in Chap. 3 can be confirmed in the case of Benalist Tunisia.

A further problem about the entrepreneurial potential among young Tunisians mentioned during interviews seems to be that a considerable part of higher-education graduates interested in entrepreneurship are leaving the country and establish their ventures – presumably opportunity-based ones – abroad, notably in European countries. While economic framework conditions are a major problem for the resulting lack of innovative entrepreneurship in Tunisia, the small size of the domestic markets is another, structural reason. One interviewee suggested the government establish a support scheme for Tunisian entrepreneurs to access markets in sub-Saharan Africa.

4.1.5 After the Revolution: A New Mode of Regulation?

When thinking about how a new, internally, and externally consistent and sustainable Arab social contract in postrevolutionary Tunisia could look like, the discussion in Sect. 3.4 is generally applicable. In particular, the scenario for such a new, consistent, and sustainable regulation regime depicted in Fig. 3.4 is equally valid for Tunisia, but some points are worth highlighting in the idiosyncratic case of Tunisia.

It is not surprising that policy recommendations found in the literature largely parallel those given for other core Arab economies. For example, because firms are exposed to volatile international markets and competition, Achy (2010: 21) calls for more flexibility in the labor market but also for compensation schemes for laid-off workers to prevent them from having to bear completely the risks of shocks. Another example is the OECD's (2018: 13) recommendation to reduce public-sector employment over time. Yet, implementing such recommendations requires overcoming mutually consistent aspirations for stable (public) employment and policy reactions towards providing government or SOE employment and thus the circular and cumulative causation process between rules and institutions on the Tunisian labor market. In the current postrevolutionary political situation, such a fundamental change in the interplay of rules and institutions conditioning the functioning of the Tunisian labor market is neither evident nor easy to achieve. Protests in rural governorates in 2016 and 2017 consistently featured calls for the creation of public-sector employment, as did the 2017 protests in the governorate of Tataouine and the reaction by government to provide new employment in the SOE sector (Marzouk 2017). Recommendations for subsidy cuts (e.g., OECD 2018: 13) are likely to be confronted with comparable popular resistance. Indeed, interviewees stressed the social climate after the 2010/2011 revolution characterized by widespread calls for social interventions including salary increases and public-sector employment. Under this political pressure, the postrevolutionary government continued to inflate public-sector employment, adding to a burdensome public wage bill exacerbated by the impact of subsidies. This policy dilemma implies that structural reforms will have to be complemented by long-term institutional change.

Institutional change takes time, and instigating it through downward causation presupposes a comprehensive, institution-sensitive policy mix (Benner 2017a; Glückler and Lenz 2016). For example, as in other core Arab economies, accepting the widely held preference for tertiary education over TVET in vocational schools and confronting the skills mismatch in the labor market with dual-study programs in HEIs such as Tunisia's ISETs could be part of such an institution-sensitive policy mix.

Developing an institution-sensitive policy mix could offer Tunisian policymakers a way out of the quandary between reform necessities and implementation problems they find themselves in. On the political level, there seems to be a willingness to undertake structural economic reforms but interviewees saw several problems in the reform process. First of all, both parliamentary decision-making processes and implementation are slow. Hence, the impact of reform steps decided on (such as the new investment code) is not yet tangible. Second, a prioritization of reform steps seems to be missing, leading policymakers to undertake a number of complex reforms at once without ensuring the necessary conditions for successful implementation such as administrative capacity on the local level. Third, resistance to reforms such as privatization by trade unions or popular resistance to subsidy cuts makes the decision-making process even more difficult. In addition, policymakers' desire to achieve a consensus prevents them to make reform decisions against political, societal, or popular opposition. At the same time, popular trust in the political system seems to have suffered due to economic instability.

While these factors apparently slow the reform process during Tunisia's current economic transition, they can be seen as evidence for the uneasy move towards a new regime of socioeconomic regulation. The fact that policymakers seek a social consensus is particularly interesting in this regard. While making decisions even more complicated to reach, this approach to opposition by the population or by trade unions suggests emerging decision-making routines known from CMEs and may in the long term contribute to the formation of a new and stable regulation regime. However, the friction between such a consensus-seeking approach and economic realities such as budgetary pressures or IFI-sponsored structural adjustment requiring quick political responses even against strong political or societal opposition is obvious.

Where institutional change is required, transnational transformative processes can give an impulse to establish and maintain institution-circumventing or even institution-competing rules. While institution-competing rules generally have low prospects of success, when it comes to public employment or subsidies, policies to reduce the scale of public recruitment and subsidies are likely to cause institutional change as popular expectations may eventually adapt to the new realities. A prerequisite for this to happen is that policies establishing institution-competing rules are maintained, which is not guaranteed as public opposition can be expected. Tunisia's "bread revolt" in the early 1980s (Hazboun 2008: 41–42; Richards and Waterbury 2008: 222) is an example of the political difficulties attached to maintaining institution-competing rules. However, transnational transformative processes such as IMF-sponsored structural adjustment and the underlying economic and fiscal realities a small, export-driven economy such as Tunisia is facing can provide a policy anchor making the maintenance of institution-competing rules more likely. Indeed, under the current IMF-sponsored structural adjustment program, the Tunisian government attempted to gradually cut back subsidies and freeze public procurement (Barnell 2017), although contrary announcements by the country's finance minister in view of the 2018 budget (Amara and Laessing 2017) suggest an ongoing process of back-and-forth policymaking and provide a recent example for the inherent political difficulty in establishing and maintaining institution-competing rules. The wave of protests against consequences of the government's 2018 budget with tax hikes and other austerity measures in the wake of rising prices in January 2018 (Dahmani 2018a, b) are another reminder that establishing and maintaining rules needed for a new and sustainable regulation regime will not be an easy task. These events suggest that institution-competing rules alone will not suffice to treat two of the major obstacles towards a sustainable and consistent new regulation regime. Institution-circumventing rules will be needed to complement the fiscal consolidation that requires institution-competing rules. Such institution-circumventing rules might include a system of targeted, need-based demand-side cash transfers replacing the supply-side subsidy system as well as facilitating employment growth in the private sector and in civil society. Comprehensive entrepreneurship policies designed to strengthen entrepreneurial attitudes among young people and particularly higher-education graduates will be effective only in the long term but might establish institution-circumventing rules by making entrepreneurial activity a viable alternative to increasingly unrealistic expectations of stable public-sector employment.

The emergence of the independent entrepreneurial association CONECT (*Confédération des Entreprises Citoyennes de Tunisie*) that has become an alternative to the traditional business association federation UTICA could indicate the emergence of a politically conscious and independent entrepreneurial class, or give them stronger voice and political clout. According to results from the interviews, CONECT was established after the 2011 revolution for several reasons. First, UTICA was perceived as too close to government and static. Second, the private sector had a negative reputation among the population. The establishment of CONECT was therefore an attempt both to set up an independent organization voicing companies and particularly SMEs' needs to the government and to improve SMEs' reputation by emphasizing the image of socially responsible business conduct (hence the term *entreprise citoyenne*). CONECT is seen to actively voice its positions to policymakers and thus may have contributed to a more confident and independent stance of the entrepreneurial class in postrevolutionary Tunisia. In this regard, economic policymaking has become more inclusive. However, it is important to note that the informal sector by definition lacks representation, thus leaving a considerable part of the economy out of more inclusive policymaking structures and processes.

Even in the postrevolutionary era, burdensome bureaucratic prescriptive rules, or burdensome implementation of prescriptive rules on the institutional level, remain a major problem for Tunisian businesspeople (OECD 2018: 67–69). In the interviews, the bureaucratic burden encountered by companies notably by slow administrative procedures was expressed, as was the need for policymakers and government officials to redefine the role of government from being interventionist to becoming a facilitator for private-sector development and entrepreneurship.

On the level of prescriptive rules, since 2017 the Tunisian government is implementing the new investment code that aims at liberalizing the authorization regime and at easing market access and investment. In particular, the new law sets incentives for investments in priority industries such as ICT, textiles and garments, and electronics. Under the framework of the new investment regime, new organizations were created such as the High Council on Investment (*Conseil Supérieur de l'Investissement*), the Tunisian Investment Authority (*Instance Tunisienne de l'Investissement*), and the Tunisian Investment Fund (*Fonds Tunisien de l'Investissement*), but pre-existing organizations such as API, APIA, CEPEX, or ONTT remain. Thus, the creation of new bodies could possibly add to the complexity of the support landscape. Furthermore, the system of regional development investment incentives was refined under the new law (OECD 2018: 74–76; 117–118).

While the new investment code changes prescriptive rules for the private sector, it remains to be seen if changes do materialize as hoped for. Given the prevalence of arbitrary and burdensome implementation of prescriptive rules as an important institutional legacy of the old Arab social contract in Tunisia, changing prescriptive rules may not be sufficient to significantly improve the framework conditions for private-sector growth. In addition to new prescriptive rules, institutional change within the government and administration will be necessary.

In the interviews, the prospect of a DCFTA between the EU and Tunisia as a possibly important transnational transformative process was considered a mixed blessing. While the PMN is perceived to have significantly contributed to upgrading in the manufacturing sector and to the emergence of new industries, there is still ample room for further upgrading under the framework of an eventual DCFTA. However, the liberalization of the service sector under a DCFTA is considered a threat because of the likely and asymmetric competition by European companies.

In any case, EU *rapprochement* will remain an important driver of the further development of the Tunisian economy. One might eventually expect Tunisia to follow Turkey's path of far-reaching economic de-facto integration into the EU. In the case of Tunisia, even without the prospect of EU accession, this could mean an eventual customs union and a strong degree of alignment in terms of economic structures, organizations, and policies (Benner 2015).

In terms of regional development, policy transfer from the EU (a transnational transformative process), if and when adapted sensibly to the institutional context found in Tunisia and its regions, could include applying the smart specialization concept and thus bring regional policy and innovation policy closer together. Different from the *pôle de compétitivité* scheme with its top-down design and possibly weak sensitivity to the regional institutional context, Tunisian regions could develop smart specialization strategies in a bottom-up way and by drawing on localized assets found in the regional knowledge base, micro-level entrepreneurial dynamics, and institutional specifics of the regional economy. Doing so could provide a more comprehensive policy approach than the *pôles* but still critically build on them as existing structures and backbone agents in implementing smart specialization strategies and resulting action plans. In more peripheral regions, CITs could play a similar role. In this way, an integrated model of endogenous regional development could be elaborated and supported by national government and international donors. For rural regions, a less innovation-focused but similarly participatory model of endogenous regional development could use the LEADER/CLLD method and tools developed under the umbrella of the EU's cohesion policy (Benner 2014b, 2017b, d, forthcoming).[8]

However, the typical constraints particularly encountered by weaker regions applying a participatory and strategic approach of regional policymaking such as smart specialization have to be considered and addressed. The obstacles the smart

---

[8] Strictly speaking, the LEADER approach originated under the EU's Common Agricultural Policy.

specialization approach is confronted with in weaker European regions such as distrust among agents, missing government capacities in public-private coordination, hierarchical policymaking traditions, and weak intermediate organizations (Trippl et al. 2018) are certainly not less prevalent in Tunisia. These constraints may be most severe in Tunisia's peripheral regions. Applying the smart specialization approach to Tunisian governorates will certainly be a long and difficult process. On the other side, considering the opportunities of the approach in mobilizing collective dynamism and changing the institutional context of a regional economy (Benner 2018), the smart specialization method could be particularly beneficial for Tunisian regions. Given the participatory nature of the process and its intricate relationship with institutional context (Benner 2018; Glückler and Bathelt 2017), the assumption that the smart specialization approach could drive changes in socioeconomic regulation on the regional level and possibly on the national level through bottom-up dynamics seems plausible. While the problems mentioned by Trippl et al. (2018) will be difficult to overcome in peripheral areas of Tunisia, regions such as Bizerte, Sousse, or Sfax might benefit from the approach by prioritizing areas of comparative advantage or promising trajectories in their regional economies (Benner forthcoming).

In the interviews, an interesting case for endogenous regional development related to regional institutional context and smart specialization was brought up. Apparently, the Sfax region enjoys advantages in the medical sector such as an exceptionally high share of medical doctors per inhabitant. As a part of the regional institutional context, parents' expectations for their children to study medicine and to become medical doctors seem widespread. Building on this institutional characteristic of the Sfax regional economy and the focus of the Sfax *pôle de compétitivité* on medical applications of ICT, a cluster initiative for e-health technologies was formed. In this context, one interviewee mentioned these efforts as a starting point for smart specialization. Within Tunisia, Sfax might serve as an example of an intermediate region and possibly benefit from the widened involvement of regional-level agents found by Trippl et al. (2018: 15) in European intermediate regions as an outcome of the implementation of smart specialization.

Older initiatives designed top-down to promote regional innovation such as the *cyberparcs* were judged less successful during interviews. It seems as if the *cyberparcs* are currently looking for a new business model more adapted to the specifics of regional economies and including the participation of regional stakeholders, which would indeed call for a process similar to the European smart specialization approach.

In general terms, the current postrevolutionary context found in Tunisia offers a window of opportunity for changing both prescriptive rules and institutions, but at the same time economic, fiscal, and political pressures make changes even more pressing than in previous periods. As in other core Arab economies, establishing and maintaining new prescriptive rules and causing institutional change through downward causation and aptly reacting to processes of upward causation to arrive at a new, consistent, and sustainable regulation regime are enormous policy challenges in a highly complex context of pressure from stakeholders, citizens, and external forces such as IFIs and, particularly in the case of Tunisia, the EU. It is by no means sure that the process of a new, consistent, and sustainable regulation regime crystallizing in a complicated and multifaceted negotiation process between policymakers and their polity will eventually succeed. What can be assumed, however, is that the postrevolutionary democratic arena of today's Tunisia offers an environment for such a process to take place through the complex but peaceful mechanisms of a pluralistic society.

4.2   Jordan

Analogously to the Tunisia case study, the case study on Jordan gives an overview on the specific structural challenges the country is confronted with, highlighting both similarities and differences to the general tendencies found in core Arab economies. Then, the case study focuses on specific policy areas before sketching the major elements of the present Jordanian regulation regime with a specific focus on the dynamics of Schumpeterian creative destruction. The case study concludes with an outlook on prospects of possible new ways of regulation in Jordan.

4.2.1   Jordan's Economic Challenges

The wave of demonstration in the wake of the "Arab Spring" touched upon Jordan in 2011 (Muasher 2011: 3). However, in contrast to Tunisia, regime change was not a widely shared goal of the protest movement. In general, the status of the king was not challenged. Rather than regime change, reform within the existing constitutional monarchy was the commonly shared goal of protesters (Josua 2016: 11).

Therefore, other than Tunisia whose current transitional state was set off by a revolution, Jordan is a case for evolutionary change of a fairly stable political regime responding to public dissatisfaction by gradual and incremental reform. The present chapter attempts to shed light on the implications of such an evolutionary policy approach for socioeconomic regulation.

Jordan's economic challenges to a considerable extent parallel those found in other core Arab economies such as high unemployment specifically among tertiary-educated youth and among young females (e.g., Amin et al. 2012: 57; International Labour Organization 2016: 9; Smadi and Tsipouri 2012: 3; World Bank 2013: 10; 2014b: 12–14). For instance, the country's unemployment rate in the first quarter of 2017 stood at 18.2% overall and at 13.9% for males and 33.0% for females. Unemployment among university graduates is particularly high at 21.4%. Unemployment among university-educated males was 20.8% compared to a staggering 53.9% for university-educated females. Youth unemployment stood at 39.5% for those aged 15–19 and at 35.4% for those aged 20–24 years. Economic participation among the labor force aged 15 and over stood at 63.0% for men and 18.3% for women (Department of Statistics 2017).

Still, the country's economy features some specifics due to its geopolitical situation and historical development. The circumstances of the country's formation and geopolitical events in its neighborhood strongly shaped the economic and demographic structure of Jordan. After 1948, the emerging merchant class came to be dominated by citizens from Palestinian origin. While estimates vary widely, it is assumed that more than half of the current Jordanian population may be of Palestinian origin (Ryan 2010: 323). Jordanians from tribal, non-Palestinian origin, so-called East Bankers, tend to hold public-sector, government, or military jobs, while Palestinians dominate the private sector (Ryan 2010: 324). Further, Jordan today exhibits the special situation of hosting a large number of Syrian refugees (International Labour Organization 2016: 5, 17; Smadi and Tsipouri 2012: 3; World Bank 2015: 32). In particular, the divide between Palestinian-origin citizens dominating the private sector and East Bankers dominating the public sector arguably led to a certain hesitation of the state to encourage growth of the private sector. However, in the wake of economic crisis towards the end of the 1980s and subsequent IMF/World Bank-supported structural adjustment, the private sector was given more freedom, trade was liberalized, and the role of the public sector was limited (Rivlin 2009: 166–169).

Generally, Jordan suffers from a scarce endowment in natural resources and a weak industrial base (Kanaan and Hanania 2009: 145–146). It is worth noting that the country is the second-largest exporter of phosphates, making the phosphate and potash mining industries very important for the country's economy (Mahroum et al. 2013: 78). Still, Jordan essentially is a service-based economy with little agriculture or manufacturing (Ryan 2010: 321–322) within a framework of international openness and important links to neighboring countries and notably Gulf states in trade, tourism, FDI, and remittances (Smadi and Tsipouri 2012: 3). Jordan's relatively far-reaching trade openness in regional comparison is underscored by the country's WTO accession in 2000 (OECD 2013: 119). Jordan's economic model relies on its relative political stability and comparatively well-developed human capital which enabled the emergence of some productive sectors such as the ICT, pharmaceuticals, healthcare, or light manufacturing industries (Smadi and Tsipouri 2012: 3). Jordanian exports in manufactured products include notably fertilizers, pharmaceuticals, textiles and apparel, as well as ICT, while tourism is another important outward-oriented industry. These relative strengths in exports are driven by the Jordanian economy's comparative advantages in clean technologies, transport, ICT, pharmaceuticals, and tourism (OECD 2013: 119–120).

Yet, Jordan's economic model faces questions on sustainability. Ryan (2010: 322) calls Jordan a "semi-rentier economy" because it strongly relies on indirect oil rents through remittances from emigrants to GCC countries and foreign aid, e.g., from the United States (Brand 2014: 576, 579–580; World Bank 2009: 183). Historically, the role of rents from foreign aid was apparent from the fact that until 1990, foreign aid reached almost a fifth of Jordan's GNI (World Bank 2009: 183).

Despite the role of rents for the Jordanian economy and state, the country has achieved some success in economic development. Structural change is comparatively advanced in Jordan (in contrast to Egypt and Morocco), but still, labor tends to move primarily into lower-productivity sectors (World Bank 2013: 95, 98–100). Looking at Jordan's progress towards becoming a knowledge-based economy, GERD in Jordan is considerably lower than in Tunisia. Nevertheless, as Tunisia, Jordan has numbers of researchers in R&D exceptionally high among comparable emerging countries (Rodríguez-Pose and Hardy 2014: 89–90).

Despite the comparative strength of human capital in Jordan, the skills mismatch typically found in core Arab economies is prevalent in Jordan, too (Mahroum et al. 2013: 68). A specificity of the Jordanian case is a brain drain towards GCC countries (Smadi and Tsipouri 2012: 3).

In terms of Jordan's spatial structure, population and industry are clustered in the country's major urban centers, with one fifth of the population living in the capital Amman and approximately half of the country's industry being located in Zarqa (Seidel et al. 2009: 23). In terms of regional socioeconomic conditions, the differential in poverty rates between urban and rural regions can serve as a prima facie indicator for spatial disparities. According to data presented by the World Bank (2011: 37), the poverty rate in rural areas in Jordan in 2002 stood at 18.7% compared to 12.9% for urban areas, suggesting a considerable urban-rural gap. However, disparities between governorates in terms of household consumption are rather small in Jordan and largely attributable to demographic factors. When controlling for education, intergovernorate disparities in per capita consumption almost vanish (World Bank 2011: 86–88).

These insights lead the World Bank (2011: 88) to conclude that "urban-rural disparities in economic opportunity should not be considered a priority policy challenge for Jordan." However, unemployment rates do diverge significantly between governorates. For instance, during the first quarter of 2017, the unemployment rate in Ma'an governorate stood at 26.2% compared to 15.5% in Jerash governorate (Department of Statistics 2017), suggesting indeed a need for specific regional policies of economic development.

In sum, the structural economic difficulties Jordan is confronted with are generally comparable to those found in other core Arab economies, but with the added dimensions of a high dependence on foreign funding, an economic structure demographically segmented according to origin, and the country's location in a geopolitically volatile neighborhood with possibly severe economic repercussions.

4.2.2   Jordan's Economic Policies: Past and Present

Jordan is an example for a small, comparatively open economy with some success in industrialization. Comparing the Jordanian case with the previous Tunisian case study is interesting because, generally, orientations of economic policy in Tunisia and Jordan appear fairly similar. However, Tunisia has apparently achieved more progress so far on industrialization and on making its economy more knowledge-based. Mahroum et al. (2013: 12) consider Jordan to have become a "semi-industrialized economy" from the 1960s to the 1990s. While in the 1960s Jordan's industrialization push was aided by an ISI policy, the country has in recent decades opened up to international trade. In the 1970s, the Jordanian government began to focus on developing medical and healthcare industries. In the wake of liberalization of the telecommunications sector where Jordan was the pioneer among Arab countries and within the framework of WTO accession, the Jordanian economy witnessed the emergence of an ICT sector in the early 2000s. Indeed, the Jordanian ICT sector has developed fairly well and given birth to a number of indigenous ICT companies, aided by low barriers to entry. In the medical sector, too, Jordan has gained a reputation as a regional leader, particularly in medical tourism. Both in ICT and in medical tourism, Jordan has managed to position itself as a regional hub, benefiting from the fast growth of the Arabic language and the small share of Arabic content on the Internet so far as well as the spatial location of the country for medical treatments. Jordan's pharmaceuticals industry, as the country's second-largest exporting industry, is highly focused on exporting to regional markets. The industry's development was aided by patent legislation that allows for generic drug producers to develop generic drugs before patent expiration, but now seeks ways to diversify its product range. Thus, both of the country's salient nonnatural resource-based exporting sectors, ICT and pharmaceuticals, seem to have benefited from policy measures allowing for their development such as, notably, early liberalization of the telecommunications sector and advantageous intellectual property legislation (Mahroum et al. 2013: 12, 46–53, 121).

When comparing the export structures of Tunisia and Jordan, Diop and Ghali (2012) find differing patterns. While Tunisian exports became technologically more sophisticated, the share of low-technology manufacturing products in Jordanian exports increased (Diop and Ghali 2012: 13). This pattern was largely driven by a rise of textiles and garments manufacturing (Diop and Ghali 2012: 13–14). In particular, the setup of the Qualified Industrial Zones (QIZ) regime attracted foreign FDI in textiles and garments manufacturing. Nevertheless, an important fact about the Jordanian textiles and garments industry is that "most of the 60,000 workers in this sector in Jordan are foreigners" (Diop and Ghali 2012: 15).

Jordan's high-technology exports rely almost exclusively on pharmaceuticals that appear comparatively competitive, with high value added included through branding and relevant linkages into the domestic economy for R&D, packaging, and other inputs (Diop and Ghali 2012: 17). Although the rise in low-technology (particularly textiles and garments) manufacturing raises questions for Jordan's pathway towards continued industrialization, international benchmarking of the country's export structure reveals a comparatively well-developed state of industrial development since Jordanian exports exhibit a higher share of high-technology products (particularly pharmaceuticals) than comparable emerging economies (Diop and Ghali 2012: 19).

This relative success in industrialization occurred within the framework of an economic policy that left comparatively much room for the private sector (Cammett

2014). As a conservative monarchy, Jordan's economic policy since independence was not marked by explicit, comprehensive, and ideologically driven Arab socialist experiments. The role of the significant part of the population with Palestinian origins that specialized in private-sector work because of the public sector being dominated by East Bankers (Rivlin 2009: 166–169) can be seen as another component of Jordan's relatively free private sector. Still, state-led growth was a major part of Jordan's economic development strategy through public investments and government stakes in industrial ventures in fields such as mining (notably phosphate), manufacturing, tourism, or transport. Contrary to other core Arab economies particularly during their Arab socialist periods, Jordanian economic policy seems to have shown little outright distrust towards the private sector and even let it develop in other fields than those dominated or heavily influenced by government (Richards and Waterbury 2008: 201).

Another feature of Jordan's general economic policy orientation is its relative openness to the global economy, as witnessed by Jordan's WTO accession in 2000 and its free-trade agreement (FTA) with the United States (Muasher 2011: 5; OECD 2013: 119, 122) as well as the EU-Jordan association agreement (AA) signed in 1997 and in force since 2002 and upcoming negotiations for a DCFTA (OECD 2013: 96, 122–123). Jordan entered another FTA with Turkey and is member of the Agadir FTA together with Morocco, Tunisia, and Egypt (OECD 2013: 121–122; Seidel et al. 2009: 9). Noland and Pack (2007: 221–222) stress the high relevance of Jordan's preferential trade agreement with the United States that seems more important to the country than its FTA with the EU, although a future DCFTA might eventually upgrade European-Jordanian trade relations. In any case, Jordan's economic policy has demonstrated a long-term commitment to a free-market orientation in international trade and to a certain degree in its domestic economy (Brand 2014: 577–580).

Within these general orientations of Jordan's economic policy since independence characterized by a comparatively high degree of freedom for the private sector, the role of citizens with Palestinian origins in the private sector, and the country's international openness, Jordan's industrial policy strives to build on the country's relative strengths in terms of human capital, pockets of industrialization such as pharmaceuticals and ICT, and its natural and cultural assets feeding the tourism sector. The next sub-section provides more details on approaches and structures guiding Jordan's industrial policy.

4.2.2.1   Industrial Policy

In 1989, Jordan embarked on an IMF-sponsored stabilization and structural adjustment program (Ryan 2010: 314). Since then, economic liberalization (*infitah*) picked up and gained further drive under the current king Abdullah II, focusing on international openness to trade through WTO membership and bilateral free-trade agreements, and a focus on making Jordan a regional center for the ICT industry (Ryan 2010: 322–323).

However, as in other core Arab economies, the *infitah* process was not smooth. The 1989 structural adjustment program led to riots (Hazboun 2008: 80), and in the second half of the 1990s, a second wave of IMF-sponsored structural adjustment occurred in the wake of a deteriorating tourism sector, sinking living standards, and a popular sentiment of exclusion when aspirations towards inclusive growth and prosperity that were originally attached to the Israel-Jordan peace treaty proved unrealistic (Hazboun 2008: 169–170).

Geopolitical realities including the importance of the Israel-Jordan peace treaty represent major framework conditions for Jordan's industrial policy. This fact is particularly evident in the setup of the Qualified Industrial Zones (QIZ), an instrument that combines the two motivations of supporting industrial development in Jordan and creating an economic anchor and thus an economic constituency for peace between Israel and Jordan. Manufacturers located in a QIZ benefit from streamlined customs procedures as well as tax and tariff exemptions, provided they meet defined local-content requirements for joint Israeli and Jordanian produce. As an external incentive for economic cooperation, products manufactured in a QIZ enjoy duty-free access to the US market (Noland and Pack 2007: 222–232; OECD 2013: 113, 116).

Together with the US-Jordan FTA, the QIZ scheme underscores the important role of trade with the United States for Jordan (Noland and Pack 2007: 230). According to Noland and Pack (2007: 231), QIZs may have generated 40,000 jobs mainly in the textiles and apparel sector with 26,000 Jordanian workers and many other from South Asia including notably Bangladesh. The high share of foreigners in the workforce employed in QIZs is assumed to be due to the low competitiveness of local producers, a lack of appropriate TVET and thus basically the labor market skills mismatch, and low degrees of technology transfer (Noland and Pack 2007: 231). Rivlin (2009: 171) highlights that the QIZs have increased Jordanian exports to the United States particularly in garments and contributed to a certain degree of diversification of the Jordanian economy, but more than 60% of employment provided in the QIZs were accounted for by foreign labor. In sum, while the QIZs have led to a boom of the textiles and garments industry in Jordan, due to low shares of local ownership and employment, value added for the Jordanian economy has been rather low (OECD 2013: 116).

On a broader level, tax incentives for investments are a part of Jordanian industrial policy although they tend to suffer from being intransparent and bureaucratic (World Bank 2014a: 62). The OECD and IDRC (2013: 94) stress that SME finance is an even more severe constraint in Jordan than in other Arab economies such as Morocco, Tunisia, Egypt, or the UAE.

In terms of the organizational landscape of industrial policy in Jordan, relevant agencies include the Jordan Investment Commission, the Development and Free Zones Commission (DFZC), the Ministry of Trade and Industry with its SME strategy, or the Jordanian Central Bank in terms of allocating credit to SMEs (World Bank 2014a: 62).

According to Jordan's National Investment Strategy, the Jordan Investment Commission (formerly: Jordan Investment Board) is charged with investment promotion and offers a one-stop shop, as does the Jordan Development and Free Zones Commission. However, the Jordan Investment Commission is not mandated with issuing all approvals needed by investors. The Jordan Investment Commission specifically focuses on four priority sectors: ICT, renewable energies, pharmaceuticals, and tourism (OECD 2013: 22, 108–110).

Further agents relevant to industrial relations include the General Federation of Jordanian Trade Unions with its 17 member trade unions (OECD 2013: 29). Free zones such as the Aqaba Special Economic Zone (ASEZ) are another feature of Jordan's industrial policy (OECD 2013: 23) and will be further characterized in Sect. 4.2.2.3.

The Jordan Enterprise Development Corporation (JEDCO) is the central business promotion agency in Jordan. The agency was established in 2003 as a replacement of the former Jordan Export Development and Commercial Centers Corporation founded in 1972 and today puts its focus on support for entrepreneurship and SMEs and provides services such as mentoring and consultancy, market research and analytics, and financial and technical support to companies. In promoting internationalization, the agency specifically focuses on countries Jordan has FTAs with, reflecting the country's general orientation towards international openness to trade and towards export development. However, the promotion of export development was transferred to the Jordan Investment Commission in 2014 (Jordan Enterprise Development Corporation 2018a).

In 2008, JEDCO took over two major programs for industrial upgrading, the Jordan Upgrading and Modernization Program (JUMP) supported by EU funds and the Euro-Jordanian Export Program (EJEP). In 2012, JEDCO was charged with managing the Governorate Development Fund (GDF) that seeks to promote entrepreneurship in areas of the country outside of Amman (Jordan Enterprise Development Corporation 2018a).

Chambers of commerce or industry as well as the Jordan Engineers Association play a significant role in Jordan's economic tissue. These organizations offer one-stop shops for administrative issues and provide business development services as well as training programs to their members (Seidel et al. 2009: 30; Sultan and Soete 2012: 323).

Further relevant agents in industrial policy and, more broadly, in the country's NIS include the Higher Council for Science and Technology (HCST), the Royal Scientific Society (RSS), and the range of HEIs the country hosts (Smadi and Tsipouri 2012: 4) which will be introduced in more detail in the following subsection on innovation policy.

Jordan's position as a resource-poor "watchmaker" economy, similar to Tunisia and neighboring Israel (Richards and Waterbury 2008: 68), effectively requires the Jordanian economy to become more knowledge-based and implies a need for targeted policies to support innovation and entrepreneurship. The next sub-section therefore provides more details on Jordan's science, technology, and innovation policy.

4.2.2.2 Science, Technology, and Innovation Policy

Consistently with Jordan's "watchmaker" status (Richards and Waterbury 2008: 68), there seems to be an awareness among Jordanian policymakers that the country's economic development in the long run depends on its ability to become more knowledge-based and that the country's young and highly educated population offers an opportunity to do so since the educational level in Jordan is high in comparison with other countries with similar levels of income (Smadi and Tsipouri 2012: 3).

Ryan (2010: 322) confirms the availability of a comparatively highly skilled workforce due to a relatively good state of general education in Jordan, leading both to the export of skilled workers particularly to Gulf states and to the import of unskilled labor particularly from Egypt, Sudan, and pre-war Syria. This combination of a brain drain to GCC countries and the import of unskilled labor implies a skills mismatch on the Jordanian labor market (Smadi and Tsipouri 2012: 3) and underscores the need for knowledge-based industrial development in Jordan. For example, Kharabsheh et al. (2011) provide qualitative evidence for the skills mismatch evident in lacking soft skills and notably lacking entrepreneurial skills (Kharabsheh et al. 2011: 222).

Due to the country's scarcity of natural resources and its lacking industrial base, human capital is highly relevant for Jordan. Indeed, the country has become a leading reformer in education within the MENA region, for instance, through curriculum reforms encompassing, inter alia, soft skills and information management for new economic activities such as e-commerce (Kanaan and Hanania 2009: 145–146).

Within the education system, some fundamental problems persist. For instance, "the system is built on memorizing textbook facts instead of creative learning systems or explorative research," and "only a few dedicated courses to innovation management and entrepreneurship can be found in public universities" (Sultan and Soete 2012: 322). Furthermore, in line with other core Arab economies, Jordan's education system is oriented more towards higher education than towards TVET (Sultan and Soete 2012: 323).

In the same vein, Mahroum et al. (2013: 30) argue that despite the generally good education indicators Jordan exhibits in regional comparison, TVET suffers from its inability to address the skills mismatch and from adverse reputational effects by referring to a "low employability of graduates and a persistent cultural stigma that vocational education leads to limited career opportunities" (Mahroum et al. 2013: 30). TVET suffers from a lower reputation than academic education, is often unable to convey the skills demanded on the labor market, and educational quality is considered low (Mahroum et al. 2013: 30).

In spite of these difficulties, Jordan's education system is fairly well developed in international comparison, but knowledge output as measured in terms of scientific publications is rather weak but increasing (Mahroum et al. 2013: 41; Smadi and Tsipouri 2012: 16–22). The patent output of the Jordanian NIS is low (Kharabsheh et al. 2011: 222). Innovation in Jordan seems to suffer from several systemic weaknesses inherent to the NIS such as a lacking innovation culture, weak university-industry linkages, and a lacking awareness for the opportunities inherent to the country's strong human capital base evident from the brain drain (Smadi and Tsipouri 2012: 33).

Jordan's share of GERD in GDP stood at a mere 0.34% in 2007–2008, significantly lower than the level found in Tunisia (1.03%) and lower than the levels found in other comparator countries such as Morocco or Turkey, but still higher than the levels found in other core Arab economies including Egypt (Mahroum et al. 2013: 38). Jordan's GERD is concentrated in the public sector with a share of 58% in total GERD compared to 36% for the private sector (Smadi and Tsipouri 2012: 13). Considering the dominance of government in R&D in Jordan, governmental priorities such as energy and water technologies shape the country's R&D system (Smadi and Tsipouri 2012: 19). The OECD and IDRC (2013: 93) hint at the paradox that although Jordan's R&D spending is high when compared to other Arab economies, the country's share of high-technology products in total manufactured exports stands at only 1%. These structural features and outcomes of the Jordanian NIS provide a clear rationale to pursue an innovation policy aimed at upgrading the innovative potential of the country's economy.

In terms of Jordan's NIS, Seidel et al. (2009: 21–44) see a lack of strategic policymaking that might have been alleviated by the National Innovation Strategy 2013–2017 (Higher Council for Science and Technology 2013; Smadi and Tsipouri 2012). The strategy focused on priority areas such as the medical and pharmaceuticals industries, ICT, clean technologies, as well as services in engineering and architecture, education, and financial services (Higher Council for Science and Technology 2013; Smadi and Tsipouri 2012: 12). The strategy allocated a budget of nearly JD 14.5 million for a total of 52 activities or projects including, inter alia, studies, entrepreneurship training courses, the introduction of new study tracks, or the setup of a fund promoting ICT innovation (Higher Council for Science and Technology 2013). Mahroum et al. (2013: 22) criticize the Jordanian government's approach to innovation policy marked by 5-year strategies as sector-oriented instead of systemic or aiming at the innovation ecosystem. This critique is consistent with the project-driven character visible in the 2013–2017 innovation strategy.

The Jordanian NIS is characterized by a number of relevant agents shaping and implementing the country's innovation policy (Sultan and Soete 2012: 322). To start with, the Higher Council for Science and Technology (HCST) is a major agent in the Jordanian NIS and is responsible for the National Innovation Strategy as well as related programs (Smadi and Tsipouri 2012: 14). Further, the HCST was charged with setting up research centers (Smadi and Tsipouri 2012: 4, 14). The HCST was created in 1987 as an overarching agency to plan, coordinate, and implement S&T policies (Mahroum et al. 2013: 16–17).

The Royal Scientific Society (RSS) is another important agent in Jordan's NIS. The society was established in 1970 as an applied research entity. The RSS provides R&D, testing, certification, and related services. The society works through 38 laboratories and focuses on thematic priorities such as energy, water and environment, industrial development, construction and sustainable buildings, and ICT (Mahroum et al. 2013: 16; Royal Scientific Society 2017).

JEDCO's services and programs are relevant for promoting entrepreneurship and for upgrading the innovative capabilities of SMEs. For instance, together with other public and private agents, JEDCO established a network of innovation centers and incubators since 2005 which today consists of six centers (Ajloun, Irbid, Jerash, Karak, Madaba, Mafraq) and three affiliates (Ma'an, Tafilah, Wadi Musa). New centers were planned in Aqaba, Balqa, and Tafilah. These centers aim towards increasing university-industry technology transfer and capacity building among entrepreneurs through consulting on subjects such as strategy, marketing, market research, and legal framework conditions. JEDCO strives to raise awareness for opportunities in entrepreneurship among youth and, inter alia, provides mentoring and consulting services to entrepreneurs aged 16–34 years and assists them in drafting business plans (Jordan Enterprise Development Corporation 2018b, c).

Rodríguez-Pose and Hardy (2014: 57–58) briefly discuss the state of science and technology parks (STPs) in Jordan. At the time of their writing, the authors count a total of eight STPs in early stages of their development, with half of them being linked to universities (Kharabsheh et al. 2011; Rodríguez-Pose and Hardy 2014: 57–58). STPs set up in Jordan so far include the Cyber City for ICT close to Irbid, El Hassan Business Park (EHBP), and El Hassan Science City (EHSC), with the latter hosting organizations such as HCST, RSS, and the Queen Rania Center for Entrepreneurship as well as HEIs such as Princess Sumaya University of Science and Technology (PSUT) and incubators. EHBP hosts the Intellectual Property Commercialization Office (IPCO) that acts as the central node of the Jordan Technology Transfer Offices Network (JTTON) (Mahroum et al. 2013: 18, 25; Seidel et al. 2009: 28–29; Smadi and Tsipouri 2012: 34).

Amman's King Hussein Business Park (KHBP) is an interesting case because this science and technology park, apart from hosting academia such as Al Hussein Technical University as well as the "Oasis 500" accelerator, managed to attract multinational anchor tenants such as Bayer, Cisco, Ericsson, Microsoft, Oracle, Samsung, or Unilever (King Hussein Business Park 2018). The park is thus an example of an anchor tenant strategy, as was discussed by Rodríguez-Pose and Hardy (2014) as a possibly promising approach for science and technology parks in developing and emerging economies.

Jordan features 10 public and 19 private universities as well as national research centers such as the National Center for Human Resources Development, the National Center for Diabetes, Endocrine and Inherited Diseases, the National Center for R&D, and the National Center for Agricultural Research and Extension (Smadi and Tsipouri 2012: 15). Mahroum et al. (2013: 16) mention in particular the University of Jordan (UoJ) set up in 1962. Another important public university is the Jordan University of Science and Technology (JUST) located in the northern city of Irbid. JUST focuses on subjects such as healthcare and ICT and includes the King Abdullah University Hospital as well as research centers in the fields of pharmaceuticals, biotechnology, and agricultural research (Mahroum et al. 2013: 81). Further important public universities include Irbid's Yarmouk University, the Hashemite University in Zarqa, and the Mu'tah University in Karak (Mahroum et al. 2013).

In terms of universities' performance, Seidel et al. (2009: 37) see a focus on theoretical education with a comparatively high quality of teaching but a smaller role of (applied) research. Karahbsheh et al. (2011) criticize Jordanian universities' lacking focus on commercialization of research results and absence of modern, experimental teaching methods (Kharabsheh et al. 2011: 222). Furthermore, students seem to aim towards public-sector employment instead of developing their innovative skills (Seidel et al. 2009: 37–38). The latter point suggests wider societal aspirations and preferences for public-sector employment, a typical feature of the regulation regime under the old Arab social contract found in core Arab economies.

Seidel et al. (2009: 41) mention a number of approximately ten incubators in Jordan and consider their work fairly successful. The incubator landscape includes university incubators or business parks, EHBP's iPark for ICT (Smadi and Tsipouri 2012: 34), and JEDCO's network of incubators and innovation centers under the *Al Urdonia lil Ebda* initiative such as the Irbid ICT Business Incubator, and UoJ's Agro-Industry Business Incubator (Mahroum et al. 2013). Sultan and Soete (2012: 324), however, judge the outcome of Jordanian incubators in terms of innovation to be moderate, notably because of the tendency of successful entrepreneurs to emigrate to Gulf states.

A remarkable element of Jordan's NIS is the "Oasis 500" accelerator that focuses on the ICT industry and provides support to early-stage entrepreneurial activities (Mahroum et al. 2013: 80). Further, a private biotechnology incubator called Copiatec is being set up in the Irbid Development Zone (Mahroum et al. 2013: 54).

While Jordan does not have an explicit cluster policy, some geographical clusters exist, and bottom-up cluster initiatives have formed, notably in the pharmaceuticals and ICT industries (Mahroum et al. 2013: 23; Seidel et al. 2009: 29–30). These clusters will be introduced in more detail in Sect. 4.2.2.3.

The setup of EHSC in 2007 can be understood as a form of innovation-driven cluster policy. Since EHSC is designed to host HEIs and research entities including PSUT, RSS, and HCST, as well as technology-based enterprises and startups, it can be understood as a similar science and technology park scheme as the Tunisian *pôles'* backbone technoparks such as Elgazala. Indeed, EHSC exhibits a comparable top-down orientation of policy design (Mahroum et al. 2013: 23).

It is remarkable that despite the formally strong position of HCST and RSS, the Jordanian NIS seems to be fragmented into a host of relevant agents and to suffer from a lack of coordination. Mahroum et al. (2013: 17–20) map relevant stakeholders in Jordan's NIS including, among others, bodies within the HCST and affiliated with it, several national ministries, as well as chambers and associations. Further, foreign donors such as the EU, USAID, JICA, and their programs play a role. The high number of agencies appears to cause some confusion among entrepreneurs and further stakeholders in search of R&D or innovation support (Mahroum et al. 2013: 20).

Jordan's innovation policies in recent years witnessed a number of initiatives and projects striving to promote innovation. One of these initiatives is the "Faculties for Factory" program seeking to stimulate university-industry technology transfer (Smadi and Tsipouri 2012: 33). However, the program is more an awareness-raising program than a device for genuine innovation support (Mahroum et al. 2013: 27). Another relevant initiative was the SRTD project that can be understood as a project promoting industrial upgrading through innovation somewhat similar to Tunisia's PMN. The program included, inter alia, the setup of technology transfer offices (TTOs) in HEIs and research centers (Smadi and Tsipouri 2012: 32). The SRTD project was supported by EUR 4 million of EU funding and aimed at enhancing the Jordanian private sector's innovative potential including through the promotion of startups and R&D commercialization. Other international donor-funded programs relevant for the Jordanian NIS include, notably, the Enterprise Development Program established by UNIDO with Italian governmental funds, USAID's long-term program to support economic development in Jordan which includes an innovation clusters initiative, or JICA's support program to various fields including human resources. The Graduate Internship and Employment Programme is an example for an initiative supported by USAID that aims at using the ICT sector as a vehicle for job creation for youth by temporarily subsidizing HEI graduates' salaries during employment in private-sector ICT companies (Mahroum et al. 2013: 23, 37, 63).

Another relevant initiative is the Jordanian government's *Kulluna al Urdun* initiative. While *Kulluna al Urdun* is the outcome of a larger national consensus process aimed at careful political reform (Muasher 2011: 15–18), it included dimensions relevant for the Jordanian NIS such as the setup of business or technology incubators (Smadi and Tsipouri 2012: 14).

Several public funding schemes for R&D projects exist under the umbrella of the Jordanian Ministry of Higher Education and Scientific Research and HCST. These funding schemes focus on priorities such as energy, water, healthcare, or food security (Smadi and Tsipouri 2012: 16). Furthermore, legislation designed to raise the economy's innovative performance has been introduced. Laws require companies to pay a 1% tax on net profit to fund a governmental R&D fund and to allocated a defined amount to R&D (Sultan and Soete 2012: 324).

4.2.2.3 Regional Structural Policy

While regional development appears to be less of a necessity in Jordan than in Tunisia, the economic dominance of Amman, Zarqa, and Irbid implies a certain need for regional policy to facilitate endogenous regional development in other, more peripheral parts of the country.

Jordanian regional policy has designated development areas (OECD 2013: 113–114; World Bank 2011: 253) and offers fiscal incentives to investments there. These incentives include corporate tax breaks differentiated into three classes according to the level of economic activity in regions (World Bank 2011: 253). Further, free zones to support export-oriented manufacturing and trade are managed by the Development and Free Zones Commission (DFZC) and offer tenant companies tax and customs exemptions (OECD 2013: 115).

Industrial estates are an instrument of regional development managed by the Jordan Industrial Estates Corporation (JIEC). According to Mahroum et al. (2013:

87), industrial estates exist in Irbid (Al-Hassan Industrial Estate and Cyber City), Karak, Amman, Aqaba (ASEZ), and Zarqa. Enterprises located in the industrial estates benefit from tax exemptions and incentives (Mahroum et al. 2013: 87; OECD 2013: 115).

Apart from these traditional approaches, the influx of Syrian refugees in the wake of the Syrian civil war creates a renewed and urgent need for regional development in specific parts of the country that are not necessarily the most remote or lagging ones. For instance, the International Labour Organization (2016) suggests a comprehensive economic development strategy for Irbid governorate. Located in the north of the country close to the border to Syria, Irbid governorate is confronted with the special situation of hosting almost a quarter of the registered Syrian refugee population present in Jordan, thus increasing the pressure on the regional labor market (International Labour Organization 2016: 5, 17–18).

Irbid governorate hosts one development area with concomitant incentives for investments such as tax exemptions and the Al-Hassan Industrial City. Similar to Jordan in general (as is the case in other core Arab economies), demand for TVET is low in Irbid governorate and exacerbates the shortage of practical skills demanded in the labor market (International Labour Organization 2016: 34, 47–48).

The regional development strategy proposed by the International Labour Organization (2016: 57–71) includes an action plan to promote agriculture, industry, tourism, crafts, education, and other sectors with measures such as awards for student innovators in schools, the establishment of an incubator to support successful student innovators, the setup of another incubator with Yarmouk University targeting youth, an innovation awareness-raising campaign, or support to research in nanotechnology, physics, and chemistry at Yarmouk University and JUST.

Mahroum et al. (2013: 81) take stock of two incubators in Irbid in fields such as ICT, electronics, agriculture, and education. The authors report on efforts to promote the ICT and healthcare industries through the setup of the Northern Development Corporation (NDC) in 2007 and the development of the Irbid Development Area (IDA). IDA is an interesting example of how to pursue a regional cluster policy under the umbrella of a development zone. On its website, IDA presents five regional clusters such as healthcare, education, IT and commerce, pharmaceuticals, and advanced engineering and lists support structures and agents for these clusters (Irbid Development Area 2018).

In general, QIZs might play a role in regional innovation policies, but since technology transfer typically does not occur on a large scale in QIZs and since a significant part of the workforce employed in the QIZs is accounted for by foreign workers, the potential of the QIZs to reinforce regional innovation limited (Seidel et al. 2009: 23). In addition, given the low degree of local value added by QIZs (OECD 2013: 116), the systemic potential of QIZs to stimulate the emergence of functional relations within the regional economies surrounding them appears low.

Various investment incentives exist, including preferential economic zones such as the Aqaba Special Economic Zone (ASEZ) with its free-zone status, a low and flat income tax, and a specific investment regime. Among the country's various free-trade zones, ASEZ is the largest. ASEZ was setup by the Aqaba Development

Corporation (ADC) under USAID's support, managed by the autonomous Aqaba Special Economic Zone Authority (ASEZA), and is attributed a model character for industrial development in Jordan. ASEZ has a special legal status because special provisions for ASEZ override general Jordanian law (OECD 2013: 116). ASEZ focuses on sectors such as tourism, logistics, and light industry and allows for up to 70% of the workforce to be foreign nationals (Mahroum et al. 2013: 83; OECD 2013: 23, 116).

Further, the science and technology parks (Kharabsheh et al. 2011; Rodríguez-Pose and Hardy 2014: 57–58) that were introduced in the previous sub-section complement the picture of spatial development in Jordan, although their rationale appears to follow primarily a growth-driven innovation logic rather than an equity-based regional development logic.

Regarding cluster initiatives, Seidel et al. (2009: 29) report that some cluster initiatives have emerged in a bottom-way and are driven primarily by industry (Seidel et al. 2009: 29). Geographical clusters exist notably in the pharmaceuticals and ICT industries (Seidel et al. 2009: 29–30). Mahroum et al. (2013: 23) state that the Jordanian government does not have a national cluster policy, neither within the framework of its industrial policy nor within the framework of its regional policy. Nevertheless, Seidel et al. (2009: 26) stress that Jordan's industrial policy promoting the pharmaceuticals industry is strongly cluster-driven. In any case, bottom-up cluster initiatives are formed during the early 2000s, notably in the pharmaceuticals and ICT industries. Further to these bottom-up cluster initiatives, a cluster for fertilizer chemicals is promoted within ASEZ (Mahroum et al. 2013: 23).

From the discussion above, it becomes apparent that Jordanian regional policy has experimented with a wide array of special economic regimes involving tax exemptions, regulatory easing, and preferential customs conditions. While integrated into Jordan's general economic orientation of international trade openness, these schemes at the intersection of industrial policy and regional policy are marked by a significant degree of selectivity. In addition to their selectivity, or maybe because of it, the impact of some of these schemes and notably of the QIZs in terms of regional development so far seems to be limited. What appears to be lacking is a pattern of regional policy striving to promote endogenous and systemic regional growth, for example, through regional innovation policies. The lack of a formal, top-down cluster policy, however, is not necessarily a disadvantage. Given that cluster initiatives designed in a top-down way are often less successful than those set up by industry in a bottom-up way (Benner 2012), Jordan's industrial and regional policy may be well advised to promote the existing, industry-driven cluster initiatives where needed instead of embarking on a top-down cluster policy of its own.

Apart from the schemes to promote trade and manufacturing in Jordan's regions that were highlighted in the discussion above, tourism plays a highly important role for Jordan and some of its regions, particularly for the southern governorates of Aqaba and Ma'an that host the country's most prominent tourist attractions Petra, Wadi Rum, and Aqaba. The next sub-section turns to the tourism policy Jordan has pursued in recent decades.

4.2.2.4   Tourism Policy

Tourism is important in several of Jordan's regions. In particular, the southern governorates of Aqaba with the country's only destination on the Red Sea and Ma'an with the famous archaeological site of Petra and the adjacent modern tourist town Wadi Musa as well as the Wadi Rum desert area offer touristic assets, but so do the capital Amman, the country's Dead Sea shore, the Roman archaeological site of Jerash, and other locations.

In contrast to Tunisia, no large-scale mass tourism development efforts are apparent in Jordan despite the country's attempts to develop the tourism sector in the late 1970s and 1980s. In the 1990s, after the signature of the Israel-Jordan peace treaty, a short boom of tourism under the "New Middle East" geopolitical imaginary of regional economic cooperation led to the rapid expansion of supply, notably in Amman and Wadi Musa/Petra, but limited government capacities in tourism planning and short-term rent-seeking behavior by new tourism entrepreneurs lacking sufficient management skills and experience led to unsustainable and undesirable outcomes most visible in Wadi Musa. When the Oslo peace process collapsed at the turn of the century, the Jordanian tourism sector faced problems of oversupply and insufficient demand. It became apparent that the hoped-for "peace dividend" did not materialize on a broad and inclusive basis. When popular support for peace between Israel and Jordan and concomitant economic normalization waned in Jordan, the country's tourism policy was compelled to change its course. Eventually, Jordanian tourism policy came to focus on promoting Jordan as a tourist destination in international markets independent of regional schemes of cooperation (Hazboun 2008).

It is particularly interesting to note the role of international donors in Jordan's tourism policy. For instance, USAID was active in supporting Jordan's tourism development in Petra, Jerash, and Amman (Hazboun 2008: 85). In addition, USAID supported plans to establish a Jordan Tourism Board (JTB) steered primarily by the private sector. When the original plan failed due to differing visions held by private-sector stakeholders, the Jordanian government, and USAID, the donor agency withdrew its support for tourism projects in Jordan, leaving space for the World Bank and JICA. Eventually, the JTB was established on terms preferred by the Jordanian government terms with the Ministry of Tourism and Antiquities (MOTA) steering the organization (Hazboun 2008: 139–141).

In 2016, Jordan registered 3.858 million international tourist arrivals, down from more than 4.2 million in 2010 (World Tourism Organization 2017: 12). Average spending per international tourist in Jordan (1080.80 USD) is high in comparison with other Mediterranean destinations (World Economic Forum 2017). Hence and in contrast to Tunisia, Jordan is not a low-cost tourist destination. Tourism development in the country's major destination, Wadi Musa/Petra, followed unsustainable boom-and-bust patterns, implying a lack of long-term planning (Hazboun 2008). A policy similar to Tunisia's approach to develop and plan integrated tourism complexes is not observable in Jordan to date. However, there is a potential for further developing the tourism sector and for diversifying the country's tourism product.

For instance, promoting ecotourism opportunities in Jordan seems promising (OECD 2013: 204).

4.2.3   Regulation in the Jordanian Economy

After the presentation of Jordan's major structural economic challenges and policies in the previous sub-sections, this sub-section characterizes the main features of how the old Arab social contract plays out in Jordan. Different from Tunisia's situation, Jordan did not witness any revolutionary changes during the "Arab Spring" in 2010/2011 but is characterized by a remarkable degree of political stability against the background of highly volatile neighborhood. Consequently, regulation-related change in the Jordanian economy and society is evolutionary, often slow, and sometimes even retrogressive. In the case of Jordan, one may prima facie assume that the old Arab social contract did not significantly change in the wake of the demonstrations and political reactions in 2010/2011. However, in terms of economic reforms, the two cases are more comparable because in both countries, fundamental economic reform is an incremental process that is to some degree conditioned by revolutionary or evolutionary political change but still needs to be negotiated between government and polity and, typically, with transnational agents such as IFIs. The latter in particular exert pressure that, combined with the underlying structural problems stemming from the inherent unsustainability of the old Arab social contract, is likely to lead to some changes in the regulation regime even in the absence of considerable political change.

Thus, the present sub-section presents stylized facts about regulation in Jordan in a longer-term perspective. As an approximation, the stylized facts presented below apply at least to the reign of the current king Abdullah II so far. Even as revolutionary change is absent in Jordan, evolutionary changes in socioeconomic regulation are either occurring or being negotiated, thus confirming to a certain degree the assumption that the old Arab social contract is dissolving in Jordan, too. These evolutionary changes are discussed particularly in Sect. 4.2.5.

While Jordanian economic policy left considerable room for the private sector compared to other core Arab economies and has pursued a rather liberal economic policy (Cammett 2014), many of the structural deficiencies and challenges characterizing the regulation regime of the old Arab social contract (see Sect. 3.4) are observable in Jordan, too, although the country's peculiar geopolitical situation yields some specificities not typically found in other core Arab economies.

For example, on economic participation among the labor force aged 15 and over, a large gap between males (63.0%) and females (18.3) can be observed, suggesting a very low rate of female labor-force participation (Department of Statistics 2017; International Labour Organization 2016: 9). Sultan and Soete (2012: 321) state that "Jordan's active-to-total population ratio is one of the lowest in the world, with an average of four non-active individuals depending on a single worker."

Similar to other core Arab economies, Jordan's government sector is inflated (Muasher 2011: 21), as is evident in a share of the public sector in total employment even significantly higher than in Tunisia (World Bank 2015: 12). This finding suggests that despite having pursued long-term policies more accommodating to private-sector development than were pursued in other core Arab economies, over the long run Jordanian governments responded to labor market pressures by providing government employment for constituent groups. Given the dominance of East Bankers in the public sector (Brand 2014: 568; Rivlin 2009: 166–169), such a strategy can be explained with the Hashemite regime's interest to secure loyalty from among the tribally structured East Bank society (Muasher 2011: 22) and can therefore be seen as an expression of the authoritarian bargain in the form of the crypto-welfare policy of public employment provision in a context of selective inclusion of the East Bank constituency while excluding Palestinian-origin citizens from this kind of bargain.

Consistent with general institutional realities typically found in core Arab economies, a preference for public-sector employment can be stated in Jordan (Mahroum et al. 2013: 98, 124). In a 2010 survey, 54% of Jordanian youth stated their willingness to work in government, while only 16% were willing to work in the private sector (World Bank 2014b: 13). Yet, this finding needs to be differentiated between East Bankers and citizens of Palestinian origin who dominate the private sector. It is reasonable to assume that expectations towards public-sector employment among Palestinian-origin citizens are less pronounced than among the East Banker population. Consistently, Brand (2014: 576) argues that economic benefits (notably public-sector jobs) were reserved for members of tribal structures and clans to establish a regime tribe symbiosis and thus a loyal support base for the Hashemite regime among East Bankers.

Mahroum et al. (2013: 96) consider Jordan a "tribal-based society" and ascribe a continuing role to the phenomenon of *wasta*. Interviewees largely confirmed this insight. The Jordanian society was described as marked by tribal traditions. That does not necessarily mean that society was structured among tribal lines which are not true for urban regions anymore. But tribal traditions underlie the importance of *wasta* and thus decision-making in favor of societal units such as extended families. For instance, jobs are often filled with relatives regardless of their qualification. Thus, tribal traditions prevent more merit-based decision-making processes in the economy. At the same time, Mahroum et al. (2013: 96) convey a statement that the impact of tribal institutions may be decreasing due to a combination of exposure to other, notably Western, cultural trends and the technological possibilities afforded by ICT or what can be understood as transnational transformative processes rooted in technological developments and cross-border flows of cultural expressions.

The skills mismatch on the labor market is observable in Jordan (Mahroum et al. 2013: 68; Smadi and Tsipouri 2012: 3), as it is in other core Arab economies. However, the brain drain of qualified human capital to GCC countries and the influx of unskilled workers from Egypt, Sudan, and Asia makes Jordan a special case. The combination of a labor market with a fairly well-developed base of human capital that apparently does not correspond to the structure of the national economy with its limited degree of industrialization in competitive pockets such as ICT and pharmaceuticals and larger labor demand in low-skilled activities such as textiles and garments manufacturing may be the reason why the Jordanian labor market is squeezed between an import of lower-skilled labor from Egypt, Sudan, and Asia and an export of higher-skilled human capital to GCC countries while being confronted with high youth unemployment particularly among higher-education graduates (Amin et al. 2012: 57; Department of Statistics 2017; International Labour Organization 2016: 9; Smadi and Tsipouri 2012: 3; World Bank 2013: 10; 2014b: 12–14).

Kanaan and Hanania (2009: 149–150) state that TVET suffers from a "social stigma" and claim that "most students and parents [are, M.B.] obsessed with the social esteem of university education." In a similar vein, Mahroum et al. (2013: 30) confirm the low reputation and stigma of TVET in Jordan that can be regarded as rule-competing institutions in the sense that political efforts to promote and strengthen TVET face institutions held among the population (i.e., low reputation and stigma) that make the policy efforts a priori less promising. Higher education is highly regarded, and many students are keen on achieving either public-sector jobs in Jordan or private-sector jobs in other countries (Seidel et al. 2009: 38). These imply three institutional features in the Jordanian economy and society. First, aspirations of students and their families are geared towards academic education and less towards alternative educational tracks such as TVET. Second, graduates tend to prefer public-sector employment to domestic private-sector employment. While these two points are fairly common in most core Arab economies, the third point appears somewhat peculiar for the case of Jordan. Next to domestic public-sector employment, graduates aspire towards employment abroad, notably in GCC countries, providing an institutional rationale for the brain drain of highly skilled human capital from Jordan to the Gulf. Aspirations for employment in the Gulf have repercussions for unemployment in Jordan by raising reservation wages and presumably exacerbating the problem of queuing (Seidel et al. 2009: 37, 40; Smadi and Tsipouri 2012: 3, 33).

In the interviews, the level of education in Jordan was considered relatively good in comparison to other Arab countries. Yet, interviewees stated that university education is theoretical, not responding to labor market demands, and contributing to the skills mismatch because graduates are seen to lack the soft skills demanded by employers. There are a large number of university graduates, implying that while the best-performing ones seek to emigrate to GCC countries due to higher salaries, there is still a sufficient number of graduates to fill vacancies. Lower-skilled work is performed by immigrants from Egypt or, in the case of the textile industry in QIZs, Indian or Bangladeshi immigrants because Jordanian jobseekers are unwilling to perform these manual industrial jobs under the conditions offered. TVET schemes do exist but their success is mixed. Usually company participation in curricula development does not succeed, and TVET contents are judged outdated by companies. Therefore, companies have to train graduates on the job. In middle management, companies often prefer to hire experienced staff than to train younger staff. This applies, for instance, to the tourism sector where TVET graduates seem to lack soft skills such as an appropriate service mentality or customer orientation. While there is a large number of craftspeople (including many immigrants from Egypt), there is no formal training and quality is mixed. The reputation of craftsmanship seems to be rather low. In general, the higher reputation of academic education over TVET and the stigma of TVET education as being an inferior choice to university studies was confirmed by interviewees, as were parents' expectations that their children study at university. There are, however, efforts to enrich academic education with practical content such as the German-Jordanian University whose study model includes company internships and cooperative bachelor theses, inspired by the German system of universities of applied sciences. Al Hussein Technical University is another example of an HEI currently trying to establish dual-study programs. During interviews, the hope was expressed that dual-study schemes might ultimately change the image of vocationally oriented education if it is offered at universities. However, for these programs to be set up successfully, a change in attitudes on the firms' side was deemed necessary since firms would need to understand the long-term benefit of participating in dual-study programs and be prepared to pay students a salary.

Other than public employment, supply-side subsidies are a traditional component of the crypto-welfare policies pursued. The relevance of these crypto-welfare policies for the authoritarian bargain is clear from the fact that in the wake of demonstrations during the "Arab Spring" in 2011, the Jordanian government raised both civil servants' salaries and subsidies for fuel (OECD 2013: 36). The extent of subsidies and their increase as a political response to popular dissatisfaction and as a crypto-welfare policy (Josua 2016: 17) is evident from the fact that from 2010 to 2011, the burden of energy subsidies in Jordan increased from 1% to 6% of the country's GDP (OECD 2013: 36). Similar to the Tunisian case, cost-of-living riots in Jordan in 1989 demonstrated the political sensitivity of subsidy cuts and their impact on the cost of living (Richards and Waterburs 2008: 283).

When it comes to institutions underpinning industrial organization, specifics in corporate culture and management styles can be discerned. These specifics apply notably to the large share of SMEs, many of them being family-owned. Mahroum et al. (2013: 124) state that these firms "are generally run in a conservative manner, and the culture of risk taking necessary for R&D and innovation is limited." In the interviews, too, the Jordanian economy was characterized as relying on micro and small enterprises with many of them being family businesses. In this labor environment, a professional "culture" with clear growth perspectives and career paths as well as transparent rules and procedures is lacking. Companies often seem to lack a corporate culture open to employee-driven innovation and new ideas. While jobseekers often look for public-sector employment and the preference for government jobs continues to be prevalent, there is also an aspiration to work for respectable private-sector companies that ensure transparent working conditions.

Various transnational transformative processes affect socioeconomic regulation in Jordan. First of all, the AA between Jordan and the EU signed in 1997 and in force since 2002 provides a framework for aligning processes in economic policies and rules (European Commission 2017a; OECD 2013: 96, 122–123), although the relevance of the country's relationship with the EU politically and economically appears somewhat less dominant than in the case of Tunisia. With Jordan, too, the

EU is seeking a new agreement meant to establish a Deep and Comprehensive Free Trade Area (DCFTA) since 2011. Such an agreement would cover additional fields such as trade in services, investment protection, and public procurement and lead to a closer alignment and *rapprochement* of Jordan to the EU in a wide range of fields related to the structure of production and economic policies in general. In this sense, a DCFTA agreement can be expected to exert considerable influence on prescriptive rules (European Commission 2017a).

In general, Jordan's web of FTAs and its commitment to openness to international trade provides a window for transnational transformative processes, as does its WTO membership (Muasher 2011: 5; OECD 2013: 119, 122). Further, the role of international donors in shaping economic policies and particularly prescriptive rules appears fairly prominent. For example, the EU was involved in Jordanian innovation policymaking with the SRTD project, and further donors such as USAID, UNIDO, and JICA have been active in Jordan (Mahroum et al. 2013: 37). For instance, USAID supported Jordan's tourism development in Petra, Jerash, and Amman (Hazboun 2008: 85). A particularly interesting episode is USAID's assistance for the setup of JTB that eventually revealed differing visions held by different stakeholders (Hazboun 2008: 139–141). In hindsight, it seems as if prescriptive rules suggested by USAID as an international donor conflicted with organizational and institutional realities, preferences, and interests held by the Jordanian government and by the private sector. In sum, the involvement of international donors appears to shape transnational transformative processes through transnational policy transfer and competition among donors and has to be viewed under the lens of their relationship with organizations and institutions existing in Jordan. Finally, waves of IFI-sponsored structural adjustment and related reform efforts (Rivlin 2009: 166–169) condition socioeconomic regulation in Jordan as another form of transnational transformative processes.

While Jordan is an economy based to a certain degree on rents, the role of well-established elites seems to be somewhat different from the one observable in Benalist Tunisia. In the case of Jordan, the well-established and connected elite seems entrenched not so much in protected parts of the private sector (as was the case in Tunisia under the Ben Ali regime) but rather in decision-making positions in government. It is likely that the main structural reason lies in the dichotomy of East Banker domination of the public sector and Palestinian-origin citizen domination of the private sector. Through this dichotomy, the relationship between political power and economic activity seems less pronounced than in Benalist Tunisia. Despite these different structural features, the role of entrenched elites in the Jordanian public sector does engender structural inefficiencies. Despite the king's often-expressed willingness to pursue a reform agenda, entrenched interests by groups resisting reform continuously contradicted or obstructed the king's reform policies (Muasher 2011: 3–4). As a consequence, "in most cases, the king's directives were ignored, diluted, and, at times, directly opposed" (Muasher 2011: 4). In spite of the king's directives for political and economic reform, resistance to reform by entrenched elites is possible because of the monarchy's dependence on the loyalty of its tribal

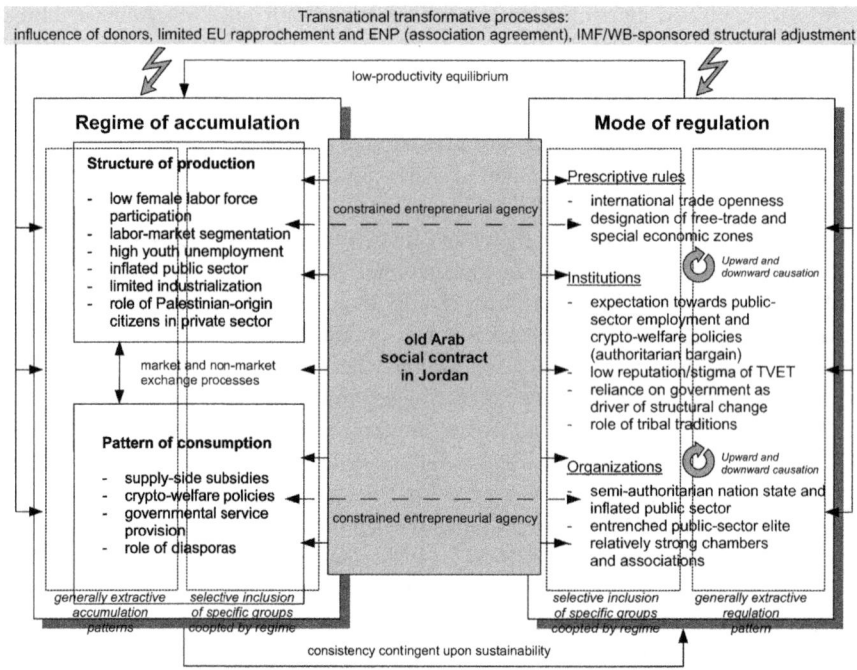

Fig. 4.2 Stylized regulation framework under the old Arab social contract in Jordan (Source: own work based on Bathelt 1994: 66)

constituency and the necessity to co-opt elites from among the tribal East Banker society (Muasher 2011: 22).

Based on the discussion of elements of socioeconomic regulation above, Fig. 4.2 gives a stylized overview on the major components of the long-standing Arab social contract in Jordan within the terms of the regulation framework developed in Chap. 3.

Figure 4.2 summarizes the following salient features of socioeconomic regulation in Jordan, based on the previous discussion.

The *structure of production* within the regime of accumulation in the Jordanian economy witnesses some features typically found in core Arab economies. The high degree of labor market segmentation is evident notably along age and gender lines through high (youth) unemployment (Amin et al. 2012: 57; Department of Statistics 2017; International Labour Organization 2016: 9; Smadi and Tsipouri 2012: 3; World Bank 2013: 10; 2014b: 12–14) as well as the low female labor force participation and low ratio of economically active population (Department of Statistics 2017; International Labour Organization 2016: 9; Sultan and Soete 2012: 321). Furthermore, the public sector is inflated (Muasher 2011: 21; World Bank 2015: 12). A particular feature of Jordan's structure of production is the peculiar form of segmentation between East Bankers dominating the public sector and citizens of Palestinian origin dominating the private sector (Brand 2014: 568; Rivlin 2009:

166–169). The skills mismatch is a salient feature of the labor market (Kharabsheh et al. 2011: 222; Mahroum et al. 2013: 30, 68; Smadi and Tsipouri 2012: 3) that underscores labor market segmentation and particularly youth unemployment. The brain drain to GCC countries (Ryan 2010: 322; Smadi and Tsipouri 2012: 3, 33) is a phenomenon peculiar to the Jordanian case that combines with the skills mismatch and with immigration of lower-skilled labor into a highly complex picture of the Jordanian labor market. Industrialization of the Jordanian economy is advanced in limited pockets of competitiveness such as the ICT and pharmaceuticals sectors, essentially making Jordan a "semi-industrialized economy" (Mahroum et al. 2013: 12). Similar to the long-standing pattern in Tunisia, low value-added textiles and garments manufacturing is widespread, and the economy is particularly integrated into global value chains in this industry. These trends are underscored by the general thrust of Jordanian economic policy towards international trade openness and in particular by the QIZ scheme (Diop and Ghali 2012: 13–14; OECD 2013: 119–120).

For the *pattern of consumption* in the old Arab social contract in Jordan, too, most of the common trends identified for core Arab economies in Sect. 3.3.1 apply. Untargeted supply-side subsidies, for example, for food and energy, are a part of the crypto-welfare policies pursued by the Jordan government and a common approach to soothe public unrest (Josua 2016: 17; OECD 2013: 36). Given the Jordanian diaspora, particularly in the Gulf, remittances play a significant role for the country's economy (OECD 2013: 34). While Jordan under the Hashemite regime can be classified as a socially conservative and economically comparatively liberal monarchy in contrast to other core Arab economies organized as secular republics that at some point followed more of less extended experiments of Arab socialism, the reliance on the state as provider of public services is part of the state-driven development model that has been prevalent in much of the Middle East and North Africa (Richards and Waterbury 2008). It seems, however, as if the Jordanian state's peculiar situation as an economy dependent on foreign rents, remittances, and aid, as well as its sensitive geopolitical situation, its exposition to various waves of massive immigration by Palestinian, Iraqi, and Syrian refugees at different times, somewhat limited the capability of the Jordanian state to provide public services to its citizens to a large degree when compared to other core Arab economies. Still, the inflated public sector implies a significant role of government service provision, as does the role of the state in education.[9] In any case, Jordan did adopt a state-driven growth model as did other core Arab economies (World Bank 2009: 25).

When it comes to the *mode of regulation* under the old Arab social contract in Jordan, it is interesting to note the comparatively liberal orientation of Jordanian economic policy. Within the Global Innovation Index, Jordan is ranked first interna-

---

[9] However, there are different regimes for public service provisions for refugees organized separately from the Jordanian state. In particular, for a part of registered Palestinian refugees or their descendants, the United Nations Relief and Works Agency for Palestine Refugees (UNRWA) in the Near East provides healthcare and educational services, for example, through schools and TVET centers (UNRWA n.d.).

tionally on the ease of dismissing workers (measured in terms of the notice period and severance pay), a place the country shares with a number of industrialized and emerging economies including, inter alia, Austria, Denmark, Hong Kong (China), Italy, Japan, New Zealand, Singapore, the UAE, or the United States (Cornell, INSEAD and WIPO 2017: 323). However, elsewhere, the labor law in Jordan is considered highly restrictive when it comes to dismissing workers (World Bank 2013: 148). This contradiction may be due to segmentation. As became clear in the interviews, labor laws mirror the segmentation of the labor market by granting comparatively high protection to Jordanian workers. Remarkably, a system of sectoral barriers to entry and protective prescriptive rules for the benefit of a politically well-connected business elite, as existed in Benalist Tunisia, is not evident in Jordan. The dichotomy between the East Banker elite dominating the public sector and Palestinian-origin citizens dominating the private sector – arguably not because of political clout but because of them having seized opportunities of comparatively free entrepreneurship – can be assumed to be a major structural reason for this marked difference to other core Arab economies. Still, this does not mean that prescriptive rules are set in economically efficient ways. The entrenched public-sector elite's resistance to reforms (Muasher 2011: 3–4) probably creates a different but somewhat comparable set of inefficiencies as in the case of Tunisia. Similarly, a survey reported by the World Bank (2009: 86–93) suggests that for entrepreneurs in Jordan, inconsistent and unpredictable implementation of prescriptive rules is a problem, although the time spent by managers dealing with the implementation of prescriptive rules appears to be less than in other core Arab economies, implying a lower bureaucratic burden.

In any case, as for prescriptive rules distinguishing Jordan from other core Arab economies, the clear policy of opening the country to international trade and thereby effectively anchoring its domestic economic policies to a certain degree of liberalism affected by transnational transformative processes makes Jordan a special case among Arab countries. Consistent with this generic orientation of Jordanian economic policy, a number of liberalization schemes have been implemented through the various special economic or free-trade zones (including the QIZs), but these schemes are by their very nature selective because of their legal regimes separate from the general legal regime applying to the rest of the economy. In a sense, Jordan's liberalization policy bears some resemblance to the onshore/offshore dichotomy in Benalist Tunisia and may reflect a policy of selective and careful liberalization, using special economic or free-trade zones as laboratories for economic reform in a way somewhat evocative of the gradual opening of the Chinese economy under Deng Xiaoping. However, Jordan's use of special legal regimes – defined not sectorally as was the method of selective liberalization in Benalist Tunisia but regionally – appears so vast that it allows for the hypothesis that the exception has effectively become the rule.

Guarantees for public-sector employment to university graduates may not have been made explicit at all times in Jordan, but the role of public employment as a crypto-welfare policy and as a means to secure loyalty of East Bankers to the Hashemite regime is still evident. Popular expectations and preferences are clearly geared towards public employment (Mahroum et al. 2013: 124; World Bank 2014b: 13), at least among the tribally structured East Banker society (Brand 2014: 576). Supply-side subsidies such as those for food and energy (Josua 2016: 17; OECD 2013: 36) are another component of the crypto-welfare policies pursued in Jordan as in other core Arab economies. The role of crypto-welfare policies in securing loyalty to the regime is evident in the relief package introduced as a reaction to protests in the wake of the "Arab Spring" (Brand 2014: 580).

Further, institutions within the mode of regulation of the old Arab social contract in Jordan include a preference for academic, higher education and the low reputation and stigma of TVET (Kanaan and Hanania 2009: 149–150), again a rather typical institutional component of the old Arab social contract in core Arab economies. These institutions give policies to strengthen vocational schools the character of institution-competing rules likely to encounter significant obstacles because of the strength and persistence of underlying institutional realities.

Further, tribal traditions play a role, notably through the institution of *wasta* (Jamal and Khatib 2014: 256–257; Mahroum et al. 2013: 96), but their precise influence on socioeconomic regulation notably among the East Banker society is unclear and merits more research. In any case, tribal patterns in the East Banker society are intricately related to the political foundations of the country's stability despite being located in a volatile neighborhood. Given Jordan's complicated demographic situation, the Hashemite regime's power is based on its long-standing alliance with East Banker tribes that dominate the public sector and specifically the military (Brand 2014: 566).[10]

Among the salient characteristics of organizations governing the mode of regulation under the old Arab social contract in Jordan is a nation-state that is inflated in terms of its public sector and centralized in terms of the monarchy's power but that is still somewhat different from the strongly authoritarian nation-state in Benalist Tunisia. In some regard, the Jordanian nation-state could be classified as weak or at least vulnerable. Among the reasons for this vulnerability are first Jordan's precarious geopolitical situation in an unstable neighborhood; second, the demographic pressures the country faces because of subsequent waves of refugee immigration from neighboring countries; third, the demographic segmentation of the population primarily in East Bankers and Palestinian-origin citizens; fourth, the reliance of the regime on its alliance with East Banker tribes; and fifth, the government's economic dependence on rents (Brand 2014). The entrenched public-sector elite hostile to reform (Muasher 2011: 3–4) is another building block of the organizational tissue of the mode of regulation, but its role is markedly different from the well-established and politically well-connected business elite that existed in Benalist Tunisia. All of these aspects suggest one might call the Jordanian nation-state semi-authoritarian. This partial weakness of the Jordanian state may be one of the reasons why in terms of economic policy, government has left the private sector with a comparatively high degree of freedom in comparison to other core Arab economies. In addition,

---

[10] Still, some Palestinian-origin businesspeople are part of the monarchy's support base (Josua 2016: 9).

the relative weakness of the Jordanian state may be a reason why chambers and associations could secure a comparatively prominent role for themselves in the Jordanian economy (Seidel et al. 2009: 30; Sultan and Soete 2012: 323).

Consequently, the characterization of the regulation regime in Jordan as extractive or inclusive is not as clear-cut as it may be in other core Arab economies. Indeed, patterns of inclusion and exclusion seem to be more complex, although overall trends are largely similar. Given high youth unemployment and low female economic participation, labor market segmentation is obvious, implying a pattern of non-inclusivity on the labor market. The crypto-welfare policy of public employment provision is non-inclusive first because it benefits those who happen to get a government job and, second, because in Jordan the policy is meant for East Bankers but not for Palestinian-origin citizens. However, the private sector does seem to offer opportunities for economic participation and thus a certain degree of inclusiveness since Palestinian-origin citizens were able to seize opportunities in entrepreneurship. In contrast to other core Arab economies with their legacies of former Arab socialist periods and extractive economic rules designed specifically to benefit the well-connected business elite, we might assume an economically more inclusive and less extractive pattern of socioeconomic regulation in Jordan. Nevertheless, it is important to stress that this somehow higher economic inclusiveness does not translate into political inclusiveness, both because of the Jordanian regime's incremental or hesitant approach to granting political freedoms in general (Josua 2016) and because of the East Banker-Palestinian-origin dichotomy.

The role of *entrepreneurial agency* seems somewhat different in Jordan than in the model of socioeconomic regulation under the old Arab social contract in core Arab economies as it was proposed in Sect. 3.3.1. In other core Arab economies such as Benalist Tunisia, entrepreneurial agency and related Schumpeterian creative destruction were more or less limited by policies that protected the business interests of a well-established and politically connected business elite from competition. In Jordan, the situation appears different, probably due in part to the vulnerability and weaknesses of the Jordanian nation-state but maybe also due to the pragmatic economic policy approach of the Hashemite regime. The Jordanian approach to economic policy differed from other core Arab economies' more or less extensive experiments with import substitution and Arab socialism in earlier decades. The demographic divide between East Bankers dominating the public sector and Palestinian-origin citizens dominating the private sector and seizing economic opportunities arising from the regime's relatively liberal economies policies may be the most relevant reason behind the seemingly greater degree of entrepreneurial freedom in Jordan. A possible hypothesis is that the East Banker dominance of the public sector prevented the rise of a politically connected business elite with sufficient political clout to push for restrictive legislation to protect itself from competition. While, within the private sector, a Palestinian-origin business elite of a certain size has formed and that some members of this elite are part of the Hashemite regime's support base (Josua 2016: 9), their support was presumably less critical to political stability than regime support by East Banker elites. Thus, in comparison with other core Arab economies, the link between political influence and economic power appears to be significantly weaker in Jordan because of the split between political/administrative power wielded by East Bankers and economic power attained by Palestinian-origin citizens.

Transnational transformative processes relevant for socioeconomic regulation in Jordan include IMF/World Bank-supported structural adjustment; a considerable influence of international donors such as the EU, USAID, or JICA; and limited but still relevant EU *rapprochement* through the AA. Some of these processes are presumably and to a certain degree motivated by Jordan's geopolitical position both in relation to the Israeli-Palestinian conflict and the instability in its neighbors Syria and Iraq.

Despite the gradual differences between the regulation regime in Jordan and other core Arab economies, the Jordanian case still exhibits major characteristics of the old Arab social contract. As other core Arab economies, the country suffers from severe structural deficiencies such as high youth unemployment and labor market segmentation with related inequities. Similar to other core Arab economies, the Jordanian economy seems trapped in a low productivity equilibrium that for some time was internally consistent but has become increasingly unsustainable. For instance, the reliance of the Jordanian state on rents and the characterization of the Jordanian economy as "semi-rentier" (Ryan 2010: 322) are reasons to question the sustainability of the country's traditional socioeconomic regulation regime. Furthermore, high unemployment among youth, women, and the educated is a socially unsustainable situation, even more so given the need for the Jordanian economy to cope with the consequences of the influx of refugees from neighboring countries. IMF-sponsored structural adjustment aimed at stabilizing the country's precarious fiscal situation, subsidy cuts, and tax hikes (Al-Khalidi 2018) demonstrates the urgency of curing the most pressing aspects of the unsustainability of the regulation regime.

Beyond the surface, however, dynamic structural characteristics of socioeconomic regulation are among the most fundamental aspects to look at in terms of the ability of the Jordanian economy to solve structural deficiencies. While the present sub-section ends with the conclusion that in terms of economic policymaking, the conditions for entrepreneurship and Schumpeterian creative destruction may be somewhat better than in other core Arab economies, the next sub-section takes a closer look at the state of entrepreneurship and innovation as drivers of dynamic efficiency in the Jordanian economy.

4.2.4 Entrepreneurship and Creative Destruction in the Jordanian Institutional Context

While the degree of entrepreneurial freedom in Jordan seems to be somewhat larger than in other core Arab economies, entrepreneurship and innovation as critical drivers for Schumpeterian creative destruction are subject to constraints that may render the country's eventual development into a knowledge-based economy more difficult. As a first indication, Jordan is placed 83rd among 127 countries in the Global Innovation Index. More specifically, the Jordanian economy is judged better on the index's dimension of "institutions," i.e., macro-level conditions (political stability, regulatory environment, and the business environment), innovation linkages (including particularly good ratings on university-industry research collaboration and cluster development), knowledge absorption, knowledge creation (particularly on scientific and technical articles), knowledge diffusion, creative goods and services, and online creativity. In contrast, Jordan is ranked below its overall rank on the dimensions of access to credit, investment, and knowledge workers (Cornell, INSEAD and WIPO 2017: 242).

The Global Entrepreneurship Monitor 2016/2017 assessed the state and challenges of entrepreneurship in Jordan. In expert ratings of the entrepreneurial ecosystem, the Jordanian economy was considered roughly on par with average values for comparator countries in Asia and Oceania but below average on entrepreneurship education indicators. While entrepreneurs are accorded a comparatively high status in Jordan, the ratio of female to male total early-stage entrepreneurial activity is the lowest of all 64 countries surveyed (Global Entrepreneurship Research Association 2017: 72).

While interviewees stated a generally low level of entrepreneurial attitudes particularly among East Bankers and their preference for long-term, stable government employment, a relatively vibrant entrepreneurial scene has emerged in urban regions, driven to a significant extent by the ICT sector and by support programs implemented by government agencies such as JEDCO or accelerators such as Oasis 500. Interestingly, these programs have created new perspectives to raise the low levels of female labor market participation. Since the families of married women often prefer them not to work outside their home, establishing a startup and working from home has become easier for women under these support schemes. This is important given the innovative and entrepreneurial potential of women, many of them highly educated, hitherto not economically active.

Seidel et al. (2009: 39–40) paint a rather cheerful picture of innovative and entrepreneurial attitudes in Jordan. In contrast, Mahroum et al. (2013: 98) do not see sufficient entrepreneurial potential in Jordan, both in terms of entrepreneurs and their business skills, which the authors explain primarily with institutional realities such high-risk adversity within Jordan's society and the stigma of failure both for the individual and for his or her family. Seidel et al. (2009: 36) confirm that the stigma of business failure is severe for the entrepreneur's whole family even if the stigma may be decreasing. However, these insights will probably differ between East Bankers and citizens of Palestinian origin, with the latter's dominance in private-sector entrepreneurship suggesting the prevalence of considerable entrepreneurial attitudes among this demographic group.

Interviewees confirmed the relatively higher entrepreneurial spirit among Palestinian-origin citizens which is presumably due to a significant extent to restrictions to government employment or regulations favoring employment for East Bankers in formal private-sector employment. Successful entrepreneurs are often from among the demographic group of Palestinian-origin citizens. Interestingly,

Syrian refugees (e.g., in Irbid province) seem to have a somewhat higher willingness to engage in entrepreneurial activities than East Bankers, too. It seems plausible to assume that need-based entrepreneurship is a coping strategy among Syrian refugees confronted with difficulties to engage in the segmented Jordanian labor market and resulting problems of exclusion.

Generally, on the institutional level "social or cultural barriers to risk taking, and the importance of financial security and social status play an important role in influencing entrepreneurship in Jordan" (Mahroum et al. 2013: 89). Therefore, one can hypothesize that Schumpeterian creative destruction through entrepreneurship is constrained in Jordan by institutional factors such as high-risk aversion, possibly leading entrepreneurially spirited people to look towards leaving the country. The result is a diaspora with significant entrepreneurial potential that generates remittances and facilitates access by entrepreneurs from Jordan to international innovative networks. At the same time, returning migrants may contribute their skills and experience gained abroad to innovative or entrepreneurial activity in Jordan (Mahroum et al. 2013: 72–74).

Jordan therefore is a case for a country with a comparatively liberal regulatory environment for entrepreneurship and innovation (somewhat different from other core Arab economies) but with institutionally grounded barriers to entrepreneurship, although constraints on the level of prescriptive rules such as the lack of innovation-stimulating tax incentives or constraints for university faculty members to engage in entrepreneurial activity do exist (Mahroum et al. 2013: 89–90). The barriers to entrepreneurship, innovation, and hence Schumpeterian creative destruction rooted both in prescriptive rules and institutions underscore the limited entrepreneurial agency in the Jordanian regulation regime. Thus, the barriers contribute to the low productivity equilibrium the Jordanian economy finds itself in, despite the comparatively higher freedom of entrepreneurial activity and tolerance of independent economic activity than found in other core Arab economies. Reforming the Jordanian regulation regime towards a more sustainable and efficient equilibrium will have to include efforts to lift barriers to entrepreneurship and innovation, both on the level of prescriptive rules and institutions. The next section discusses how a more sustainable and efficient regime of socioeconomic regulation in Jordan could be brought about, given the context of evolutionary and incremental reform currently present in Jordan.

4.2.5 Perspectives for Regulation in Jordan: Continuity or Change?

Although Jordan offers a context of regime stability and evolutionary and incremental change in contrast to Tunisia's context of revolutionary political change, in economic terms the two countries' challenges in transitioning towards a new, internally and externally consistent and sustainable regulation regime are remarkably similar.

Again, the discussion in Sect. 3.4 is generally applicable. In particular, the stylized framework for such a new, consistent, and sustainable regulation regime as depicted in Fig. 3.4 is generally valid for Jordan. However, some peculiarities have to be pointed out. Since Jordan appears to have a partly liberal but selective labor law and an investment environment characterized by a host of spatially defined special economic regimes, reforming prescriptive rules may not necessarily necessitate generic liberalization but rather focus on extending liberal special economic regimes to wider parts of the economy, thus reducing segmentation. Rather than further liberalizing legislation, assuring predictable and equal enforcement may be more relevant in the Jordanian case, but doing so is likely to touch upon the institutional level of the economy, possibly requiring institution-circumventing rules within the public sector to improve the quality of rule enforcement. Meritocratic government recruitment should play a role in this regard but to a certain extent may touch upon the dominance of the tribal East Banker elite in the public sector by opening it up to other parts of the society.

Indeed, the current transitional period seems to be marked by uncertainty related to patterns on the institutional level of the Jordanian economy. In the interviews, the policy environment in Jordan was considered unstable due to frequent changes, leading to unstable expectations on behalf of private-sector companies and investors. The current IMF-sponsored structural adjustment program with the income tax increases planned was cited as a major example. While governmental strategies to tackle structural problems such as unemployment exist, implementation is lacking. Interviewees addressed the problem of the challenging business environment companies face. While there are a large number of support agencies or programs to encourage investments and entrepreneurship, regulatory decisions are seen to be made in an arbitrary and often surprising manner. For instance, new laws or tax increases are not communicated to companies, and their sudden implementation thus comes as a surprise to firms. Information from government agencies is often contradictory and competences overlap. Due to these difficulties, a significant part of successful entrepreneurs seem willing to emigrate abroad if they had the chance to do so. Similarly, young graduates with ideas for entrepreneurship may end up disappointed with the existing limits to realizing their ideas. Still, most graduates apparently stay in Jordan due to the proximity of family and friends, a clear indication of embeddedness (Granovetter 1985).

As in other core Arab economies, the institutional foundations of the state-driven growth model including expectations towards public employment and supply-side subsidies and unsustainable prescriptive rules establishing and maintaining selective crypto-welfare policies to accommodate publicly held preferences and expectations are at the heart of the structural deficiencies of the old Arab social contract in Jordan. This relationship between policy and institutions is evident, for example, in the government reaction to public discontent by offering yet another wave of crypto-welfare policies (Brand 2014: 580; Josua 2016: 17). In particular, Brand (2014: 580) stresses that the Jordanian government reacted to demonstrations during the "Arab Spring" with economic relief packages for the poor and middle classes. Given the continued fiscal stress, the country finds itself confronted with (Brand 2014:

581); however, one may ask whether such a strategy can be sustainable in the long term. Breaking this mechanism presupposes a different growth model based on private-sector initiative, vibrant entrepreneurship, and effective policies to counter the labor market skills mismatch. To be successful, these policies will have to be developed in an institution-sensitive way and will have to find ways to provoke institutional change through processes of downward causation.

Recommendations proposed by Mahroum et al. (2013: 127–128) include shaping institutions towards more entrepreneurial vibrancy, e.g., through education reforms for more problem-solving and critical-thinking skills, business and management skill courses, awareness-raising activities, or an "innovation festival." Doing so might eventually strengthen the conditions for Schumpeterian creative destruction, but this kind of institutional change, if successful, will take time.

The relatively high number of engineers in Jordan and significant unemployment among them, combined with a scarcity of technicians with mid-level skills, suggests the need for extending the TVET system (Mahroum et al. 2013: 97–98). However, the reputational bias in favor of higher education and against TVET (Mahroum et al. 2013: 30) is an institutional fact that cannot be ignored by rule-setting policymaking. Instead of setting up institution-competing rules by promoting TVET, pursuing a policy built on institution-reinforcing rules such as enriching higher education with practical skills demanded on the labor market through dual-study courses at universities in collaboration with enterprises, as is being pursued to some degree at the German-Jordanian University, seems more promising. Such a dual-study approach can serve to create closer linkages between higher education and workplace needs (Kharabsheh et al. 2011: 222) and may thus provide a way to reduce the skills mismatch without competing with firmly anchored institutions such as preferences for academic education.

Reforming the subsidy system will be highly difficult because doing so touches upon questions of political stability. Nevertheless, subsidy reform is not only a question of fiscal sustainability but a question of the external consistency of the Jordanian regulation regime with transnational transformative processes in the form of IFI-sponsored structural adjustment. In early 2018, the Jordanian government lifted subsidies on one type of bread (but not on others), marking the first major bread price hike since 1996, and introduced cash transfers to offset the impact on poor parts of the population. In addition, the government announced tax increases in the wake of an IMF-sponsored stabilization package designed to curb the Jordanian state's high public debt that has accumulated, in part, due to expansionist policies such as public job creation and subsidies in previous years. Yet, in mid-2018, austerity measures under the IMF-sponsored structural adjustment program such as tax increases and subsidy cuts led to protests and the resignation of the country's prime minister (Al-Khalidi 2018; France 24 2018a, b).

In terms of Jordan's regional policy, adapting policymaking more to the context of regional-level socioeconomic regulation seems worthwhile. The thoughts on regional development through the smart specialization approach used in European regions apply by analogy (see Sect. 4.1.5). In particular, the institutional and governance-related problems found in lagging European regions (Trippl et al. 2018) can be expected to be found in Jordan and maybe even more severely so. However, given the opportunities of the smart specialization approach in improving the institutional context of regional economies (Benner 2018), it is likely that some regions of the country might benefit from implementing the approach. In particular, a region such as Irbid with its Yarmouk University could provide an interesting case to pioneer the approach, similar to Tunisia's Sfax region. Paralleling the role of intermediate organizations in mediating the necessary public-private prioritization and policymaking process found by Benner (2018) in some European economies, JEDCO could function as a major driver of the approach in Irbid and other suitable regions.

Interviewees stressed that the emergent entrepreneurial dynamic is limited to urban regions. Extending it to rural regions of the country was considered necessary by interviewees, given that labor market problems such as high unemployment among youth and low female labor market participation are even more severe there than in urban regions. In addition, interviewees saw a widespread unwillingness of inhabitants of rural regions to move to another region to find a job. Hence, there seems to be a need for rural programs to foster entrepreneurship that will have to address broader questions of socio-institutional regulation and notably entrepreneurial attitudes.

Reforming the Jordanian regulation regime both in terms of prescriptive rules and in terms of institutions will be a long, uncertain, and politically difficult process. Given the Jordanian economy's weaknesses (such as its dependence on foreign rents and the government's difficult fiscal situation) as well as its strengths (such as the comparatively liberal approach towards the private sector and pockets of competitive industries such as ICT and pharmaceuticals), there may be a possibility to do so through evolutionary and incremental change. Overcoming the entrenched public-sector elite's hostility to reform will be imperative though. Here, too, institution-sensitive policy reforms will be necessary.

4.3 Learning from the Tunisian and Jordanian Cases

While the case studies in Tunisia and Jordan generally confirmed the major elements of the regulation framework for core Arab economies proposed in Chap. 3, each of the two cases revealed some peculiarities. On a conceptual level, these peculiarities emphasize the need to refine the regulation framework for each national case (and maybe even for subnational, i.e., regional cases) and highlight that the generic regulation framework is indeed a framework that requires adaptation to the specific case at hand. Nevertheless, both cases studied confirm the validity of the most salient elements and tendencies in socioeconomic regulation in core Arab economies.

Comparing the generic, stylized regulation framework for core Arab economies (Fig. 3.3) with the refined regulation frameworks for Benalist Tunisia (Fig. 4.1) and Jordan (Fig. 4.2) yields the following observations:

- Within the *structure of production*, structural deficiencies such as labor market segmentation, low female labor-force participation, high youth unemployment particularly among higher-education graduates, and an inflated public sector and limited industrialization are elements of the generic regulation framework that are well supported by the Tunisian and Jordanian cases.
- The *pattern of consumption* characterized by crypto-welfare policies including supply-side subsidies for goods such as energy and foodstuffs as well as government service provision is another set of components of the regulation regime confirmed in both Tunisia and Jordan. While both cases share the importance of their diaspora, trends are different in that Europe is the main destination of the Tunisian diaspora while the Jordanian diaspora is to a large degree oriented towards GCC countries.
- On *prescriptive rules*, the tendencies identified in the generic regulation framework are confirmed to some degree, but notable differences exist between the two cases studied. With its stringent labor laws, Tunisia confirms the generic regulation framework in this regard, while Jordan features somewhat more liberal but selective labor legislation. Both countries exhibit some pattern of segmentation in their investment regimes. Public employment guarantees in both countries were rather implicit, but in Jordan they were effectively restricted to the East Banker part of the population. A major difference is the protectionist legislation effectively shielding the business interests of the politically connected business elite in Benalist Tunisia from competition, an element of crony capitalism that may be found in other core Arab economies but not in Jordan, arguably due to the fact of the relatively clear-cut dichotomy of a politically connected East Banker elite dominating the public sector and a Palestinian-origin elite dominating the private sector. While connections between these two elites may exist, they are arguably much weaker than was the case under the intricate nexus between political and economic power found in Benalist Tunisia.
- On the level of *institutions*, expectations towards crypto-welfare policies including supply-side subsidies and public-sector employment, as well as preferences for public-sector over private-sector employment, are at the core of the generic regulation regime in core Arab economies and are to a large degree confirmed in the cases of Tunisia and Jordan, although aspirations for public employment in Jordan are effectively limited to the East Banker population. Further, a preference for higher education over TVET is observable. Despite the different political systems and historical traditions in Benalist Tunisia and Jordan, respectively, both countries witness the tendency of seeing the state as the main driver of development rather than the private sector, although one might expect that this was less the case over time in Jordan due to the relative freedom left to the private sector there.
- One detail of the case studies is noteworthy for the transition towards an eventual new regulation system. In both countries, entrepreneurial dynamics seem to gain ground. Even if the emerging entrepreneurialism is limited to pockets of urban youth in agglomerations such as Tunis and Amman and to sectors such as ICT, there is reason to believe that the unideological, pragmatic, and opportunity-

driven approach Amin et al. (2012: 16) suggest contributes to long-term institutional change through upward causation. The insights gained in the case studies that expectations towards private-sector employment are becoming somewhat weaker points into the same direction. However, even if these phenomena imply nascent processes of institutional change, they will have to be sustained and reinforced to be able to contribute to the establishment of a more private-sector-led regulation regime.

- Finally, in terms of *organizations*, both cases confirm the generic regulation framework but with gradual differences. The authoritarian nation-state under Ben Ali was fairly strong and related to a well-established business elite connected to the regime. The Jordanian nation-state, however, was marked by a less secure position that may have limited the state's ability to extend its power into the economy to a degree comparable to Benalist Tunisia. This may be a reason why, in contrast to co-opted business associations in Benalist Tunisia, economic chambers and business associations in Jordan could secure a fairly strong position. The public sector in both countries – as in core Arab economies in general – can be seen as inflated. The Jordanian case, however, is particular due to the comparatively isolated role of the East Banker elite in the public sector that does not extend to the private sector.

In terms of policy, parallels between the Tunisian and Jordanian cases are visible and may be due in part to the two countries' similar situation as semi-industrialized small open economies seeking to deepen their knowledge and innovation intensity. One of these parallels is that in both countries, programs supporting innovative upgrading of the economy (PMN in Tunisia, SRTD in Jordan) were pursued and were supported by the EU. Another parallel is that both countries are pursuing some kind of territorial innovation policy, Tunisia with its *pôles de compétitivité* and constituent *technopôles* as well as its CITs and Jordan with its technology parks such as EHSC and KHBP. When it comes to detailed policy design, however, different approaches are observable. While the Tunisian *pôles de compétitivité* scheme was basically a comprehensive cluster policy designed in a top-down way (Lehmann and Benner 2015), cluster initiatives in Jordan have grown through bottom-up industrial initiative (Mahroum et al. 2013: 23; Seidel et al. 2009: 29–30). Still, "cluster" networks in Tunisia are somewhat of a bottom-up complement to top-down designed technoparks (Benner forthcoming). In Jordan, EHSC and KHBP can be understood as a top-down technopark policy similar to the Tunisian *pôle* architecture (Mahroum et al. 2013: 23).

On the regional level, both case studies show that there is a certain potential for anchoring newer approaches of regional innovation policy based on regional knowledge bases (Asheim et al. 2017) and the diversification of regional economies along the lines of related variety (Asheim et al. 2011; Frenken et al. 2007). While simply transferring policies from abroad is not advisable, learning from the European experience with the smart specialization approach could prove valuable for regions marked by a relatively dynamic regional innovation system. The approach is basically a method for using public-private collaboration to set regional policy priorities according to the regional socioeconomic context and can be combined with horizontal policies in the broader notion of smart experimentation (Benner 2014b, 2017b, 2018, forthcoming). Suitable regions to introduce the approach in a context-specific and institution-sensitive way could be those marked by comparatively strong universities and bottom-up cluster initiatives. In Tunisia, Sfax could serve as a pilot region, while in Jordan, prima facie Irbid seems suitable.

On the macro-level, both countries are characterized by a general *infitah* policy orientation, although in historically different contexts. While in Tunisia, *infitah* was a policy turn after a less-than-successful and rather short period of Arab socialism, the Hashemite regime in Jordan pursued a general penchant for relative economic liberalism over time and may have found that the country's precarious situation marked by its lack of natural resources, its location in a geopolitically unstable environment, and its reliance on rents required international trade openness. While Tunisia's international opening went along with far-reaching reliance on European markets, Jordan's trade policy was somewhat more diversified and consistent with its geopolitical orientation towards the United States, not least in the context of the Israel-Jordan peace treaty and concomitant economic support schemes such as the QIZs. Still, in both countries, international trade and investment policies exhibit some kind of segmentation, in the case of Tunisia the onshore/offshore dichotomy and in the case of Jordan the mosaic of various special economic and free-trade zones.

Both countries are under fiscal pressure and subject to transnational transformative processes within the framework of IFI-sponsored structural adjustment. The underlying fiscal pressures underscore the fundamental unsustainability of the old Arab social contract and are thus compatible with the insights gained through the generic regulation framework. Both Tunisia and Jordan find themselves in a situation where they will have to limit public employment provision and supply-side subsidies, effectively ending crypto-welfare policies pursued for decades, and both countries find it politically difficult to do so. Hence, the transition towards a new, more sustainable and internally and externally consistent regulation regime will be a challenging process in both countries. Still, some incipient changes on the institutional level of both economies give reason for careful optimism, provided that institution-sensitive reform policies adapted to the peculiar context of both countries can be designed and implemented to support the institutional changes needed.

References

Achy L (2010) Trading high unemployment for bad jobs: employment challenges in the Maghreb. Carnegie Papers. Carnegie Endowment for International Peace, Washington, DC. http://carnegieendowment.org/files/labor_maghreb.pdf. (10.10.2013)

Adly A, Khatib L (2014) Reforming the entrepreneurship ecosystem in post-revolutionary Egypt and Tunisia. Center on Democracy, Development and the Rule of Law/Center for International Private Enterprise, Stanford/Washington, DC. http://cddrl.fsi.stanford.edu/sites/default/files/

Reforming_the_Entrepreneurship_Ecosystem_in_Post-Revolutionary_Egypt_and_Tunisia-_
   Amr_Adly.pdf. (13.04.2015)
Agence de Promotion de l'Industrie et de l'Innovation (ed) (2016) Les Technopoles en Tunisie.
   http://www.tunisieindustrie.nat.tn/fr/doc.asp?mcat=16&mrub=157. (09.11.2016)
Agence de Promotion de l'Industrie et de l'Innovation (ed) (n.d.) Guide de l'innovation: Nous
   vous accompagnons pour réussir. http://www.tunisianindustry.nat.tn/fr/download/innovation.
   pdf. (09.11.2016)
Al-Khalidi S (2018) Jordan ends bread subsidy, doubling some prices, to help state finances.
   https://www.reuters.com/article/us-jordan-economy-subsidies-bread/jordan-ends-bread-sub-
   sidy-doubling-some-prices-to-help-state-finances-idUSKBN1FF2CP. (27.01.2018)
Altenburg T (2011) Industrial policy in developing countries: overview and lessons from seven
   country cases. DIE Discussion Paper 4/2011. Deutsches Institut für Entwicklungspolitik,
   Bonn.   http://www.die-gdi.de/CMS-Homepage/openwebcms3.nsf/(ynDK_contentByKey)/
   ANES-8EAHQ3/$FILE/DP%204.2011.pdf. (20.08.2012)
Amara T, Laessing U (2017) Tunisia resists calls to cut public wage bill and subsidies in 2018.
   https://af.reuters.com/article/africaTech/idAFL8N1MS3UA. (02.01.2018)
Amin M, Assaad R, Al-Baharna N, Derviş K, Desai RM, Dhillon NS, Galal A, Ghanem H, Graham
   C, Kaufmann D, Kharas H, Page J, Salehi-Isfahani D, Sierra K, Yousef TM (2012) After the
   spring: economic transformations in the Arab world. Oxford University Press, Oxford
Asheim B, Boschma R, Cooke P (2011) Constructing regional advantage: platform policies based
   on related variety and differentiated knowledge bases. Reg Stud 45(7):893–904
Asheim B, Grillitsch M, Trippl M (2017) Smart specialization as an innovation-driven strategy
   for economic diversification: examples from Scandinavian regions. In: Radosevic S, Curaj A,
   Gheorgiu R, Andreescu R, Wage I (eds) Advances in the theory and practice of smart specialization. Elsevier, London, pp 74–99
Aubert J-E, Taha T, Utz A (2013) Local innovation dynamics: examples and lessons from the
   Arab world. In: Cornell University, INSEAD, World Intellectual Property Organization
   (eds) The global innovation index 2013: the local dynamics of innovation. World Intellectual
   Property Organization/Cornell University/INSEAD, Geneva/Ithaca/Fontainebleau, pp 99–106.
   http://www.wipo.int/export/sites/www/freepublications/en/economics/gii/gii_2013.pdf.
   (29.08.2014)
Barnell O (2017) Seven years after Arab Spring revolt, Tunisia's future remains uncertain. http://
   www.france24.com/en/20171217-tunisia-seven-years-after-arab-spring-revolution-protests-
   economic-uncertainty. (02.01.2018)
Bathelt H (1994) Die Bedeutung der Regulationstheorie in der wirtschaftsgeographischen
   Forschung. (The significance of regulation approaches for economic geography). Geogr Z
   82(2):63–90
Ben Abdessalem H, El Elj M (2011) Innovation in Tunisia: sectorial analysis. Paper presented
   at the Journées de Microéconomie de Sousse, 2–3 June 2011, Sousse. http://jma2014.fr/fich-
   iers2011/136/Innovation%20in%20Tunisia-%20JMA%202011.pdf. (12.12.2013)
Ben Miled-M'rabet N (n.d.) Dossier: Le système national d'innovation en Tunisie. http://www.
   tunisianindustry.nat.tn/fr/download/ci/innovation.pdf. (10.10.2013)
Benner M (2012) Clusterpolitik: Wege zur Verknüpfung von Theorie und politischer Umsetzung.
   (Cluster policy: ways to link theory and political implementation). LIT, Münster
Benner M (2014a) Decentralised regional development policy in Tunisia: a new beginning after
   the "Arab Spring"? In: International Reports 06/2014, pp 31–50. http://www.kas.de/wf/doc/
   kas_38099-544-2-30.pdf?140618133239. (21.06.2014)
Benner M (2014b) From smart specialisation to smart experimentation: building a new theoret-
   ical framework for regional policy of the European Union. Z Wirtsch (Ger J Econ Geogr)
   58(1):33–49
Benner M (2015) Europa und der Maghreb: Von der Nachbarschaft zur Wirtschaftspartnerschaft.
   (Europe and the Maghreb: from neighborhood to economic partnership). In: Neuss B, Nötzold

A (eds) The Southern Mediterranean: challenges to the european foreign and security policy. Nomos, Baden-Baden, pp 57–82

Benner M (2017a) From clusters to smart specialization: tourism in institution-sensitive regional development policies. Economies 5(3):26. http://www.mdpi.com/2227-7099/5/3/26/pdf. (29.07.2017)

Benner M (2017b) Smart specialisation and cluster emergence: building blocks for evolutionary regional policies. In: Hassink R, Fornahl D (eds) The life cycle of clusters: a policy perspective. Edward Elgar, Camberley, pp 151–172

Benner M (2017c) The legacy of Sidi Bouzid: overcoming spatial inequalities in Tunisia. In: Krížek D, Záhorík J (eds) Beyond the 'Arab Spring' in North Africa: macro and micro perspectives. Lexington, Lanham, pp 47–65

Benner M (2018) Smart specialization and institutional context: towards a process of institutional discovery and change. Papers in Economic Geography and Innovation Studies 2018/03. http://www-sre.wu.ac.at/sre-disc/geo-disc-2018_03.pdf. (14.11.2018)

Benner M (forthcoming) Cluster policy in Tunisia: from institutional voids to smart specialization. In: Knedlik T, Wohlmuth K (eds) African Development perspectives yearbook 2018: science, technology and innovation policies for inclusive growth in Africa. In preparation

Brand LA (2014) Jordan. In: Lust E (ed) The Middle East, 13th edn. CQ Press, Thousand Oaks, pp 564–589

Cammett M (2007) Business-government relations and industrial change: the politics of upgrading in Morocco and Tunisia. World Dev 35(11):1889–1903

Cammett M (2014) The political economy of development in the Middle East. In: Lust E (ed) The Middle East, 13th edn. CQ Press, Thousand Oaks, pp 161–208

Cornell University, INSEAD, WIPO (2017) The global innovation index 2017: innovation feeding the world. Cornell University/INSEAD/WIPO, Ithaca/Fontainebleau/Geneva

Dahmani F (2017) Après avoir longtemps tergiversé, la Tunisie ouvre son ciel. http://www.jeuneafrique.com/501290/economie/apres-avoir-longtemps-tergiverse-la-tunisie-ouvre-son-ciel. (05.05.2018)

Dahmani F (2018a) L'augmentation de la TVA provoque un tollé en Tunisie, (TVA increase provokes an outcry in Tunisia). http://www.jeuneafrique.com/507291/economie/laugmentation-de-la-tva-provoque-un-tolle-en-tunisie (10.01.2018)

Dahmani F (2018b) Tunisie: les manifestations contre la cherté de la vie tournent à l'affrontement violent, (Tunisia: protests against the cost of living turn violent). http://www.jeuneafrique.com/508376/politique/tunisie-les-manifestations-contre-la-cherte-de-la-vie-tournent-a-laf-frontement-violent. (10.01.2018)

Department of Statistics (ed) (2017) Press/1st Q. 2017. http://dos.gov.jo/dos_home_e/main/archive/Unemp/2017/1stQ.pdf. (08.01.2018)

Diop N, Ghali S (2012) Are Jordan and Tunisia's exports becoming more technologically sophisticated? analysis using highly disaggregated export databases. The World Bank, Washington, DC. http://documents.worldbank.org/curated/en/716281468312890526/pdf/672480NWP00PUB07863B00FEBRUARY15NEW.pdf. (20.05.2017)

Erdle S (2011) Industrial policy in Tunisia. DIE Discussion Paper 1/2011. Deutsches Institut für Entwicklungspolitik, Bonn. http://www.die-gdi.de/CMSHomepage/openwebcms3.nsf/(ynDK_contentByKey)/ANES-8DEE7C/$FILE/DP%201.2011.pdf. (20.08.2012)

European Commission (ed) (2017a) Trade: policy: countries and regions. Jordan. http://ec.europa.eu/trade/policy/countries-and-regions/countries/jordan. (18.02.2018)

European Commission (ed) (2017b) Trade: policy: countries and regions. Tunisia. http://ec.europa.eu/trade/policy/countries-and-regions/countries/tunisia. (20.12.2017)

France 24 (ed) (2018a) Jordan PM Mulki resigns amid anti-government protests. http://www.france24.com/en/20180604-jordan-king-abdullah-resign-summons-pm-mulki-over-anti-government-protests. (04.06.2018)

France 24 (ed) (2018b) Jordan's next PM vows to withdraw controversial tax bill. http://www.france24.com/en/20180607-jordan-next-pm-omar-al-razzaz-vows-withdrawal-controversial-tax-bill-protests. (07.06.2018)

Frenken K, van Oort F, Verburg T (2007) Related variety, unrelated variety and regional economic growth. Reg Stud 41(5):S. 685–S. 697

Ghali S, Rezgui S (2015) Structural transformation and industrial policy in selected Southern Mediterranean countries: Tunisia. In: Forum Euroméditerranéan des Instituts de Sciences Économiques (ed) Structural transformation and industrial policy: a comparative analysis of Egypt, Morocco, Tunisia and Turkey and case studies. European Investment Bank, Luxembourg, pp 39–68. http://www.femise.org/wp-content/uploads/2015/06/femip_study_structural_transformation_and_industrial_policy_en1.pdf. (10.06.2015)

Global Entrepreneurship Research Association (ed) (2017) Global entrepreneurship monitor: global report 2016/17. http://www.gemconsortium.org/report/49812. (18.05.2017)

Glückler J, Bathelt H (2017) Institutional context and innovation. In: Bathelt H, Cohendet P, Henn S, Simon L (eds) The Elgar companion to innovation and knowledge creation. Elgar, Cheltenham, Northampton, pp 121–137

Glückler J, Lenz R (2016) How institutions moderate the effectiveness of regional policy: a framework and research agenda. Invest Reg – J Reg Res 36(2016):255–277

Granovetter M (1985) Economic action and social structure: the problem of embeddedness. Am J Sociol 91(3):481–510

Hazboun W (2008) Beaches, ruins, resorts: the politics of tourism in the Arab world. University of Minnesota Press, Minneapolis

Hertog S (2016) Is there an Arab variety of capitalism? Economic Research Forum Working Paper No. 1068. https://erf.org.eg/wp-content/uploads/2016/12/1068.pdf. (02.03.2017)

Higher Council for Science and Technology (ed) (2013) National innovation strategy 2013–2017. http://www.hcst.gov.jo/sites/default/files/national_innovation_strategy_final.pdf. (12.01.2018)

International Labour Organization (ed) (2016) Local economic development strategy for Irbid Governorate: 2016–2018. International Labour Organization, Beirut. http://www.ilo.org/wcmsp5/groups/public/%2D%2D-arabstates/%2D%2D-ro-beirut/documents/publication/wcms_456503.pdf. (19.01.2018)

International Monetary Fund (ed) (2016) Tunisia: selected issued. IMF Country Report No. 16/47. http://www.imf.org/external/pubs/ft/scr/2016/cr1647.pdf. (12.02.2016)

Irbid Development Area (ed) (2018) Irbid Development Area (IDA). http://www.ida.jo/default.aspx. (10.02.2018)

Jamal A, Khatib L (2014) Actors, public opinion, and participation. In: Lust E (ed) The Middle East, 13th edn. CQ Press, Thousand Oaks, pp 246–286

Jordan Enterprise Development Corporation (ed) (2018a) About JEDCO: about us. http://www.jedco.gov.jo/Pages/viewpage.aspx?pageID=147. (15.01.2018)

Jordan Enterprise Development Corporation (ed) (2018b) Projects and projects for emerging enterprises: JEDCO 2016. http://www.jedco.gov.jo/Pages/viewpage.aspx?pageID=293. (15.01.2018)

Jordan Enterprise Development Corporation (ed) (2018c) Projects and projects for new entrepreneurs: JEDCO 2016. http://www.jedco.gov.jo/Pages/viewpage.aspx?pageID=291. (15.01.2018)

Josua M (2016) If you can't include them, exclude them: countering the Arab uprisings in Algeria and Jordan. GIGA Working Paper No. 286. https://www.giga-hamburg.de/de/system/files/publications/wp286_josua.pdf. (30.05.2016)

Kanaan T, Hanania M (2009) The disconnect between education, job growth, and employment in Jordan. In: Dhillon N, Yousef T (eds) Generation in waiting: the unfulfilled promise of young people in the Middle East. Brookings, Washington, DC, pp 142–165

Kelley D, Singer S, Herrington M (2016) Global entrepreneurship monitor: 2015/16 global report. http://www.gemconsortium.org/report/49480. (18.05.2017)

Kharabsheh R, Magableh IK, Arabiyat TS (2011) Obstacles of success of technology parks: the case of Jordan. Int J Econ Fin 3(6):219–226

King Hussein Business Park (ed) (2018) Tenants. http://www.businesspark-jo.com/en-us/KHBP-Community/Tenants. (17.12.2018)

Lehmann T, Benner M (2015): Cluster policy in the light of institutional context – a comparative study of transition countries. Adm Sci 5(4):188–212. http://www.mdpi.com/2076-3387/5/4/188/pdf. (05.11.2015)

M'Henni H, Deniozos D (2012) Erawatch country reports 2012. Tunisia. http://erawatch.jrc.ec.europa.eu/erawatch/export/sites/default/galleries/generic_files/file_0432.pdf. (26.08.2014)

M'Henni H, Ben Youssef A, Elaheebocus N, Ragni L (2013) Are technoparks high tech fantasies? lessons from the Tunisian experience. MPRA Paper No. 46183. https://mpra.ub.uni-muenchen.de/46183/1/MPRA_paper_46183.pdf. (11.07.2016)

Mahroum S, Al-Bdour JM, Scott E Shouqar S, Arafat A (2013) Jordan: the atlas of islamic world science and innovation country case study. https://royalsociety.org/~/media/policy/projects/atlas-islamic-world/atlas-jordan.pdf. (12.01.2018)

Marzouk H (2017) Tataouine: recrutement de mille agents au sein de la Société d'environnement, (Tataouine: recruitment of one thousand staff at the environment company). http://www.leconomistemaghrebin.com/2017/06/13/tataouine-recrutement-mille-agents-societe-environnement. (30.12.2017)

Mattes H (2016) Entwicklung der tunesischen Binnenregionen: Hohe Erwartungen – schwierige Umsetzung. (The development of Tunisian interior regions: high expectations – difficult implementation) GIGA Focus Nahost No. 1. https://www.giga-hamburg.de/de/system/files/publications/gf_nahost_1601.pdf. (28.04.2016)

Medinilla Aldana A, El Fassi S (2016) Tackling regional inequalities in Tunisia. ECDPM Briefing Note No. 84. http://ecdpm.org/wp-content/uploads/BN-84-Tackling-regional-inequalities-Tunisia-ECDPM-2016.pdf. (24.06.2016)

Ministère de l'Industrie, de l'Énergie et des Mines (ed) (2014) Parcs d'activités industrielles et technologiques en Tunisie. http://www.parcs-activites.tn/parcs-activites.html. (15.11.2016)

Muasher M (2011) A decade of struggling reform efforts in Jordan: the resilience of the rentier system. Carnegie Papers. Carnegie Endowment for International Peace, Washington, DC. http://carnegieendowment.org/files/jordan_reform.pdf. (10.05.2014)

Noland M, Pack H (2007) The Arab economies in a changing world. Peterson Institute for International Economics, Washington, DC

Observatoire National de l'Emploi et des Qualifications (ed) (2013) Rapport Annuel sur: Le Marché du Travail en Tunisie: Novembre 2013, (Annual report on the labor market in Tunisia: November 2013). http://www.emploi.gov.tn/uploads/tx_elypublication/Rapport_annuel_decembre_2013.pdf. (11.10.2017)

OECD (ed) (2012a) OECD investment policy reviews: Tunisia. Organisation for Economic Cooperation and Development, Paris

OECD (ed) (2012b) Promoting graduate entrepreneurship in Tunisian universities. OECD Local Economic and Employment Development (LEED) Working Papers 2012/18. Organisation for Economic Co-operation and Development, Paris

OECD (ed) (2013) OECD investment policy reviews: Jordan. Organisation for Economic Cooperation and Development, Paris

OECD (ed) (2014) Women in business 2014: accelerating entrepreneurship in the Middle East and North Africa region. Organisation for Economic Co-operation and Development, Paris

OECD (ed) (2015) Tunisia: a reform agenda to support competitiveness and inclusive growth. Organisation for Economic Development and Cooperation, Paris. http://www.oecd.org/countries/tunisia/Tunisia-a-reform-agenda-to-support-competitiveness-and-inclusive-growth.pdf. (02.06.2015)

OECD (ed) (2018) OECD economic surveys: Tunisia: economic assessment. Organisation for Economic Development and Cooperation, Paris

OECD, IDRC (2013) New entrepreneurs and high performance enterprises in the Middle East and North Africa. Organisation for Economic Cooperation and Development, Paris

Peck J, Theodore N (2007) Variegated capitalism. Prog Hum Geogr 31(6):731–772

Richards A, Waterbury J (2008) A political economy of the Middle East, 3rd edn. Westview Press, Boulder

Rijkers B, Freund C, Nucifora A (2014) All in the family: state capture in Tunisia. Policy Research Working Paper No. 6810. The World Bank, Washington, DC. http://www-wds.worldbank. org/external/default/WDSContentServer/IW3P/IB/2014/03/25/000158349_20140325092905/ Rendered/PDF/WPS6810.pdf. (28.03.2014)

Rivlin P (2009) Arab economies in the twenty-first century. Cambridge University Press, New York

Rodríguez-Pose A, Hardy D (2014) Technology and industrial parks in emerging countries: panacea or pipedream? Springer, Cham, Heidelberg, New York, Dordrecht, London

Royal Scientific Society (ed) (2017) Welcome. http://www.rss.jo. (16.01.2018)

Ryan CR (2010) Jordan. In: Angrist MP (ed) Politics and society in the contemporary Middle East. Lynne Rienner, Boulder, pp 311–333

Seidel U, Domröse W, Meier zu Köcker G (2009) Study on the National Innovation System in Jordan: final report. VDI/VDE Innovation + Technik GmbH, Berlin. http://www.jedco.gov. jo/joomla/images/international_reports/Innovation%20Study%20-%20Jordan%20-%20Final. pdf. (01.12.2014)

Smadi R, Tsipouri L (2012) Erawatch country reports 2012: Jordan. http://erawatch.jrc.ec.europa. eu/erawatch/export/sites/default/galleries/generic_files/file_0454.pdf. (26.08.2014)

Sultan SS, Soete L (2012) Innovation for development: the case of Jordan. Dirasat: Admin Sci 39(2):321–327

Trippl M, Zukauskaite E, Healy A (2018) Shaping smart specialisation: the role of place-specific factors in advanced, intermediate and less-developed European regions. Papers in Economic Geography and Innovation Studies 2018/01. http://www-sre.wu.ac.at/sre-disc/geo-disc-2018_01.pdf. (14.11.2018)

UNRWA (ed) (n.d.) Where we work: Jordan. https://www.unrwa.org/where-we-work/jordan. (20.02.2018)

World Bank (ed) (2009) From privilege to competition: unlocking private-led growth in the Middle East and North Africa. The World Bank, Washington, DC. http://siteresources.worldbank.org/ INTMENA/Resources/Privilege_complete_final.pdf. (08.12.2013)

World Bank (ed) (2011) Poor places, thriving people: how the Middle East and North Africa can rise above spatial disparities. The World Bank, Washington, DC. https://openknowledge. worldbank.org/bitstream/handle/10986/2255/589970PUB0ID181UBLIC109780821383216. pdf?sequence=1. (19.02.2014)

World Bank (ed) (2013) Jobs for shared prosperity: time for action in the Middle East and North Africa. The World Bank, Washington, DC. http://www-wds.worldbank.org/external/default/ WDSContentServer/WDSP/IB/2013/04/12/000445729_20130412114115/Rendered/PDF/724 690v40Full00Prosperity0full0book.pdf. (09.11.2013)

World Bank (ed) (2014a) Jobs or privileges: unleashing the employment potential of the Middle East and North Africa. The World Bank, Washington, DC. http://www-wds.worldbank.org/ external/default/WDSContentServer/WDSP/IB/2014/07/16/000333037_20140716151958/ Rendered/PDF/888790MNA0Box382141B00PUBLIC0.pdf. (10.10.2014)

World Bank (ed) (2014b) MENA quarterly economic brief: predictions, perceptions and economic reality. The World Bank, Washington, DC. http://www-wds.worldbank.org/external/default/ WDSContentServer/WDSP/IB/2014/08/06/000470435_20140806105353/Rendered/PDF/898 440REVISED00ue030JULY020140FINAL.pdf. (09.08.2014)

World Bank (ed) (2014c) The unfinished revolution: bringing opportunity, good jobs and greater wealth to all Tunisians. The World Bank, Washington, DC. http://www-wds.worldbank.org/ external/default/WDSContentServer/WDSP/IB/2014/09/16/000456286_20140916144712/ Rendered/PDF/861790DPR0P12800Box385314B00PUBLIC0.pdf. (27.09.2014)

World Bank (ed) (2015) MENA economic monitor: towards a new social contract. The World Bank, Washington, DC. http://www-wds.worldbank.org/external/default/WDSContentServer/WDSP/IB/2015/04/09/000456286_20150409170931/Rendered/PDF/956500PUB0REVI0201 50391416B00OUO090.pdf. (16.04.2015)

World Economic Forum (ed) (2017) The travel and tourism competitiveness report 2017: paving the way for a more sustainable and inclusive future. World Economic Forum, Geneva. http://www3.weforum.org/docs/WEF_TTCR_2017_web_0401.pdf. (26.05.2017)

World Tourism Organization (ed) (2017) UNWTO tourism highlights: 2017 edition. https://www.e-unwto.org/doi/pdf/10.18111/9789284419029. (13.02.2018)

Chapter 5
Towards Integrated Strategies to Promote Private-Sector Growth

Abstract The chapter summarizes the results, proposes answers to the research questions, and provides suggestions for further research.

Keywords New Arab social contract · Policy implications · Research agenda

The preceding chapters have attempted to propose answers to the research questions introduced in Chap. 1 and applied the conceptual perspectives proposed in Chap. 3 to the cases of Tunisia and Jordan. The present, concluding chapter summarizes these findings, draws stylized conclusions, and discusses policy implications for institution-sensitive reform agendas in core Arab economies based on the wider socioeconomic regulation perspective taken in this book. The chapter closes by summarizing what the previous chapters contributed to answering the research questions introduced in Chap. 1 and by laying out needs and fields of further research.

5.1 From Old to New Modes of Socioeconomic Regulation in Core Arab Economies

The need for core Arab economies to develop a new Arab social contract is a conclusion frequently found in the literature on economic policy and reforms in the Middle East and North Africa (e.g., World Bank 2015). However, what precisely this means is much less clear.

The literature on Middle Eastern political economy and reports by international organizations and think tanks are full of reform proposals which typically include, inter alia, liberalizing labor markets, limiting public employment, and abolishing supply-side subsidies while introducing need-based cash transfers in exchange and encouraging private-sector growth and entrepreneurship through entrepreneurship training and improved access to finance for start-ups (e.g., African Development Bank 2011; OECD 2012a, b, 2013, 2014, 2015; OECD and IDRC 2013; World

© Springer Nature Switzerland AG 2020

M. Benner, *A New Arab Social Contract?*, Economic Geography,
https://doi.org/10.1007/978-3-030-19270-9_5

Bank 2007, 2009, 2011, 2012a, b, 2013, 2014a, d). While many of these proposals may be well-founded and do indeed feature as parts of the policy menu elaborated in Sect. 3.4 aimed at moving core Arab economies towards a new, more sustainable, and efficient regulation regime, isolated reform proposals often lack sensitivity to institutions and socioeconomic context. What is needed is a process of policy design that considers institutional realities in the regulation regime of the old Arab social contract in general and in its specific shape in the country (or even region) in question. Such a policy process would need to define adequate and effective policies to institute more efficient and sustainable prescriptive rules that are either consistent with existing institutions (such as widely held preferences or expectations) or able to change institutions, at least in the long run. Policy reforms might therefore particularly focus on institution-reinforcing rules or institution-circumventing rules. For example, in the case of institutionally anchored low reputation and stigma of TVET, policies aiming to strengthen vocational schools qualify as institution-competing rules and can be expected to have low chances of success. The alternative policy of establishing dual-study courses in HEIs may provide a more institution-sensitive reform policy because it is consistent with institutions and qualifies as an example for an institution-reinforcing rule. Another example for the point made here is that offering entrepreneurship trainings for graduates or students may not be enough to significantly raise the propensity for entrepreneurship in core Arab economies as long as institutions such as high-risk adversity and a preference for public-sector employment persist. Tackling institutional change through processes of downward causation should be considered as part of a comprehensive reform agenda but will be difficult to achieve, require indirect and abstract measures such as awareness-raising, and take time. Further research applying approaches taken from behavioral economics may be useful to identify policy options to embark upon downward causation of institutional change if and where appropriate.

The nascent but still limited processes of institutional change on the microlevel that became apparent during the case studies, notably the emerging entrepreneurial dynamism among urban youth or weakening expectations towards public employment, could eventually lead to a gradual and limited readjustment of the regulation regime even in the absence of major reform policies. Given the dangers of political sclerosis and inertia, this is a realistic scenario that calls for careful optimism even under difficult circumstances. Nevertheless, policy-driven reforms to complement and support nascent processes of upward causation of institutional change are preferable.

Reform policies aimed at the transition towards a new, more sustainable, and efficient regulation regime should build on the strengths and opportunities available in the economies of core Arab countries. For instance, the availability of large shares of students in the social sciences and humanities in Tunisia can be a point of departure for the emergence of social innovations and growth trajectories based on a knowledge base in social sciences and humanities. Designing platform policies to seize the opportunities of the specific kind of knowledge base available in a country such as Tunisia or Jordan could achieve more context sensitivity of reform agendas (Asheim et al. 2011). A regulation perspective that acknowledges contextual specifics of an economy calls for seizing the economic opportunities inherent to the economy's peculiar knowledge base instead of applying generic, one-size-fits-all recommendations. For example, rather than calling on students to change their interests from the social sciences and humanities towards engineering, policy should turn its attention to how to use cultural and creative skills inherent to knowledge bases built on humanities or social sciences as a driver of economic development (Benner 2017). Such a policy that facilitates the commercialization of assets in the specific knowledge base available in a cross-sectoral perspective, i.e., a platform policy (Asheim et al. 2011), would be more sensitive to prevailing institutional patterns such as students' preferences or attitudes.

The peculiarities that were evident from the Tunisian and Jordanian cases in comparison to the generic regulation framework for core Arab economies, as well as other peculiarities one might find when applying the regulation framework to other national cases, suggest that generic reform agendas to be applied uniformly across core Arab economies are likely to be too undifferentiated. Considering the similarities in general trends of socioeconomic regulation, policies aimed at reforming elements of the regulation regime in core Arab economies may follow a certain policy framework responding to the major socioeconomic regulation challenges prevalent across the Arab world. But how precisely to adapt and fine-tune concrete policy designs to a particular national or even regional case depends on the idiosyncratic context at hand, and this idiosyncratic context will often differ more or less clearly on some elements of the regime of accumulation or of the mode of regulation including prescriptive rules, institutions, organizations, or several of these components. In particular, institutional peculiarities are important because they are not visible at first sight. Instead of applying a uniform reform agenda across the Arab world, defining a policy menu and selecting the appropriate specific policy designs after applying the regulation framework as a lens to identify both general trends and context-specific peculiarities of the case at hand are a more sensible and institution-sensitive (Glückler and Lenz 2016) approach.

A further aspect to consider when discussing the transition towards new regulation regimes in core Arab economies is the variety of political and social contexts. Tunisia and Jordan can serve as an illustration. While Tunisia offers a case of revolutionary political change currently followed by incremental but urgent economic reform, Jordan is characterized by general political stability marked by incremental and evolutionary, though generally very careful, political reform. Still, the context of economic transition in Jordan is remarkably different to the Tunisian case. In Jordan, too, economic reform is urgent, incremental, and evolutionary and conditioned by transnational transformative processes such as IFI-sponsored structural adjustment and international trade openness. Given these similarities of the countries' approach towards economic transition and reform, we might hypothesize that the chances of successful reform of the regulation system may not be all that different when it comes to more technical economic issues. However, in a wider perspective of socioeconomic regulation, purely technical economic issues are rare because of the intricate link between the political, economic, and social spheres of a regulation regime. Chances of successful transition to new regimes of socioeconomic regulation might vary between political regimes marked by the possibility of regular changes of those in power and those marked by higher regime stability. How exactly these differences affect the chances and outcomes of the transition to new regulation regimes cannot be predicted and will have to be observed over the coming years.

5.2   A New Arab Social Contract?

The preceding chapters and sections have attempted to answer the research questions introduced in Chap. 1. The stylized conclusions and insights can be briefly summarized under each research question as follows:

1. How does regulation between economic action and institutional context work in Arab economies, notably in relation to drivers of private-sector growth such as entrepreneurship?

Based on major economic challenges and structural efficiencies commonly found in core Arab economies as assessed in Chap. 2, Chap. 3 proposed a stylized framework of socioeconomic regulation in core Arab economies (Sect. 3.3) through a synthesis of regulation approaches. This regulation framework combines policies and structures governing the economies of core Arab economies with institutions such as expectations, preferences, and aspirations held among agents. In Chap. 4, the generic regulation framework was applied to the specific cases of Tunisia and Jordan, and the framework's axioms were generally found valid, although triangulation through a limited number of expert and stakeholder interviews cannot provide a comprehensive empirical testing but a prima facie validation only.

2. Which new modes of regulation could help Arab countries in addressing structural economic and social difficulties by facilitating private-sector-led growth?

The generic regulation framework proposed in Sect. 3.3 is a positive model. The model describes socioeconomic regulation in core Arab economies as it was or is under the old Arab social contract. Considering the prima facie empirical validation of the model in the cases of Tunisia and Jordan (Chap. 4), the model qualifies as a positive theory, that is, a system linking assumptions with predictions through axioms. When combined with politically preset postulates or normative first principles exogenous to the model, a positive theory can yield recommendations for policies based on the axioms and predictions of the model to achieve the preset postulates or first principles. This is what was undertaken in Sect. 3.4. The regulation framework was modified to represent the scenario of an idealized regulation regime for core Arab economies that fulfills the assumed exogenous postulates of internal and external consistency, higher static and dynamic efficiency, and long-term sustainability. Going into further detail, Sect. 3.4 proposed a set of reform policies to drive or facilitate the transition from the present regulation regime towards such a scenario of a new regulation regime satisfying the assumed postulates.

3. What role can entrepreneurship play in such new modes of regulation?

As a major driver of dynamic efficiency through Schumpeterian creative destruction, Sect. 3.4 puts particular emphasis on the role entrepreneurship (and innovation) can play in the idealized new regulation regime addressing the postulates of consistency, higher efficiency, and sustainability. Based on the assessment of the state of entrepreneurship, innovation, and consequent Schumpeterian creative destruction undertaken in Sect. 2.3 for core Arab economies generally and in Sects. 4.1.4 and 4.2.4 for Tunisia and Jordan specifically, the menu of reform policies proposed in Sect. 3.4 focused specifically on how to improve conditions defined by socioeconomic regulation for mechanisms behind Schumpeterian creative destruction. In so doing, the present book took the position that for core Arab economies to follow a new growth model based more strongly on private-sector dynamism, isolated policies to promote entrepreneurial activity are not sufficient. Rather, when seen under the wider lens of socioeconomic regulation, institutions have to be taken into account. In particular, widely held preferences for state-driven growth and public employment prevalent in core Arab economies require policies either consistent with these institutions or, more likely under the assumed postulates of consistency, efficiency, and sustainability, policies attempting to modify these institutions in the long run by instigating processes of downward causation of institutional change. This intricate link between the preconditions set by institutional context and the outcomes in terms of entrepreneurship, innovation, and resulting Schumpeterian creative destruction is central to the comprehensive perspective of socioeconomic regulation taken here.

4. Which implications does the current transitional context in Arab economies hold for regulation, including opportunities implicit in the current regulation crisis?

The inherent unsustainability and inefficiency of the old Arab social contract, or what can be called the low-productivity equilibrium it engenders with its concomitant structural deficiencies such as high unemployment particularly among youth and higher-education graduates, labor market segmentation, inflated public sectors, and fiscal imbalances, call for a transition towards some kind of new, more sustainable, and efficient as well as internally and externally consistent regulation regime. Prima facie the political movements commonly subsumed under the popular but problematic label "Arab spring" may offer a window of opportunity for the mid- to long-term transition towards a new regulation regime. However, some years after the Tunisian revolution in 2010/2011 that is said to have sparked the "Arab spring," the reality looks much more complex. Core Arab economies have developed in highly diverse ways since. Even when excluding extreme cases of countries that have slipped into cruel civil wars such as Syria, Yemen, and Libya, the spectrum of trajectories ranges from little political change to far-ranging democratization, with cases of evolutionary, careful, and incremental reform steps in between.

The cases presented here, Tunisia and Jordan, offer two different approaches to political reform. Tunisia witnessed far-reaching democratization after its popular revolution, while in Jordan, the Hashemite regime attempted some limited top-down reform without significantly altering political decision-making processes. Therefore, both cases offer very different contexts for a transition towards a new regulation regime that could be classified as revolutionary and evolutionary approaches.

These different approaches to change refer to political decision-making. When it comes to economic reform, both countries nevertheless exhibit significant similarities. Both are subject to mostly similar structural difficulties, an urgent need to address fiscal imbalances, and transnational transformative processes such as international trade openness and IFI-sponsored structural adjustment. The similarity in both countries' approaches to economic reform is evident, for instance, in their attempts to cut supply-side subsidies, one of the major components of the crypto-welfare policies that are so characteristic of the old Arab social contract. Under pressure from IFIs, governments in both countries repeatedly attempted to cut subsidies but found themselves confronted with public opposition or what could be understood as a confrontation between prescriptive rules and institutions that are not consistent with each other.

While it is currently impossible to predict what context offers the better chances for socioeconomic regulation reform, it is clear that economic reform policies are difficult to pursue even in the current transitionary era. It may be that the "Arab spring" and its aftermath is less relevant as a context for a transition towards new regulation regimes than is long-term institutional change that could be shaped by far-sighted comprehensive reform policies aiming at downward causation processes.

5. What types of policies are needed to put such new modes of regulation in place?

Sections 3.4, 4.1.5, and 4.2.5 proposed comprehensive socioeconomic reform menus for core Arab economies in general and Tunisia and Jordan in particular. While many of the reform options presented there are not so different from reform proposals found in the literature and specifically in reports by international donors and think tanks, it is important to stress that given the need to reform core Arab economies' regulation regimes as such, isolated reform measures run a considerable risk of failure when not taking into consideration their relationship with underlying institutional realities such as widely held preferences, aspirations, or expectations. This is why Sects. 3.4, 4.1.5, and 4.2.5 attempted to link reform policies capable of achieving higher degrees of consistency, sustainability, and efficiency with underlying institutional realities in the regulation regime and to define institution-reinforcing or institution-circumventing rules to either design reform policies in a way consistent with existing institutions or to design policies to tackle institutional change by instigating processes of downward causation. In any case, what is needed in policy design is an institution-sensitive approach to comprehensive socioeconomic regulation reform.

The research presented in this book is subject to a number of constraints. For instance, the evolving literature on institutional approaches to economic geography could not be covered in its entirety. Furthermore, socioeconomic regulation is a highly complex matter that applies to a wide range of social and economic fields.

This book could highlight a few of these fields only while others such as the configuration of financial markets in core Arab economies are highly specific and will have to be left to the future, specifically dedicated research. The most important caveat about the research presented here is that its nature is primarily conceptual. Although triangulation through a limited number of expert and stakeholder interviews served to evaluate prima facie the empirical validity of the model, any comprehensive empirical test of the model is beyond the scope of this book. Due to the complexity and breadth of socioeconomic regulation and the model presented here (although the model itself is a reduced and simplified representation of the even more complex reality of socioeconomic regulation), any comprehensive empirical test in just one country would require a high number of stakeholder interviews in each of the fields of socioeconomic regulation covered, possibly combined with complementary quantitative research. Such a comprehensive mixed methods research design would constitute a multi-year research project on its own for each country and has to be left to future research.

Further fields for future research related to socioeconomic regulation in core Arab economies abound. They include, for example, in-depth research on the following aspects:

- The role of welfare policies and their relationship with labor market needs (Hall and Soskice 2001: 50–51) is a complex field that includes questions of the concrete design of public welfare systems that could not be dealt with in detail here.
- The role of the international arena in coordination modes (Hall and Soskice 2001: 52–54) includes, for example, the relevance of continuing processes of closer integration into EU neighborhood structures in Tunisia (such as the existing AA, the "Open Skies" agreement, and the DCFTA currently being negotiated) or questions of the future international orientation of Jordan (closer EU *rapprochement*, a closer economic orientation towards the United States, or eventually closer economic alignment with GCC countries). Future research might further pursue the results of this book in a perspective of variegated capitalism (Peck and Theodore 2007), linking regulation in Arab economies to broader trends in global capitalism such as economic integration with the EU and related liberalization or WTO accession. In the case of Jordan, the role of future economic cooperation with Israel and, more broadly, the impact of the geopolitically important and sensitive relationship between the two neighbor countries affect socioeconomic regulation in Jordan in highly complex ways.
- The success stories of the East Asian NIEs (South Korea, Taiwan, Singapore, and Hong Kong) are often cited as the benchmark for industrialization and economic development for other developing regions including the Arab world (e.g., Noland and Pack 2007; Rivlin 2009: 67–81). While much could be said about the peculiar context and the historical window of opportunity these countries' industrial emergence occurred in, comparing the role of rent-seeking and the relationship between private-sector elites and government with that typically found in core Arab economies would be interesting to identify possible differences in socioeconomic regulation (e.g., Rivlin 2009: 67–81, 124–126; World Bank 1993:

167–181). The results of such an analysis might demonstrate the limitations of taking East Asian NIEs as a benchmark but also reveal possibly some governance and regulation circumstances that call for policy attention before major efficiency-enhancing economic reforms can succeed. Given the continued interests for policymakers in core Arab economies for successful role models in other world regions, comparative research identifying commonalities and differences is highly relevant.

- In the same vein, comparing the current transitional context found in core Arab economies with the socioeconomic transitions in Eastern Europe in 1989/1990 could prove relevant. While the specifics of the radical, revolutionary change of the political and economic system in Eastern Europe are obvious at first sight, it might still be interesting to analyze more subtle processes of institutional change and economic reform in Eastern European economies that might eventually provide relevant insights for core Arab economies. Given the prevalence of a state-driven model with inflated public sectors and often large SOE sectors, a comparison with the system transformation in Eastern Europe during the early 1990s could prove more relevant than it seems. Furthermore, Eastern Europe's transition was neither quick nor smooth in every case. In particular, South-East European countries are likely to offer the most interesting insights. For example, Serbia could serve as a benchmark for Tunisia due to shared challenges and a similar state of economic development (e.g., Lehmann and Benner 2015).

- Another interesting case for comparative research is Turkey, given the country's economic boom after the early 2000s that was to a large degree conditioned by its alignment with the EU market and structures under the umbrella of its EU accession process. While Southern neighborhood countries such as Morocco, Tunisia, Egypt, or Jordan do not have the perspective of joining the EU, *rapprochement* under the umbrella of the EU's neighborhood policy with its instrument of association agreements and eventual DCFTAs offers a similar framework for de facto integration, at least in the economic domain. Learning from the Turkish case could yield relevant insights on how core Arab economies could seize opportunities of this far-reaching degree of de facto economic integration.

- Another related question that warrants further research is how conditions for effective economic reforms in Middle Eastern countries with a long tradition of strong governments such as Turkey (Eder 2014) and Iran (Bouroujerdi 2014) differ from the ones found in Arab countries with their historically newer independent structures of government (Gasper 2014), although Egypt (Masoud 2014) and Morocco (Maghraoui and Zerhouni 2014) with their longer histories of centralized government might be possible exceptions. A comparative perspective on regulation might therefore be interesting not only between Arab and East Asian economies[1] but also within the Middle East and North Africa.

---

[1] Second-generation Asian industrializers and notably Indonesia and Malaysia are yet another set of comparators and are indeed attracting attention as benchmarks, especially for larger Arab countries such as Egypt (Noland and Pack 2007).

- While the present book attempted to sketch an approach to develop institution-sensitive reform agendas in a perspective of socioeconomic regulation in core Arab economies, a similar approach could be useful for other world regions and draw on the consolidated regulation framework proposed in Sect. 3.2.

When it comes to the prospects of the transition towards new regulation regimes in core Arab economies or to what could be called a new Arab social contract, the present book proposed some avenues for reform and embedded existing reform proposals into an overarching, institution-sensitive perspective of socioeconomic regulation. Reforming regulation regimes is a highly complex, indirect, uncertain, and time-consuming task even under the best of circumstances. Therefore it is by no means certain that core Arab economies will come up with new, more consistent, efficient, and sustainable regulation regimes any time soon. If they do, new regulation regimes might eventually look different from the scenario proposed in Sect. 3.4. Further, trajectories between core Arab economies will certainly vary and so will their eventual success in reforming their regulation regimes. Still, there is no reason to claim that regulation in the Arab world is static or to take a wholly pessimistic view due to the difficulties inherent to regulation crises. While calls for economic reform are not new, it seems as if a combination of popular discontent, an urgent need for reform due to acute fiscal imbalances, and pressing transnational transformative processes such as IFI-sponsored structural adjustment has left policymakers with little choice than to tackle long-needed reforms. The ability and willingness to do so will differ between countries, but this divergence may give rise to some degree of policy experimentation that could be beneficial for evolutionary processes of regulation reform. Provided that at least some of the reform policies pursued be institution-sensitive, they might be able to build on ongoing processes of institutional change through upward causation such as slowly emerging entrepreneurial dynamics or a more pragmatic outlook by younger generations. And even if policy does not support ongoing institutional change, upward causation could eventually bring about gradual modifications in socioeconomic regulation in some core Arab economies. At least in this regard, there is reason for careful optimism.

References

African Development Bank (ed) (2011) Tackling youth unemployment in the Maghreb: economic brief. African Development Bank, Tunis. http://www.afdb.org/fileadmin/uploads/afdb/Documents/Publications/North%20Africa%20ch%C3%B4mage%20Anglais%20ok_North%20Africa%20Quaterly%20Analytical.pdf. (10.10.2013)

Asheim B, Boschma R, Cooke P (2011) Constructing regional advantage: platform policies based on related variety and differentiated knowledge bases. Reg Stud 45(7):893–904

Benner M (2017) Culture in local and regional development: a Mediterranean perspective on the culture/economy nexus. MPRA Paper No. 77787. https://mpra.ub.uni-muenchen.de/77787/1/MPRA_paper_77787.pdf. (08.04.2017)

Bouroujerdi M (2014) Iran. In: Lust E (ed) The Middle East, 13th edn. CQ Press, Thousand Oaks, pp 478–506

Eder M (2014) Turkey. In: Lust E (ed) The Middle East, 13th edn. CQ Press, Thousand Oaks, pp 830–865

Gasper M (2014) The making of the modern Middle East. In: Lust E (ed) The Middle East, 13th edn. CQ Press, Thousand Oaks, pp 1–72

Glückler J, Lenz R (2016) How institutions moderate the effectiveness of regional policy: a framework and research agenda. Invest Reg – J Reg Res 36(2016):255–277

Hall PA, Soskice D (2001) An introduction to varieties of capitalism. In: Hall PA, Soskice D (eds) Varieties of capitalism: the institutional foundations of comparative advantage. Oxford University Press, Oxford, New York, pp 1–68

Lehmann T, Benner M (2015): Cluster policy in the light of institutional context – a comparative study of transition countries. Adm Sci 5(4):188–212. http://www.mdpi.com/2076-3387/5/4/188/pdf. (05.11.2015)

Maghraoui D, Zerhouni S (2014) Morocco. In: Lust E (ed) The Middle East, 13th edn. CQ Press, Thousand Oaks, pp 660–687

Masoud T (2014) Egypt. In: Lust E (ed) The Middle East, 13th edn. CQ Press, Thousand Oaks, pp 448–477

Noland M, Pack H (2007) The Arab economies in a changing world. Peterson Institute for International Economics, Washington, DC

OECD (ed) (2012a) OECD investment policy reviews: Tunisia. Organisation for Economic Cooperation and Development, Paris

OECD (ed) (2012b) Promoting graduate entrepreneurship in Tunisian universities. OECD Local Economic and Employment Development (LEED) Working Papers 2012/18. Organisation for Economic Co-operation and Development, Paris

OECD (ed) (2013) OECD investment policy reviews: Jordan. Organisation for Economic Cooperation and Development, Paris

OECD (ed) (2014) Women in business 2014: accelerating entrepreneurship in the Middle East and North Africa region. Organisation for Economic Co-operation and Development, Paris

OECD (ed) (2015) Tunisia: a reform agenda to support competitiveness and inclusive growth. Organisation for Economic Development and Cooperation, Paris. http://www.oecd.org/countries/tunisia/Tunisia-a-reform-agenda-to-support-competitiveness-and-inclusive-growth.pdf. (02.06.2015)

OECD, IDRC (2013) New entrepreneurs and high performance enterprises in the Middle East and North Africa. Organisation for Economic Cooperation and Development, Paris

Peck J, Theodore N (2007) Variegated capitalism. Prog Hum Geogr 31(6):731–772

Rivlin P (2009) Arab economies in the twenty-first century. Cambridge University Press, New York

World Bank (ed) (1993) The East Asian miracle: economic growth and public policy. Oxford University Press, New York

World Bank (ed) (2007) Youth – an undervalued asset: towards a new agenda in the Middle East and North Africa: progress, challenges and way forward. The World Bank, Washington, DC. https://openknowledge.worldbank.org/bitstream/handle/10986/19614/433720REPLACEM10Box327363B01PUBLIC1.pdf?sequence=1&isAllowed=y. (03.10.2017)

World Bank (ed) (2009) From privilege to competition: unlocking private-led growth in the Middle East and North Africa. The World Bank, Washington, DC. http://siteresources.worldbank.org/INTMENA/Resources/Privilege_complete_final.pdf. (08.12.2013)

World Bank (ed) (2011) Poor places, thriving people: how the Middle East and North Africa can rise above spatial disparities. The World Bank, Washington, DC. https://openknowledge.worldbank.org/bitstream/handle/10986/2255/589970PUB0ID181UBLIC109780821383216.pdf?sequence=1. (19.02.2014)

World Bank (ed) (2012a) Enabling economic miracles. The World Bank, Washington, DC. http://siteresources.worldbank.org/INTMENA/Resources/WEBVERSIONREPORT.pdf. (08.12.2013)

World Bank (ed) (2012b) World development report 2013: jobs. The World Bank, Washington, DC

World Bank (ed) (2013) Jobs for shared prosperity: time for action in the Middle East and North Africa. The World Bank, Washington, DC. http://www-wds.worldbank.org/external/default/

WDSContentServer/WDSP/IB/2013/04/12/000445729_20130412114115/Rendered/PDF/724
690v40Full00Prosperity0full0book.pdf. (09.11.2013)

World Bank (ed) (2014a) Jobs or privileges: unleashing the employment potential of the Middle
East and North Africa. The World Bank, Washington, DC. http://www-wds.worldbank.org/
external/default/WDSContentServer/WDSP/IB/2014/07/16/000333037_20140716151958/
Rendered/PDF/888790MNA0Box382141B00PUBLIC0.pdf. (10.10.2014)

World Bank (ed) (2014b) The unfinished revolution: bringing opportunity, good jobs and greater
wealth to all Tunisians. The World Bank, Washington, DC. http://www-wds.worldbank.org/
external/default/WDSContentServer/WDSP/IB/2014/09/16/000456286_20140916144712/
Rendered/PDF/861790DPR0P12800Box385314B00PUBLIC0.pdf. (27.09.2014)

World Bank (ed) (2015) MENA economic monitor: towards a new social contract. The World
Bank, Washington, DC. http://www-wds.worldbank.org/external/default/WDSContentServer/
WDSP/IB/2015/04/09/000456286_20150409170931/Rendered/PDF/956500PUB0REVI0201
50391416B00OUO090.pdf. (16.04.2015)

References

Acemoğlu D, Robinson JA (2012) Why nations fail: the origins of power, prosperity and poverty. Profile Books, London

Achy L (2010) Trading high unemployment for bad jobs: employment challenges in the Maghreb. Carnegie Papers. Carnegie Endowment for International Peace, Washington, DC. http://carnegieendowment.org/files/labor_maghreb.pdf. (10.10.2013)

Adly A, Khatib L (2014) Reforming the entrepreneurship ecosystem in post-revolutionary Egypt and Tunisia. Center on Democracy, Development and the Rule of Law/Center for International Private Enterprise, Stanford/Washington, DC. http://cddrl.fsi.stanford.edu/sites/default/files/Reforming_the_Entrepreneurship_Ecosystem_in_Post-Revolutionary_Egypt_and_Tunisia-_Amr_Adly.pdf. (13.04.2015)

African Development Bank (ed) (2011) Tackling youth unemployment in the Maghreb: economic brief. African Development Bank, Tunis. http://www.afdb.org/fileadmin/uploads/afdb/Documents/Publications/North%20Africa%20ch%C3%B4mage%20Anglais%20ok_North%20Africa%20Quaterly%20Analytical.pdf. (10.10.2013)

Agence de Promotion de l'Industrie et de l'Innovation (ed) (2016) Les Technopoles en Tunisie. http://www.tunisieindustrie.nat.tn/fr/doc.asp?mcat=16&mrub=157. (09.11.2016)

Agence de Promotion de l'Industrie et de l'Innovation (ed) (n.d.) Guide de l'innovation: Nous vous accompagnons pour réussir. http://www.tunisianindustry.nat.tn/fr/download/innovation.pdf. (09.11.2016)

Al-Khalidi S (2018) Jordan ends bread subsidy, doubling some prices, to help state finances. https://www.reuters.com/article/us-jordan-economy-subsidies-bread/jordan-ends-bread-subsidy-doubling-some-prices-to-help-state-finances-idUSKBN1FF2CP. (27.01.2018)

Al-Quds University (ed) (2016) Dual studies. http://www.ds.alquds.edu/en. (21.05.2017)

Altenburg T (2011a) Can industrial policy work under neopatrimonial rule? UNU-WIDER Working Paper No. 2011/41. UNU World Institute for Development Economics Research, Helsinki. http://www.wider.unu.edu/publications/workingpapers/2011/en_GB/wp2011-041/_files/86080661855076371/default/wp2011-041.pdf. (20.08.2012)

Altenburg T (2011b) Industrial policy in developing countries: overview and lessons from seven country cases. DIE Discussion Paper 4/2011. Deutsches Institut für Entwicklungspolitik, Bonn. http://www.die-gdi.de/CMS-Homepage/openwebcms3.nsf/(ynDK_contentByKey)/ANES-8EAHQ3/$FILE/DP%204.2011.pdf. (20.08.2012)

Amara T, Laessing U (2017) Tunisia resists calls to cut public wage bill and subsidies in 2018. https://af.reuters.com/article/africaTech/idAFL8N1MS3UA. (02.01.2018)

Amin M, Assaad R, Al-Baharna N, Derviş K, Desai RM, Dhillon NS, Galal A, Ghanem H, Graham C, Kaufmann D, Kharas H, Page J, Salehi-Isfahani D, Sierra K, Yousef TM (2012) After the spring: economic transformations in the Arab world. Oxford University Press, Oxford

© Springer Nature Switzerland AG 2020
M. Benner, *A New Arab Social Contract?*, Economic Geography,
https://doi.org/10.1007/978-3-030-19270-9

Asheim B, Boschma R, Cooke P (2011) Constructing regional advantage: platform policies based on related variety and differentiated knowledge bases. Reg Stud 45(7):893–904

Asheim B, Grillitsch M, Trippl M (2017) Smart specialization as an innovation-driven strategy for economic diversification: examples from Scandinavian regions. In: Radosevic S, Curaj A, Gheorgiu R, Andreescu R, Wage I (eds) Advances in the theory and practice of smart specialization. Elsevier, London, pp 74–99

Aubert J-E, Taha T, Utz A (2013) Local innovation dynamics: examples and lessons from the Arab world. In: Cornell University, INSEAD, World Intellectual Property Organization (eds) The global innovation index 2013: the local dynamics of innovation. World Intellectual Property Organization/Cornell University/INSEAD, Geneva/Ithaca/Fontainebleau, pp 99–106. http://www.wipo.int/export/sites/www/freepublications/en/economics/gii/gii_2013.pdf. (29.08.2014)

Barnell O (2017) Seven years after Arab Spring revolt, Tunisia's future remains uncertain. http://www.france24.com/en/20171217-tunisia-seven-years-after-arab-spring-revolution-protests-economic-uncertainty. (02.01.2018)

Basedau M, Gobien S, Prediger S (2017) The ambivalent role of religion for sustainable development: A review of the empirical evidence. GIGA Working Paper No. 297. https://www.giga-hamburg.de/de/system/files/publications/wp297_basedau-gobien-prediger.pdf. (08.02.2017)

Bathelt H (1994) Die Bedeutung der Regulationstheorie in der wirtschaftsgeographischen Forschung. (The significance of regulation approaches for economic geography). Geogr Z 82(2):63–90

Bathelt H, Glückler J (2012) Wirtschaftsgeographie: Ökonomische Beziehungen in räumlicher Perspektive. (Economic geography: economic relations in a spatial perspective), 3rd edn. UTB, Stuttgart

Bathelt H, Glückler J (2014) Institutional change in economic geography. Progr Hum Geogr 38(3):340–363

Ben Abdessalem H, El Elj M (2011) Innovation in Tunisia: sectorial analysis. Paper presented at the Journées de Microéconomie de Sousse, 2–3 June 2011, Sousse. http://jma2014.fr/fichiers2011/136/Innovation%20in%20Tunisia-%20JMA%202011.pdf. (12.12.2013)

Ben Miled-M'rabet N (n.d.) Dossier: Le système national d'innovation en Tunisie. http://www.tunisianindustry.nat.tn/fr/download/ci/innovation.pdf. (10.10.2013)

Ben Shitrit L (2014) Israel. In: Lust E (ed) The Middle East, 13th edn. CQ Press, Thousand Oaks, pp 537–563

Benner M (2012) Clusterpolitik: Wege zur Verknüpfung von Theorie und politischer Umsetzung. (Cluster policy: ways to link theory and political implementation). LIT, Münster

Benner M (2014a) Decentralised regional development policy in Tunisia: a new beginning after the "Arab Spring"? In: International Reports 06/2014, pp 31–50. http://www.kas.de/wf/doc/kas_38099-544-2-30.pdf?140618133239. (21.06.2014)

Benner M (2014b) From smart specialisation to smart experimentation: building a new theoretical framework for regional policy of the European Union. Z Wirtsch (Ger J Econ Geogr) 58(1):33–49

Benner M (2015) Europa und der Maghreb: Von der Nachbarschaft zur Wirtschaftspartnerschaft. (Europe and the Maghreb: from neighborhood to economic partnership). In: Neuss B, Nötzold A (eds) The Southern Mediterranean: challenges to the european foreign and security policy. Nomos, Baden-Baden, pp 57–82

Benner M (2017a) Culture in local and regional development: a Mediterranean perspective on the culture/economy nexus. MPRA Paper No. 77787. https://mpra.ub.uni-muenchen.de/77787/1/MPRA_paper_77787.pdf. (08.04.2017)

Benner M (2017b) From clusters to smart specialization: tourism in institution-sensitive regional development policies. Economies 5(3):26. http://www.mdpi.com/2227-7099/5/3/26/pdf. (29.07.2017)

Benner M (2017c) Smart specialisation and cluster emergence: building blocks for evolutionary regional policies. In: Hassink R, Fornahl D (eds) The life cycle of clusters: a policy perspective. Edward Elgar, Camberley, pp 151–172

Benner M (2017d) The legacy of Sidi Bouzid: overcoming spatial inequalities in Tunisia. In: Křížek D, Záhořík J (eds) Beyond the 'Arab Spring' in North Africa: macro and micro perspectives. Lexington, Lanham, pp 47–65

Benner M (2018) Smart specialization and institutional context: towards a process of institutional discovery and change. Papers in Economic Geography and Innovation Studies 2018/03. http://www-sre.wu.ac.at/sre-disc/geo-disc-2018_03.pdf. (14.11.2018)

Benner M (forthcoming) Cluster policy in Tunisia: from institutional voids to smart specialization. In: Knedlik T, Wohlmuth K (eds) African Development perspectives yearbook 2018: science, technology and innovation policies for inclusive growth in Africa. In preparation

Bobek H (1959) Die Hauptstufen der Gesellschafts- und Wirtschaftsentfaltung in geographischer Sicht. (The main stages in the socio-economic evolution from a geographical point of view). Erde 90(3):259–298

Bobek H (1974) Zum Konzept des Rentenkapitalismus. (On the concept of rent capitalism). Tijdschr Econ Soc Geogr 65(2):73–78

Bouroujerdi M (2014) Iran. In: Lust E (ed) The Middle East, 13th edn. CQ Press, Thousand Oaks, pp 478–506

Boyer R (1988) Technical change and the theory of "régulation". In: Dosi G, Freeman C, Nelson RR, Silverberg G, Soete LLG (eds) Technical change and economic theory. Pinter, London, New York, pp 67–94

Boyer R, Hollingsworth JR (1997a) From national embeddedness to spatial and institutional nestedness. In: Hollingsworth JR, Boyer R (eds) Contemporary capitalism: the embeddedness of institutions. Cambridge University Press, Cambridge, New York, Melbourne, pp 433–484

Boyer R, Hollingsworth JR (1997b) The variety of institutional arrangements and their complementarity in modern economics. In: Hollingsworth JR, Boyer R (eds) Contemporary capitalism: the embeddedness of institutions. Cambridge University Press, Cambridge, New York, Melbourne, pp 49–54

Brand LA (2014) Jordan. In: Lust E (ed) The Middle East, 13th edn. CQ Press, Thousand Oaks, pp 564–589

Cammett M (2007) Business-government relations and industrial change: the politics of upgrading in Morocco and Tunisia. World Dev 35(11):1889–1903

Cammett M (2014) The political economy of development in the Middle East. In: Lust E (ed) The Middle East, 13th edn. CQ Press, Thousand Oaks, pp 161–208

Chaaban J (2010) Job creation in the Arab economies: navigating through difficult waters. Arab Human Development Report Research Paper. United Nations Development Programme Regional Bureau for Arab States, New York. http://www.arab-hdr.org/publications/other/ahdrps/paper03-en.pdf. (21.05.2014)

Cornell University, INSEAD, WIPO (2017) The global innovation index 2017: innovation feeding the world. Cornell University/INSEAD/WIPO, Ithaca/Fontainebleau/Geneva

Dahmani F (2017) Après avoir longtemps tergiversé, la Tunisie ouvre son ciel. http://www.jeuneafrique.com/501290/economie/apres-avoir-longtemps-tergiverse-la-tunisie-ouvre-son-ciel. (05.05.2018)

Dahmani F (2018a) L'augmentation de la TVA provoque un tollé en Tunisie, (TVA increase provokes an outcry in Tunisia). http://www.jeuneafrique.com/507291/economie/laugmentation-de-la-tva-provoque-un-tolle-en-tunisie (10.01.2018)

Dahmani F (2018b) Tunisie: les manifestations contre la cherté de la vie tournent à l'affrontement violent, (Tunisia: protests against the cost of living turn violent). http://www.jeuneafrique.com/508376/politique/tunisie-les-manifestations-contre-la-cherte-de-la-vie-tournent-a-laffrontement-violent. (10.01.2018)

Department of Statistics (ed) (2017) Press/1st Q. 2017. http://dos.gov.jo/dos_home_e/main/archive/Unemp/2017/1stQ.pdf. (08.01.2018)

Desai RM, Olofsgård A, Yousef TM (2009) The logic of authoritarian bargains. Econ Polit 21(1):93–125

Dhillon N, Salehi-Isfahani D (2009) Looking ahead: making markets and institutions work for young people. In: Dhillon N, Yousef T (eds) Generation in waiting: the unfulfilled promise of young people in the Middle East. Brookings, Washington, DC, pp 240–251

Dhillon N, Yousef T (2009) Introduction. In: Dhillon N, Yousef T (eds) Generation in waiting: the unfulfilled promise of young people in the Middle East. Brookings, Washington, DC, pp 1–10

Diop N, Ghali S (2012) Are Jordan and Tunisia's exports becoming more technologically sophisticated? analysis using highly disaggregated export databases. The World Bank, Washington, DC. http://documents.worldbank.org/curated/en/716281468312890526/pdf/672480NWP00P UB07863B00FEBRUARY15NEW.pdf. (20.05.2017)

Eder M (2014) Turkey. In: Lust E (ed) The Middle East, 13th edn. CQ Press, Thousand Oaks, pp 830–865

Erdle S (2011) Industrial policy in Tunisia. DIE Discussion Paper 1/2011. Deutsches Institut für Entwicklungspolitik, Bonn. http://www.die-gdi.de/CMSHomepage/openwebcms3.nsf/ (ynDK_contentByKey)/ANES-8DEE7C/$FILE/DP%201.2011.pdf. (20.08.2012)

European Commission (ed) (2010) Green paper: unlocking the potential of cultural and creative industries. European Commission, Brussels. https://www.hhs.se/contentassets/3776a2d6d61c4 058ad564713cc554992/greenpaper_creative_industries_en.pdf. (20.03.2017)

European Commission (ed) (2017a) Trade: policy: countries and regions. Jordan. http://ec.europa. eu/trade/policy/countries-and-regions/countries/jordan. (18.02.2018)

European Commission (ed) (2017b) Trade: policy: countries and regions. Tunisia. http://ec.europa. eu/trade/policy/countries-and-regions/countries/tunisia. (20.12.2017)

Felsenstein D (1994) University-related science parks – 'seedbeds' or 'enclaves' of innovation? Technovation 14(2):93–110

France 24 (ed) (2018a) Jordan PM Mulki resigns amid anti-government protests. http://www. france24.com/en/20180604-jordan-king-abdullah-resign-summons-pm-mulki-over-anti-government-protests. (04.06.2018)

France 24 (ed) (2018b) Jordan's next PM vows to withdraw controversial tax bill. http://www. france24.com/en/20180607-jordan-next-pm-omar-al-razzaz-vows-withdrawal-controversial-tax-bill-protests. (07.06.2018)

Freeman C (1988) Japan: a new national system of innovation? In: Dosi G, Freeman C, Nelson RR, Silverberg G, Soete LLG (eds) Technical change and economic theory. Pinter, London, New York, pp 330–348

Frenken K, van Oort F, Verburg T (2007) Related variety, unrelated variety and regional economic growth. Reg Stud 41(5):S. 685–S. 697

Gasper M (2014) The making of the modern Middle East. In: Lust E (ed) The Middle East, 13th edn. CQ Press, Thousand Oaks, pp 1–72

Ghali S, Rezgui S (2015) Structural transformation and industrial policy in selected Southern Mediterranean countries: Tunisia. In: Forum Euroméditerranéan des Instituts de Sciences Économiques (ed) Structural transformation and industrial policy: a comparative analysis of Egypt, Morocco, Tunisia and Turkey and case studies. European Investment Bank, Luxembourg, pp 39–68. http://www.femise.org/wp-content/uploads/2015/06/femip_study_ structural_transformation_and_industrial_policy_en1.pdf. (10.06.2015)

Giddens A (1979) Central problems in social theory: action, structure, and contradiction in social analysis. University of California Press, Berkeley, Los Angeles

Global Entrepreneurship Research Association (ed) (2017) Global entrepreneurship monitor: global report 2016/17. http://www.gemconsortium.org/report/49812. (18.05.2017)

Glückler J, Bathelt H (2017) Institutional context and innovation. In: Bathelt H, Cohendet P, Henn S, Simon L (eds) The Elgar companion to innovation and knowledge creation. Elgar, Cheltenham, Northampton, pp 121–137

Glückler J, Lenz R (2016) How institutions moderate the effectiveness of regional policy: a framework and research agenda. Invest Reg – J Reg Res 36(2016):255–277

Gobat J, Kostial K (2016) Syria's conflict economy. IMF Working Paper No. 16/123. http://www.imf.org/external/pubs/ft/wp/2016/wp16123.pdf. (30.06.2016)

Granovetter M (1985) Economic action and social structure: the problem of embeddedness. Am J Sociol 91(3):481–510

Gray M (2011) A theory of "Late Rentierism" in the Arab States of the Gulf. CIRS Occasional Paper No. 7. Georgetown University School of Foreign Service in Qatar Center for International and Regional Studies, Doha. http://www12.georgetown.edu/sfs/qatar/cirs/MatthewGrayOccasionalPaper.pdf. (28.03.2014)

Hall PA, Soskice D (2001) An introduction to varieties of capitalism. In: Hall PA, Soskice D (eds) Varieties of capitalism: the institutional foundations of comparative advantage. Oxford University Press, Oxford, New York, pp 1–68

Haut Commissariat du Plan (ed) (2015) Activité, Emploi et Chômage 2013: Résultats détaillés, (Activity, employment, and unemployment 2013: detailed results). http://www.hcp.ma/file/169010/. (12.10.2017)

Hazboun W (2008) Beaches, ruins, resorts: the politics of tourism in the Arab world. University of Minnesota Press, Minneapolis

Hertog S (2016) Is there an Arab variety of capitalism? Economic Research Forum Working Paper No. 1068. https://erf.org.eg/wp-content/uploads/2016/12/1068.pdf. (02.03.2017)

Higher Council for Science and Technology (ed) (2013) National innovation strategy 2013–2017. http://www.hcst.gov.jo/sites/default/files/national_innovation_strategy_final.pdf. (12.01.2018)

Hollingsworth JR, Boyer R (1997a) Coordination of economic actors and social systems of production. In: Hollingsworth JR, Boyer R (eds) Contemporary capitalism: the embeddedness of institutions. Cambridge University Press, Cambridge, New York, Melbourne, pp 1–47

Hollingsworth JR, Boyer R (1997b) How and why do social systems of production change? In: Hollingsworth JR, Boyer R (eds) Contemporary capitalism: the embeddedness of institutions. Cambridge University Press, Cambridge, New York, Melbourne, pp 189–195

International Labour Organization (ed) (2016) Local economic development strategy for Irbid Governorate: 2016–2018. International Labour Organization, Beirut. http://www.ilo.org/wcmsp5/groups/public/%2D%2D-arabstates/%2D%2D-ro-beirut/documents/publication/wcms_456503.pdf. (19.01.2018)

International Monetary Fund (ed) (2016) Tunisia: selected issued. IMF Country Report No. 16/47. http://www.imf.org/external/pubs/ft/scr/2016/cr1647.pdf. (12.02.2016)

Irbid Development Area (ed) (2018) Irbid Development Area (IDA). http://www.ida.jo/default.aspx. (10.02.2018)

Isenberg DJ (2010) How to start an entrepreneurial revolution. Harv Bus Rev 88(6):40–50

Jamal A, Khatib L (2014) Actors, public opinion, and participation. In: Lust E (ed) The Middle East, 13th edn. CQ Press, Thousand Oaks, pp 246–286

Jordan Enterprise Development Corporation (ed) (2018a) About JEDCO: about us. http://www.jedco.gov.jo/Pages/viewpage.aspx?pageID=147. (15.01.2018)

Jordan Enterprise Development Corporation (ed) (2018b) Projects and projects for emerging enterprises: JEDCO 2016. http://www.jedco.gov.jo/Pages/viewpage.aspx?pageID=293. (15.01.2018)

Jordan Enterprise Development Corporation (ed) (2018c) Projects and projects for new entrepreneurs: JEDCO 2016. http://www.jedco.gov.jo/Pages/viewpage.aspx?pageID=291. (15.01.2018)

Josua M (2016) If you can't include them, exclude them: countering the Arab uprisings in Algeria and Jordan. GIGA Working Paper No. 286. https://www.giga-hamburg.de/de/system/files/publications/wp286_josua.pdf. (30.05.2016)

Kanaan T, Hanania M (2009) The disconnect between education, job growth, and employment in Jordan. In: Dhillon N, Yousef T (eds) Generation in waiting: the unfulfilled promise of young people in the Middle East. Brookings, Washington, DC, pp 142–165

Kelley D, Singer S, Herrington M (2016) Global entrepreneurship monitor: 2015/16 global report. http://www.gemconsortium.org/report/49480. (18.05.2017)

Kharabsheh R, Magableh IK, Arabiyat TS (2011) Obstacles of success of technology parks: the case of Jordan. Int J Econ Fin 3(6):219–226

King Hussein Business Park (ed) (2018) Tenants. http://www.businesspark-jo.com/en-us/KHBP-Community/Tenants. (17.12.2018)

Lee R, Ben Shitrit L (2014) Religion, socierty, and politics in the Middle East. In: Lust E (ed) The Middle East, 13th edn. CQ Press, Thousand Oaks, pp 209–245

Lehmann T, Benner M (2015): Cluster policy in the light of institutional context – a comparative study of transition countries. Adm Sci 5(4):188–212. http://www.mdpi.com/2076-3387/5/4/188/pdf. (05.11.2015)

Lundvall B-Å (1988) Innovation as an interactive process: from user-producer interaction to the national system of innovation. In: Dosi G, Freeman C, Nelson RR, Silverberg G, Soete LLG (eds) Technical change and economic theory. Pinter, London, New York, pp 349–369

Lundvall B-Å (1992a) Introduction. In: Lundvall B-Å (ed) National systems of innovation: towards a theory of innovation and interactive learning. Pinter, London, pp 1–19

Lundvall B-Å (1992b) User-producer relationships, national systems of innovation and internationalisation. In: Lundvall B-Å (ed) National systems of innovation: towards a theory of innovation and interactive learning. Pinter, London, pp 45–67

Lundvall B-Å, Maskell P (2000) Nation states and economic development: From national systems of production to national systems of knowledge creation and learning. In: Clark GL, Feldman MP, Gertler MS (eds) The Oxford handbook of economic geography. Oxford University Press, Oxford, pp 353–372

Lynch M (2014) Regional international relations. In: Lust E (ed) The Middle East, 13th edn. CQ Press, Thousand Oaks, pp 367–395

M'Henni H, Deniozos D (2012) Erawatch country reports 2012. Tunisia. http://erawatch.jrc.ec.europa.eu/erawatch/export/sites/default/galleries/generic_files/file_0432.pdf. (26.08.2014)

M'Henni H, Ben Youssef A, Elaheebocus N, Ragni L (2013) Are technoparks high tech fantasies? lessons from the Tunisian experience. MPRA Paper No. 46183. https://mpra.ub.uni-muenchen.de/46183/1/MPRA_paper_46183.pdf. (11.07.2016)

Maghraoui D, Zerhouni S (2014) Morocco. In: Lust E (ed) The Middle East, 13th edn. CQ Press, Thousand Oaks, pp 660–687

Mahdavy H (1970) The pattern and problems of economic development in rentier states: the case of Iran. In: Cook MA (ed) Studies in the economic history of the Middle East. Oxford University Press, Oxford, pp 428–467

Mahroum S, Al-Bdour JM, Scott E Shouqar S, Arafat A (2013) Jordan: the atlas of islamic world science and innovation country case study. https://royalsociety.org/~/media/policy/projects/atlas-islamic-world/atlas-jordan.pdf. (12.01.2018)

Marzouk H (2017) Tataouine: recrutement de mille agents au sein de la Société d'environnement, (Tataouine: recruitment of one thousand staff at the environment company). http://www.lecono-mistemaghrebin.com/2017/06/13/tataouine-recrutement-mille-agents-societe-environnement. (30.12.2017)

Masoud T (2014) Egypt. In: Lust E (ed) The Middle East, 13th edn. CQ Press, Thousand Oaks, pp 448–477

Mattes H (2016) Entwicklung der tunesischen Binnenregionen: Hohe Erwartungen – schwierige Umsetzung. (The development of Tunisian interior regions: high expectations – difficult implementation) GIGA Focus Nahost No. 1. https://www.giga-hamburg.de/de/system/files/publications/gf_nahost_1601.pdf. (28.04.2016)

Medinilla Aldana A, El Fassi S (2016) Tackling regional inequalities in Tunisia. ECDPM Briefing Note No. 84. http://ecdpm.org/wp-content/uploads/BN-84-Tackling-regional-inequalities-Tunisia-ECDPM-2016.pdf. (24.06.2016)

Ministère de l'Industrie, de l'Énergie et des Mines (ed) (2014) Parcs d'activités industrielles et technologiques en Tunisie. http://www.parcs-activites.tn/parcs-activites.html. (15.11.2016)

Moghadam VN, Decker T (2014) Social change in the Middle East. In: Lust E (ed) The Middle East, 13th edn. CQ Press, Thousand Oaks, pp 73–106

Moore PW (2010) Political economy. In: Angrist MP (ed) Politics and society in the contemporary Middle East. Lynne Rienner, Boulder, pp 69–90

Muasher M (2011) A decade of struggling reform efforts in Jordan: the resilience of the rentier system. Carnegie Papers. Carnegie Endowment for International Peace, Washington, DC. http://carnegieendowment.org/files/jordan_reform.pdf. (10.05.2014)

Nelson RR (1988) Institutions supporting technical change in the United States. In: Dosi G, Freeman C, Nelson RR, Silverberg G, Soete LLG (eds) Technical change and economic theory. Pinter, London, New York, pp 312–329

Noland M, Pack H (2007) The Arab economies in a changing world. Peterson Institute for International Economics, Washington, DC

Observatoire National de l'Emploi et des Qualifications (ed) (2013) Rapport Annuel sur: Le Marché du Travail en Tunisie: Novembre 2013, (Annual report on the labor market in Tunisia: November 2013). http://www.emploi.gov.tn/uploads/tx_elypublication/Rapport_annuel_decembre_2013.pdf. (11.10.2017)

OECD (ed) (2012a) OECD investment policy reviews: Tunisia. Organisation for Economic Cooperation and Development, Paris

OECD (ed) (2012b) Promoting graduate entrepreneurship in Tunisian universities. OECD Local Economic and Employment Development (LEED) Working Papers 2012/18. Organisation for Economic Co-operation and Development, Paris

OECD (ed) (2013) OECD investment policy reviews: Jordan. Organisation for Economic Cooperation and Development, Paris

OECD (ed) (2014) Women in business 2014: accelerating entrepreneurship in the Middle East and North Africa region. Organisation for Economic Co-operation and Development, Paris

OECD (ed) (2015a) Lessons learned from the Lüneburg Innovation Incubator. Organisation for Economic Co-operation and Development, Paris

OECD (ed) (2015b) Tunisia: a reform agenda to support competitiveness and inclusive growth. Organisation for Economic Development and Cooperation, Paris. http://www.oecd.org/countries/tunisia/Tunisia-a-reform-agenda-to-support-competitiveness-and-inclusive-growth.pdf. (02.06.2015)

OECD (ed) (2018) OECD economic surveys: Tunisia: economic assessment. Organisation for Economic Development and Cooperation, Paris

OECD, European Commission (2015) The Missing Entrepreneurs 2015: policies for self-employment and entrepreneurship. Organisation for Economic Co-operation and Development, Paris

OECD, IDRC (2013) New entrepreneurs and high performance enterprises in the Middle East and North Africa. Organisation for Economic Cooperation and Development, Paris

Peck J, Theodore N (2007) Variegated capitalism. Prog Hum Geogr 31(6):731–772

Putnam R (1995) Bowling alone: America's declining social capital. J Democr 6(1):65–78

Richards A, Waterbury J (2008) A political economy of the Middle East, 3rd edn. Westview Press, Boulder

Rijkers B, Freund C, Nucifora A (2014) All in the family: state capture in Tunisia. Policy Research Working Paper No. 6810. The World Bank, Washington, DC. http://www-wds.worldbank.org/external/default/WDSContentServer/IW3P/IB/2014/03/25/000158349_20140325092905/Rendered/PDF/WPS6810.pdf. (28.03.2014)

Rivlin P (2009) Arab economies in the twenty-first century. Cambridge University Press, New York

Rodríguez-Pose A, Hardy D (2014) Technology and industrial parks in emerging countries: panacea or pipedream? Springer, Cham, Heidelberg, New York, Dordrecht, London

Rostow WW (1959) The stages of economic growth. Econ Hist Rev 12(1):1–16

Royal Scientific Society (ed) (2017) Welcome. http://www.rss.jo. (16.01.2018)

Ryan CR (2010) Jordan. In: Angrist MP (ed) Politics and society in the contemporary Middle East. Lynne Rienner, Boulder, pp 311–333

Salem P (2014) Lebanon. In: Lust E (ed) The Middle East, 13th edn. CQ Press, Thousand Oaks, pp 609–630

Seidel U, Domröse W, Meier zu Köcker G (2009) Study on the National Innovation System in Jordan: final report. VDI/VDE Innovation + Technik GmbH, Berlin. http://www.jedco.gov. jo/joomla/images/international_reports/Innovation%20Study%20-%20Jordan%20-%20Final. pdf. (01.12.2014)

Smadi R, Tsipouri L (2012) Erawatch country reports 2012: Jordan. http://erawatch.jrc.ec.europa. eu/erawatch/export/sites/default/galleries/generic_files/file_0454.pdf. (26.08.2014)

Storper M, Walker R (1989) The capitalist imperative: territory, technology, and industrial growth. Basil Blackwell, New York, Oxford

Sultan SS, Soete L (2012) Innovation for development: the case of Jordan. Dirasat: Admin Sci 39(2):321–327

Trippl M, Zukauskaite E, Healy A (2018) Shaping smart specialisation: the role of place-specific factors in advanced, intermediate and less-developed European regions. Papers in Economic Geography and Innovation Studies 2018/01. http://www-sre.wu.ac.at/sre-disc/geo-disc-2018_01.pdf. (14.11.2018)

UNESCO Institute for Statistics (ed) (2015) Global Education Digest 2012: opportunities lost: the impact of grade repetition and early school leaving. UNESCO Institute for Statistics, Montreal. http://www.uis.unesco.org/Education/GED%20Documents%20C/GED-2012-Complete-Web3.pdf. (13.02.2016)

UNRWA (ed) (n.d.) Where we work: Jordan. https://www.unrwa.org/where-we-work/jordan. (20.02.2018)

Williamson J (1990) What Washington means by policy reform. In: Williamson J (ed) Latin American adjustment: how much has happened? Washington, Institute for International Economics

Wood S (2001) Business, government, and patterns of labor market policy in Britain and the Federal Republic of Germany. In: Hall PA, Soskice D (eds) Varieties of capitalism: the institutional foundations of comparative advantage. Oxford University Press, Oxford, New York, pp 247–274

World Bank (ed) (1993) The East Asian miracle: economic growth and public policy. Oxford University Press, New York

World Bank (ed) (2007) Youth – an undervalued asset: towards a new agenda in the Middle East and North Africa: progress, challenges and way forward. The World Bank, Washington, DC. https://openknowledge.worldbank.org/bitstream/handle/10986/19614/433720REPLACEM10 Box327363B01PUBLIC1.pdf?sequence=1&isAllowed=y. (03.10.2017)

World Bank (ed) (2009) From privilege to competition: unlocking private-led growth in the Middle East and North Africa. The World Bank, Washington, DC. http://siteresources.worldbank.org/ INTMENA/Resources/Privilege_complete_final.pdf. (08.12.2013)

World Bank (ed) (2011) Poor places, thriving people: how the Middle East and North Africa can rise above spatial disparities. The World Bank, Washington, DC. https://openknowledge. worldbank.org/bitstream/handle/10986/2255/589970PUB0ID181UBLIC109780821383216. pdf?sequence=1. (19.02.2014)

World Bank (ed) (2012a) Enabling economic miracles. The World Bank, Washington, DC. http://sit-eresources.worldbank.org/INTMENA/Resources/WEBVERSIONREPORT.pdf. (08.12.2013)

World Bank (ed) (2012b) World development report 2013: jobs. The World Bank, Washington, DC

World Bank (ed) (2013) Jobs for shared prosperity: time for action in the Middle East and North Africa. The World Bank, Washington, DC. http://www-wds.worldbank.org/external/default/ WDSContentServer/WDSP/IB/2013/04/12/000445729_20130412114115/Rendered/PDF/724 690v40Full00Prosperity0full0book.pdf. (09.11.2013)

World Bank (ed) (2014a) Jobs or privileges: unleashing the employment potential of the Middle East and North Africa. The World Bank, Washington, DC. http://www-wds.worldbank.org/ external/default/WDSContentServer/WDSP/IB/2014/07/16/000333037_20140716151958/ Rendered/PDF/888790MNA0Box382141B00PUBLIC0.pdf. (10.10.2014)

World Bank (ed) (2014b) MENA quarterly economic brief: growth slowdown heightens the need for reforms. The World Bank, Washington, DC. http://www.worldbank.org/content/dam/Worldbank/document/MNA/QEBissue2January2014FINAL.pdf. (20.02.2014)

World Bank (ed) (2014c) MENA quarterly economic brief: predictions, perceptions and economic reality. The World Bank, Washington, DC. http://www-wds.worldbank.org/external/default/WDSContentServer/WDSP/IB/2014/08/06/000470435_20140806105353/Rendered/PDF/898440REVISED00ue030JULY020140FINAL.pdf. (09.08.2014)

World Bank (ed) (2014d) The unfinished revolution: bringing opportunity, good jobs and greater wealth to all Tunisians. The World Bank, Washington, DC. http://www-wds.worldbank.org/external/default/WDSContentServer/WDSP/IB/2014/09/16/000456286_20140916144712/Rendered/PDF/861790DPR0P12800Box385314B00PUBLIC0.pdf. (27.09.2014)

World Bank (ed) (2015) MENA economic monitor: towards a new social contract. The World Bank, Washington, DC. http://www-wds.worldbank.org/external/default/WDSContentServer/WDSP/IB/2015/04/09/000456286_20150409170931/Rendered/PDF/956500PUB0REVI020150391416B00OUO090.pdf. (16.04.2015)

World Economic Forum (ed) (2017) The travel and tourism competitiveness report 2017: paving the way for a more sustainable and inclusive future. World Economic Forum, Geneva. http://www3.weforum.org/docs/WEF_TTCR_2017_web_0401.pdf. (26.05.2017)

World Tourism Organization (ed) (2017) UNWTO tourism highlights: 2017 edition. https://www.e-unwto.org/doi/pdf/10.18111/9789284419029. (13.02.2018)

Index

Printed by Printforce, the Netherlands